RECIPROCAL ETHNOGRAPHY AND THE POWER OF WOMEN'S NARRATIVES

RECIPROCAL ETHNOGRAPHY AND THE POWER OF WOMEN'S NARRATIVES

Elaine J. Lawless
Foreword by Amy Shuman

INDIANA UNIVERSITY PRESS

This book is a publication of

Indiana University Press
Office of Scholarly Publishing
Herman B Wells Library 350
1320 East 10th Street
Bloomington, Indiana 47405 USA
iupress.indiana.edu

Manufactured in the United States of America.

Cataloging information is available from the Library of Congress.

ISBN 978-0-253-04296-5 (hardback)
ISBN 978-0-253-04297-2 (paperback)
ISBN 978-0-253-04298-9 (ebook)

1 2 3 4 5   24 23 22 21 20 19

First Printing 2019

For Madison, Luke, Olivia, and Chloé,
who bless my life every day, make me proud,
and give me hope for the future

CONTENTS

FOREWORD

E LAINE LAWLESS HAS BEEN A CHAMPION FOR THE ethnographic study of women's narratives and cultural practices for her entire career. This book represents the range of her work, from her classic study of rural, white Pentecostal women to her study of women preachers and her more recent research on the narratives told by abused women who have sought refuge in shelters. Throughout her work, Lawless has listened to stories told by women whose stories are not known and not valued. She pays close attention to how they describe themselves and explores the complexity of the cultural categories they use. For example, in her study of the Pentecostal women, she turns to the term they use to describe themselves, "handmaidens of the Lord," to understand how they regard themselves as subservient to men in religious service and in daily life. Lawless's work explores how these women nonetheless sustain their own voices and sometimes defy social restrictions.

All of the women Lawless studied described an absence of stories about their lives. When they did tell their stories to Lawless, they did not see them as part of a collective narrative. Lawless was able to identify patterns in their stories about themselves; for example, she found similar ways of recounting the awareness of the calling to become a preacher. However, as Lawless notes, the stories were not only not told but often suppressed, and an important part of the shared dialogue was about the emergence of women's stories.

The suppression and emergence of women's accounts of their own experiences have been significant topics in feminist research, and much has been written about both the conditions in which narratives are told or not told and about whether telling the stories changes the larger social conditions of subjugation. As collectors of women's narrative, folklorists have been central in this enterprise. Lawless advances the project significantly by addressing the problems of the intertwined claims to truth and interpretation and by outlining the methods of reciprocal ethnography, which includes the dialogic coproduction of interpretation.

Using the methods of reciprocal ethnography, Lawless conducted extensive discussions with a group of women preachers who told her their life stories and engaged in a dialogue with her about their and her interpretations. Her work confronts one of the central issues facing folklorists, oral historians, and others who collect and study narratives about experience. The women objected to the idea that their narratives were constructed and instead insisted that they were true. Lawless explained that our narratives are based on expectations and previously existing ways of describing experience that can serve as scripts that we confirm, reject, and renegotiate. This is part of the dialogic dimension of narrative; we incorporate other voices and integrate them with our own. Not only our actual listeners but also earlier voices become part of the dialogic creation of narrative. In an age of "fake news," recognizing the validity of personal experience narratives has become even more important. Lawless's book locates truth in dialogue, even when the dialogue produces uncomfortable differences in interpretation.

Undoubtedly, readers will pore over Lawless's book for its honest discussion of the difficult problems of contested cultural interpretation when, as fieldworkers, we attempt to understand people as they understand themselves and when, inevitably, if we listen as carefully as Lawless does, we recognize the gaps and gulfs that emerge out of sustained dialogue. Lawless proposes the methods of reciprocal ethnography to address these limits. Far from suggesting that scholarly and cultural interpretations are at odds with each other, Lawless instead interrogates how her preconceptions and assumptions as a scholar are also shaped by her own personal history. She pauses to interrogate her own biases and to create and sustain an ongoing dialogue with the people she studies. This has become a central concern of feminist research, and in the field of folklore feminist studies, Lawless's work is foundational.

Lawless's book also provides important conversations among folklorists, feminists, religion scholars, sociologists, literary scholars, and others. Articulating the contribution of folklore, she demonstrates how attention to both observations of everyday experience and the aesthetics of narrative performance challenges some of the central claims in other disciplines. For example, in her discussion of essentialist claims about women's experience as relational, Lawless provides an important counternarrative. The women preachers Lawless studied contextualize claims to the relational; complicating the essentialist claims, they describe how being seen as a mother can interfere with their authority as a preacher. Attending to these situational complexities requires ethnographic observation not usually available through other modes of research.

As we move into the next generation of research on feminism and folklore, Elaine Lawless's work remains central to our enterprise. She has taken on some of the most difficult questions—theoretically, methodologically, and ethically. Reading this book, which intertwines the personal and the scholarly on so many levels, will be, for some readers, a life-changing experience.

Amy Shuman
The Ohio State University

AMY SHUMAN is Professor of English at the Ohio State University. She is author of *Other People's Stories: Entitlement Claims and the Critique of Empathy* and (with Carol Bohmer) of *Political Asylum Deceptions: The Culture of Suspicion.*

ACKNOWLEDGMENTS

EVEN THOUGH I AM DELIGHTED TO SEE THIS collection of my essays dealing with the birth and evolution of what I have called reciprocal ethnography appear in print, my true legacy as a folklorist is, and will continue to be, the brilliant graduate students I have had the pleasure of working with at the University of Missouri. Over the years, they have read my work and engaged with it, much as I have advocated that we do the same with those we study in the field. Their own field research and written ethnographies, their dedication to teaching folklore as it lives and breathes in life, literature, theater, and creative endeavors, their innovative work in the public sector arts and humanities world, and their continued influence on me and the field we love push us all to question and continue to grow as activist folklorists. I am cautious about listing the names of all of my folklore graduate students only because I might omit one person. You know who you are, and you know how much I admire each of you and what you do.

Within the American Folklore Society, I have also been blessed to have longstanding friends and colleagues who have inspired me every single day to be a good folklorist, providing a dedicated community in which to flourish and evolve. You know who you are too.

At the University of Missouri, I have been most fortunate to have Anand Prahlad as a folklore colleague devoted to the work of folklore and creative writing. I thank him for his steady support of me and my work, as well as for his dedication to our joint teaching and mentoring of our folklore students. My survival in the academic world was made possible largely by his warm friendship and his ability to help me see beyond the petty department politics and keep my eye on what really matters.

At Indiana University Press, I thank Gary Dunham and Janice Frisch for their continued confidence in my work and willingness to help get it published. Janice, especially, has worked closely with me now on two books, and I have come to appreciate her critical eye for detail and her ability to push me to improve my prose, again and again.

Thanks to Rita Reed, photojournalist extraordinaire, who traveled with me to southern Missouri in the bitter cold weeks of early 2018 to take photographs for my work with the displaced Pinhook residents. Until this year, I had no photographs of myself doing fieldwork. It just never occurred to me to have pictures taken of me. But when I saw the photo of me with Aretha Robinson, the matriarch of Pinhook, I knew it could serve as the cover of this book about my work, and I appreciate Rita allowing us to use it.

I am deeply thankful for the assistance of Jackie McGrath in undertaking the laborious responsibility of getting these articles gathered together into one volume, for reformatting them from their original journal format into the standard IU format for a book, for editing the articles and my notes, and for getting all the necessary permissions from the original publishers. Without any compensation, but with great good cheer and thoughtful suggestions, Jackie has worked tirelessly on this volume, ensuring the collection would be much better than I had ever imagined it could be.

Last, but never least, I thank Sandy Rikoon, husband, partner, friend, cheerleader, and supporter, whom I met at the beginning of this journey and stands with me every single day.

RECIPROCAL ETHNOGRAPHY AND THE
POWER OF WOMEN'S NARRATIVES

Introduction

LEARNING TO LISTEN, HEAR, AND INCLUDE WOMEN'S VOICES

The Genesis of Reciprocal Ethnography

LITERATURE AND READING WERE MY ESCAPE AND MY solace as a child. Growing up on a dirt farm with a demanding father who dominated every situation in our lives made me aware that my mother had things to say but very few spaces in which to express her opinion. As the only girl in a family of boys, I also learned to keep the peace by remaining largely silent, even as I tuned my ears, hoping to hear my mother quietly assert herself or tell me stories when the men were gone from the house. As an adult, I still cringed when she would ask my father to tell a certain story, knowing full well that her version invariably was more thrilling, colorful, and insightful. I recognized early on that she had learned to curb her voice in deference to her husband and to the societal norms in southern Missouri in the years following my father's return from World War II.

I think my mother was terrified when I defied my father and left the farm for the local state college thirty miles away, yet years later I would hear her tell a story about how she had encouraged my bravery and drove me to the campus herself. Imagine my shock when I learned that, after I graduated, she had secretly driven back to that same college to get her GED without telling my father. In college, I studied literature and continued to read vociferously, always on the lookout for texts written by women. Unfortunately, although women were definitely writing during those years and long before, the books (mostly written by dead white males) chosen by my college professors (all white males) were rarely those written by women. Of course, we read the token poems by Emily Dickenson and occasionally read an Austen novel, but, in general, whatever women were thinking, saying, and writing was not part of my undergraduate education.

In graduate school at the University of Illinois, I continued to take English department offerings but found myself less and less interested in Proust, Hawthorne, Eliot, Melville, Hemingway, and the other male writers we studied in earnest. By accident I discovered the study of folklore in courses taught by John Flannagan, Larry Danielson, and Archie Green. Judy McCullough was the graduate assistant in Archie's classes. Between them, these folklorists introduced me to folktales and ballads, epics, and, from Archie, I learned to appreciate the vibrant connections between folk tradition and activism. In one fell swoop, I dropped all my other courses and steadily enrolled in every course offered in this fascinating new field I had never known existed. With the encouragement of my folklore professors at Illinois, I eventually found my way to Indiana University to get my PhD. In 1977, there were thirty-three students in my cohort in folklore, many of whom are currently the leaders in folklore studies nationwide. At IU, I was thrilled with the offerings by Richard Dorson, Linda Degh, John McDowell, Roger Janelli, and Felix Oinas. I found my calling in field research. Listening to and recording the voices of human beings who had a unique and valuable relationship with history and their own culture resonated with me profoundly. The turning point in my graduate education came when Dick Bauman and Beverly Stoeltje came to IU to teach during the summer of 1979, introducing us to the ethnography of speaking and communication (Bauman), as well as attention to women performers (Stoeltje). Those were heady times for me. I discovered women's studies through folklorist Mary Ellen Brown, who eventually signed on as my dissertation adviser. Even then, I knew I wanted to pay attention to what women had to say. Aligned with that desire to listen to and actually "hear" women's words was my deep-seated anger that women were consistently, horribly silenced in our culture, as well as many cultures around the world. My immediate research question then emerged: how, when, and where *do* women speak, given the restrictions in place to deny them a voice? The field research Betsy Peterson and I did as graduate students for *Joy Unspeakable*, our 1981 film on a group of Pentecostals in southern Indiana, provided the foundation for my focus on women's participation in Pentecostal religious services and, eventually, a lifelong commitment to ethics in ethnographic documentation.

Fortunately for me, the turn in Folklore Studies in the late 1970s, from text(s) to context, identifying folklore as verbal art situated within the ethnography of speaking, performance, and communication, perfectly matched my enthusiasm for field research and close attention ("deep listening") to how women located spaces within Pentecostal religious contexts to speak and voice their religious and gendered concerns. My dissertation and early publications parsed the spontaneous, yet patterned, generic aspects of the Pentecostal services I witnessed and recorded, paying particular attention to the genres available to women, including prayer, testimony, singing, tongue-speaking, dancing in the spirit, and occasionally preaching. Observing when and how women could and did speak, I was able to identify the ways in which authority and power were delineated, and subverted, within this richly charismatic religion, and how women managed to claim both through their commitment to speaking their truth no matter the rules in place intended to deny them that right. I could see that women confidently claimed spiritual power, while male *authority* both recognized and feared that power, keeping close reins on a perceived female affinity for the otherworldly by allowing for, but restricting, its expression. Gradually, I came to better understand the subtle ways in which women might resist and challenge patriarchal constraints on their authority without risking alienation or censure by the men who regulated the religious context that meant so much to them.

Shifting my focus from the gendered performance spaces in the Pentecostal religious services required that I also shift my ethnographic focus to the actual words the women spoke and the narratives they told within the various genre spaces available to them, a move that continued to inform my study of women's speech in their testimonies, prayers, and sermons. My ethnographic work in the Pentecostal services was also enhanced by the interviews I was conducting with the women, seeking to flesh out a life of belief that informed their expressive religious behavior.

In 1988, with the publication of *Handmaidens of the Lord*, a book about Pentecostal women preachers and clergy in southern Missouri, my ethnographic approach came to a jolting, and painful, halt when my primary informant (and, yes, at this point I was still referring to her as my "informant") read the entire book and wrote me long letters about just how wrong my interpretations and analyses were, in her opinion. Unfortunately, I had not bothered to tell her exactly what I was writing about her and her words.

After much soul-searching and anguish over her disagreements with my published work, I set about to devise a different kind of collaborative ethnography, one that might honor and respect all points of view—those of the performers/participants in the study and the ethnographer equally. This new ethnographic approach would require that I show the participants in my studies everything I wrote, would insist upon a dialogue about my thinking and writing with all those involved, and would fashion new ways of rendering the work of the study onto the published page. Highlighting the dialogic and emergent aspects of what I saw as a viable new ethnographic approach meant my ethnographies would actually look and read differently from previously published ethnographies that focused entirely upon the ethnographer's narrative voice, illuminating instead the multiplicity of voices in our discussions together.

In many ways, the articles in this collection document my evolution as an ethnographer from my early published articles on women's speech in the Pentecostal service through the development of a new and more collaborative and feminist methodology, which I have called reciprocal ethnography. Coming as it did on the heels of the 1985 publication of the James Clifford and George Marcus edited volume, *Writing Culture*, I intentionally chose "reciprocal" to counter the "reflexive" ethnographic turn that irked feminist scholars because it seemed to provide yet another way for (male) ethnographers to turn the gaze back onto themselves rather than upon those they chose to study. It has been my hope that reciprocal ethnography can provide a scholarly space for dialogue and discussion, even disagreement and challenges, that privilege not the ethnographer but the work done collaboratively with the participants.

My work with Pentecostal women speaking evolved into several years of work with the voices of more mainline denominational clergywomen. I developed an interest in women's life stories, particularly as those stories related to a woman's claim to the pulpit, noting how her own desires for companionship and family had to be negotiated and often compromised in her quest for equal access to the pulpit and religious authority. Reciprocal ethnography found its secure home in the years I spent with clergywomen in central Missouri during the 1990s. These highly educated, thoughtful, witty, delightful, and, at times, irreverent women were willing and eager to read my writing and discuss my ideas and those of other scholars through the completion of several collaborative books and articles on their lives, sermons, and ministry. Throughout, I have continued to be interested in when, where, and how women may and do speak, with close attention to what the female body may signify when located in (contested) positions of authority, such as a religious pulpit, and how a woman in that female body makes her claims based on female spiritual power that can earn her a tentative place in the church hierarchy.

Perhaps it was not until I began ethnographic research in a women's shelter that my concerns, and hence my work, about when and where women are *not allowed to speak* came to focus more on blatant misogyny and notions of the female body as abject. While these cultural realities had been evident in my work with women in religious contexts, to be sure, the naked truth about how the female body is seen as *abject* had never been so evident as it was when talking with women who had been beaten repeatedly by men who feared, hated, and wanted to kill them. Nothing in my ethnographic research up to this point had adequately prepared me for what I encountered in the stories the women hiding in the local shelter shared with me. This situation put reciprocal ethnography to its ultimate test. While the women were willing and (sometimes) able to converse with me about what I was writing and what I heard in their stories, they were distracted by their dangerous and chaotic situations and their pain, which forced me to find other ways to discuss my findings, including asking survivors of domestic violence to read my work and discuss it with me in various settings outside the shelter. Designing the Troubling Violence Performance Project also enabled me to bring the work to a larger audience for dialogue and vetting by community and campus women who had also suffered at the hands of their partners, as well as women who had yet to escape a life of violence but were eager to imagine a different life for themselves and their children. This work also brought my research into the realm of partnership violence among teenagers and college students, an arena of abuse that has only recently been acknowledged and addressed. On the stage with the performers and in the discussions following, my colleague Heather Carver and I explored the ways women's voices and stories could provide new ways to employ a kind of reciprocal ethnography broadened and strengthened across different age groups and cultures, as evidenced in our book *Troubling Violence: A Performance Project*.

For the past eight years, I have taken my theories about how to better listen to and hear the voices of women into new territories that demand sensitivity and respect for how the former residents of Pinhook, Missouri, see the world through their strong faith in God and community, even as they respond to racism and discrimination by the government. The African American town of Pinhook was destroyed by the Army Corps of Engineers in 2011, yet the displaced residents have not been aided by the government in their efforts to rebuild their town. As with other cases of environmental racism and government disregard, it was the women of Pinhook who emerged as the leaders in the efforts to rebuild their community. For this ethnographic work, folklorist Todd Lawrence and I have been traveling regularly to southern Missouri to document the former residents' persistent work to get financial redress for the loss of their town. We have brought the tenets of reciprocal ethnography to our work in Missouri's Bootheel region by encouraging the women who speak for Pinhook to share with us their beliefs, strategies, and challenges when faced with the politics of race that first forced them to build their town in the Mississippi River spillway, and nearly a century later enabled the government to destroy what they had worked to build. In our lengthy discussions with the displaced residents, we expressed our righteous anger and shared our writing that argued for lawsuits and countermeasures, but in the process we learned from them what it actually means to stand proud and demand justice without compromising their principles of faith in God and faith in community. Our book, *When They Blew the Levee*, went to press before we stood with them and watched as good-intentioned Mennonite and Amish builders raised the walls for a few new homes for some of them in the cold weeks of January 2018, in an area far from their beloved town. Through reciprocal ethnography, we have learned to hear their claims that God has answered their prayers, even as we all agree that justice has not been done and restitution has not been offered by the very government that destroyed their property.

In the process of writing this book, we learned more than the Pinhook people did. I have come to believe this may always be the case with reciprocal ethnography: deep listening to people we respect and honor as equal participants in our work reveals the promise of a different kind of knowledge building based on long-term ethnography. We have aligned ourselves with them, working to help them locate a space to tell their story, to speak their truth, even as they seek those who are willing to listen. I have spent my career listening to the voices of women in the places and spaces where they can be heard, honoring their words and writing *with* them a story that others need to hear. The audience for this kind of effort has come to recognize reciprocal ethnography as a legitimate way to seek social justice, equality, and transformation, when the stakes are especially high and when women's voices are too easily dismissed.

1

SHOUTING FOR THE LORD

The Power of Women's Speech in the Pentecostal Religious Service

P ENTECOSTALS IN SOUTHERN INDIANA ARE QUICK TO ASSERT that theirs is a religion of equality; all members, male and female, are equal in the sight of God, and all may participate in the ecstatic behaviors that have become the trademark of this charismatic religion.[1] In fact, if anything, the

Author's note: Much of the material used for this study was collected by Elizabeth Peterson and me between 1978 and 1980 while we were graduate students at Indiana University. The field research was conducted primarily for our film, *Joy Unspeakable* (1981). I utilized the interviews and transcriptions from our research for my dissertation on women's speech in the Pentecostal Church as well as for several published articles. This article illustrates my early interest in women's religious speech, their verbal art in performance, and the distinctions between (female) power and (male) authority. This article also pays tribute to the structure of women's testimony performance and their generous use of personal narrative to support their right to speak within the religious service. At this point in my work, I utilized oral formulaic theory to explore the use of formulae, line breaks, and performance style as delineated by Albert Lord (1976). My use of line breaks based on breath pauses in performance also relied on Bruce Rosenberg's *The Art of the American Folk Preacher* and Dennis Tedlock's models for transcription. The publication of Richard Bauman's *Verbal Art as Performance* in 1977 took those theories in directions more useful for contemporary folklorists and greatly influenced this article and my subsequent work on the performed verbal arts of women. This was a heady time for the study of folklore as it flew in the face of the longstanding study of folklore "texts," with identifiable motifs that were assumed to be stable and could be codified. With new attention to both context and performance, the notion of a stable text was supplanted by the recognition that the text was emergent within different contexts and for various reasons within each performance. These innovative approaches took advantage of the work being done by Dell Hymes, Dan Ben-Amos, Kenneth Goldstein, and others in the newly emerging field of sociolinguistics that spawned the ethnography of communication and ethnography of performance scholarship that offered a great deal to folklorists working with oral performance. Although there are many sentences and assertions in this early work that I would phrase differently today, such as using the term "sex-linked" rather than "gendered," I have left this article much as it appeared in the *Journal of American Folklore* 96, no. 382 (1983): 434–459.

newcomer to a Pentecostal religious service would report that women dominate the services: they are there in greater numbers; they sing more; they march and dance around the church with tambourines more than men do; they are more likely the ones to go into a trance, jerk, fall down, and speak in tongues; and it is they who more often go forward to the altar area for special healing. For all of this, male authority and control in a Pentecostal church must not be confused with female spiritual power. Although women can be preachers in this faith, at least in name, they are rarely pastors. Men maintain the position of authority in this religion that is based squarely on a biblical hierarchy that places women below men. The traditional sex-linked roles in this religious community dictate behavior models and support only those performances that maintain and perpetuate the status quo. By recognizing this fact, it is possible to understand the differences in the artistic verbal performances of Pentecostal men and women.

This study of women's speech in the Pentecostal religious service supports I. M. Lewis's contention that ecstatic religion is most attractive to those segments of society that are politically impotent, providing them a means for expression and group identity (Lewis 1971, 32). Denying any innate tendency toward hysteria in women, Lewis correlates the "peripherality of women" in most, if not all, social systems with female possession tendencies: "It is in terms of the exclusion of women from full participation in social and political affairs and their final subjection to men that we should seek to understand their marked prominence in peripheral possession" (1971, 88). Attraction to trance and possession experiences provides a means for establishing cohesion for disjointed groups, according to Lewis, who sees such experiences as "thinly disguised protest movements directed against the dominant sex. Thus, they play a significant part in the sex-war in traditional societies and cultures where women lack more obvious and direct means for forwarding their aims" (1971, 31). The testimony performances of Pentecostal women illustrate the artful manipulation of performance rules, delivering to the performers and their audience of other women a moment of respite from the domination by the male members of their religious community.

This study is based on fieldwork done with one white, rural Pentecostal church in southern Indiana. Although this church can be recognized as representative of the rural Pentecostal churches in this area, study of religious performance is enhanced by concentration on one church community. At Johnson's Creek Church, as at other rural Pentecostal churches, women are active participants in the services. They are encouraged to sing loudly, bring special prayer requests to the pastor, testify, sing "specials," listen to the preacher, "let God have his way" in ecstatic release, and come to the altar for salvation and healing. The entire focus of a service is on the anticipation of the moment(s) when the women are released from their rather formal daily poses and begin to respond to the ecstatic nature of the service and the admonitions of their male leaders. Charismatic religious behavior is seen as evidence of God's presence in the room. Women sing; women pray; women testify; women even preach. However, for all this activity, women manipulate the creative force of their verbal art most obviously in the performances of their testimonies. This can be illustrated by first examining the way Pentecostal women preach and by contrasting their style of preaching with their style of testifying. Although women are allowed to preach, they are *not* allowed to preach "like men"; it is only in the performance of their testimonies that they are permitted the freedom to perform such that they have potential for control of the services.

Pentecostalism permits both women and men to become preachers. Women can, in fact, become licensed preachers. One female Pentecostal showed me her "card" proving she was a licensed preacher in the United Apostolic Church of Jesus Christ, Inc. She explained her role as preacher in this way: "I can just do anything my husband can do. Now, there are some organizations that don't believe in women ministers. Some won't ordain them, won't give them licenses. But I get my turn too. I haven't been put down (asked to preach) on a regular basis yet, but they've been wanting me to preach a revival" (Connie S., May 21, 1980, her home, Stinesville, Indiana, interviewed by Elizabeth Peterson and E. Lawless). About her style of preaching, she said, "Of course, women, I don't preach like my husband. Everybody has their own style. I would say I preach a lot simpler than my husband does. My husband is just, I'll have to admit it, he's deeper than I am. Now, that's just my style, I mean, I'm just simple. As far as being educated in order to use big words and things like that, now, my husband can do that" (Connie S. 1980).

Some of the conflicts surrounding the reality of how women preach are revealed by what this woman says. Even though she has been licensed, she has not been given a regular position for preaching in the church. Furthermore, she is quick to pay deference to her husband as the better preacher and to limit her own capabilities. This woman's statements, as well as subsequent statements by her husband about her, support Robin Lakoff's observation that "we can learn about the way women view themselves and everyone's assumptions about the nature and role of women from the use of language in our culture, that is to say, the language used by and about women" (Lakoff 1975, 1). The issue of women preachers in the Pentecostal religion is certainly reflective of the cultural expectations and social role behaviors of both men and women in this faith.

Pentecostal uneasiness about women preachers comes from biblically-supported beliefs about the role and status of women. Since Pentecostals claim to take the Bible literally, it is difficult for them to justify allowing women to speak in church. Paul wrote to Timothy on this point: "Let the women learn in silence with all subjection. But I suffer not a woman to teach, nor to usurp authority over the man, but to be in silence" (1 Tim. 2:11, 12). And to the Corinthians, Paul wrote, "Let your women keep silence in the churches; for it is not permitted unto them to speak; but they are commanded to be under obedience, as also saith the law. And if they learn anything, let them ask their husbands at home, for it is a shame for women to speak in church" (1 Cor. 14:34, 35).

One male Pentecostal lay preacher talked with me at length on his views about male and female roles in the church. He related a story about a church he had wanted to "take over" as pastor, but there was a family of women at that church who had become accustomed to testifying so long that he never got a chance to preach: "Yeah, they'd get up and testify for half an hour. Dance and talk, dance and talk . . . it just wasn't right. It didn't give the minister a chance to minister them the word. There was three of them. Time they all got done it was time to send everybody home. I told them, I said, 'Well, God didn't say go out and testify; he said go out and preach the word. So I will preach the word, and then you can just dance all night.' And that's what I done. I done the preaching, and then I let them testify" (Marvin M., March 4, 1981, Heltonville School, Heltonville, Indiana, interviewed by E. Lawless).

About women preachers, he confided, "I never did care too much about women preachers. God didn't have any. He told the *men* to go out and preach the gospel. He never told a woman to do that. Here's what he said: 'A woman's place is at home, rearing the children.'" Primarily, he asserted that women were not equipped to deal with the problems a Pentecostal preacher faces. He related several long, involved stories about how he and other preachers had been forced to fight off antagonistic Pentecostal haters with knives and guns. "Lord told his disciples, 'I send you amongst wolves.'

Now, do you think I'd send my wife out amongst a bunch of heathens? Sinners don't care what they do. They'll string you out. They don't care." When asked what the role of women ought to be within the church, he answered, "They are handmaidens. They should wait upon the ministers of the church. . . . A woman's got no right. She is over the house. She is not over a man. A man is over the woman, and Christ is over the man, over the church. Now, she's got a place in the church as a Sunday School teacher or maybe as advising to the women. But she can't stand up in that pulpit and tell people what to do because that makes her over the man, and that's not according to God's word" (Marvin M., May 4, 1981).

Of course, the central issue here is not the danger involved in the ministry but the symbolic implications of having a woman stand in the position of authority—behind the pulpit. This is interpreted as having the potential for usurping authority from the men and clearly makes them nervous. That the issue is a gendered one and that women are denied the right to the platform because of their "natural" role as sexual being is supported by the same man's final statement: "A woman can't pull a church together. People won't go to hear a woman preach . . . unless old men will. Just to be honest with you, the way a woman might act, squatting around, men would go. Some of them, old men, are just crazy about women preachers" (Marvin M. 1981).

In contrast, women who feel called to be preachers do find scriptural support for their calling. One female preacher's words are echoed by other women who support female preaching: "The Bible does give us women this right. It says 'in the last days'—this is in Joel and also in Acts—'I will pour out my spirit on all flesh, your sons and your *daughters* shall prophesy.' And he said, 'Upon my handmaidens I will pour out my spirit.' So the word allows us to be handmaidens, and the men have to give us that right" (Wanda N., July 2, 1980, Bloomington, Indiana). This woman recognized that in contrast to Paul's directives that women are not to teach or even to speak, this verse offers a justification for her own endeavors as a preacher. Most Pentecostals who rely on these verses as proof that women should be able to preach point out that these are the "last days" and that all the preaching possible is needed to save the world before the "end" comes.

Like the male preacher above, the female preacher is aware of her potential to be viewed as a sex object. She is careful not to present herself as anything other than a meek female who has actually had no choice in the matter.

> I always present myself as a handmaiden of the Lord. Let the men take the part of the ministry and the government of the church because they are the head. The Bible clearly says we are the weaker vessel. Sometimes I'm called to a church and I run into a hard spirit at first. I say, "Relax, I don't call myself a preacher. Let the men do that; it's all right. But you have got to give me the right to be a handmaiden of the Lord, and he has poured out his spirit unto me, and he has called me into his work, and I'm here." (Wanda N. 1980)

She is aware of the importance of her demeanor and dress while in front of a congregation, and in the following statement, she identifies what she sees as the difference between the way men and women preach.

> I have always tried to be a woman. I resent in my own heart seeing women take the platform and try to be mannish. This is the first mistake women make. We are women. We are the weaker vessel. I try to give honor to the ministry. I try to be subject to them. I never try to act mannish. I don't want to act like a man. I am a woman. I don't exhort, and I am not as rambunctious, you might say, as some men. . . . I always dress in white in the platform because I do not feel that is a place to display clothes. Many, many people watch these things. (Wanda N. 1980)

In the infrequent cases where women are allowed to preach, the male pastor of the church leads the service until the woman preacher takes the sermon slot and stands behind the pulpit. When she has finished her sermon, the pastor takes the authority back and conducts the altar call, while the woman returns to her place on a pew in the congregation. Lakoff has suggested that "women's language," that is, both language used by women and language about women, "submerges a woman's personal identity, by denying her the means of expressing herself strongly, on the one hand, and encouraging expressions that suggest triviality in subject matter and uncertainty about it, on the other" (Lakoff 1975, 7). This is often manifested in speaking of the woman as a sex object and/or by suggesting that she is not a serious person. The following introduction by a male pastor for his wife-preacher's sermon is an excellent example of what Lakoff is talking about:

> Sister Connie's going to speak for us tonight. She's been reading and studying and praying all week. I came home, you know, and found a tablet, you know, tablet sheets of paper all over the dresser, and so I knew she'd been up to something. I finally asked her what it was, and she admitted to it and told me a little of it. So I said, "Well, when are you going to do it?" "Whenever I get the chance." And I said, "How 'bout this Saturday night?" So I'm glad that she did this, reading and studying the things of God. You know, that's how we grow, and I think we ought to be about our father's business. So we're glad to have Sister Connie come. Glad to have her as a helpmate. So I want her to

come down and deliver whatever she has. (Willie S., May 28, 1980, Johnson's Creek Church)

Compare the above introduction with another given by the same pastor when introducing a visiting male preacher: "We're glad to have Brother Richards here with us tonight. We know the Lord has been good tonight; we've really felt the spirit tonight and love to feel the spirit of the Lord. Amen. I know Brother Richards; he's come now a few times to preach for us, and I know the way he preaches tonight, and I know the rest is going to be full of the same. Amen. We just want him to preach until he gets tired. Everybody that agrees, say 'Amen'" (Willie S., May 17, 1980, Johnson's Creek Church).

The pastor-husband's introduction for his wife's "sermon" is a carefully calculated speech meant to place her squarely in her place as trivial woman and his own "helpmate." His description of her activities and what he "found" upon arriving at his home are more suggestive of a parent-child relationship than that of a husband-wife. The full implication is that he "caught" her at something she really ought not to be doing. She "admitted" being "up to something" and will "do it" whenever he allows her to do it. He never uses the word "preach" in describing what she will do in the pulpit and never suggests that what she will deliver will be inspiring and likely to invoke the spirit of God as he does in introducing the male preacher.

The attitude displayed by this Pentecostal pastor appears to be inconsistent with the commonly held notion that women are more spiritual than men, closer to nature as they are and more likely to be emotional, be possessed by the spirit, and exhibit uninhibited ecstatic behaviors. The difference is that women are allowed to exhibit all these behaviors only within certain carefully bounded "frames" of the service. A woman standing behind the pulpit offers such a threat to male authority and control that in that position she is relegated to a narrowly confined role, one that cannot possibly be construed as a "preacher" role. To do so would be to usurp the authority of all the men in the room. The female preacher clearly recognizes her precarious position and plays the role of the inadequate woman sent by God to address the congregation. She is careful to reassure everyone in attendance that she will comply with all their expectations; she will play the game with the prescribed rules. Sister Connie begins her sermon this way:

Well, I kinda hope you all aren't expecting too much. He kinda put me out there on a limb. I praise the Lord tonight because truly he is so good to me.

Now I want you to know that I never thought about these things on my own. I prayed, and the Lord revealed these things to me. I have not got that much sense in my own head. The Lord has to show me things. I'm not intelligent. I never went to college. I don't have any education, learning in this world. But whatever the Lord give me, he give it to me straight from him. We'll start. Now this may be kinda like teaching, I don't know, you know, sometimes it's kinda hard to preach, but maybe a mixture of both, preaching and teaching. (Connie S., May 28, 1980, Johnson's Creek)

What Sister Connie delivered that night was a calm, thoroughly contemplated speech based on her own interpretation of the symbolism of the crucifixion of Jesus Christ. In style of delivery, this "sermon" was much more like the teaching of a Sunday School lesson; Sister Connie was teaching, not preaching. At one point in the sermon, she apologized, "I may be going kinda slow and not jumping around and being real fiery." However, I *have* seen Sister Connie jump around, and I have heard her being "real fiery," not from the pulpit, to be sure, but from her position at her pew, in the congregation, where her verbal skills are not a threat to male authority. In fact, the frame in which women are more likely to speak in ways that are stylistically closer to "preaching" is in their testimonies.

The Testimonies

Like the spontaneous fundamentalist sermons of men examined by Bruce Rosenberg in *The Art of the American Folk Preacher* (1970), the *testimonies* of the women at Johnson's Creek Church display both standardized formulaic constructions and creative, improvised materials in a carefully wedded blend. Rosenberg identifies four kinds of "memorized" formulas in folk sermons, classified according to their function within a particular sermon:

1. Stable, frequently used "refrains," e.g., "Hark Hallelujah," "I want you to know."
2. Stimulants to the congregation, e.g., "Do you know what I'm talking about?"
3. Two kinds of formulas to:
   a. introduce dialogue, e.g., "The Bible said to me," and
   b. introduce narrative, e.g., "Every now and then."
4. Characteristic phrasing for advancing narrative, e.g., "by and by" (1970, 54–57).

According to Rosenberg, the original Parry-Lord concept of "formula" depended upon repetition: "By formula I mean a group of words which is regularly employed under the same metrical conditions to express a given essential idea" (Lord 1976, 4). Formulaic expressions denoted "a line or half line constructed on the pattern of the formula" (Lord 1976, 4). Rosenberg claims that "in the matter of verbatim repetition of phrases, the [folk] sermons [he collected] are even more formulaic than any epic Parry or Lord recorded" (Rosenberg 1970, 255).

Based on this concept of "formula," the testimonies of Pentecostal women indicate a significant reliance on the use of formula and formulaic phrases, especially in certain positions of the testimonies, such as introductions and conclusions. Like the sermons, the testimonies exhibit stable, frequently used "refrains" such as "Praise the Lord," "Hallelujah," and "Thank you, Lord," which may serve the same function as the "stalls" Rosenberg discusses (1970, 53). Stimulants are in evidence in the frequent use of the rhetorical "you know?," "you know what," and "I don't care; do you?" Standard metanarrational devices, such as "Let me tell you about it," introduce dialogue and narration within the testimonies. The similarities between women's testimonies and the male sermons analyzed by Rosenberg extend from formulaic construction into the areas of content and style of delivery.

The standardized concept of a typical testimony might take the form of the following testimony delivered by a man who was visiting Johnson's Creek Church.

> I'm glad I know the Lord.
> It's been about fifty-seven years ago
> I was going blind, and I got baptized in Jesus's name.
> The power of God came down
> and healed my body,
> filled me with his spirit.
> I'm thankful tonight
> to know that he'll answer prayers,
> anything you have need of.
> (Unidentified testifier, May 24, 1980, Johnson's Creek Church, Heltonville, Indiana)

Such a testimony can be heard at nearly any Pentecostal church service. It is a standard testimony capable of being delivered in any religious setting. This man was a visitor to Johnson's Creek Church; although he was not part of that church community, his testimony is recognized by the group as satisfactory. The same type of general testimony will often be heard in revivals or camp meetings that draw from several church communities. Most Pentecostals would, in fact, define a testimony as a speech that asserts something particular that God has done for them. I asked one man to explain the difference between testifying and preaching: "Testifying is what God has done for you. Testifying is what God has done for *you*. Nobody else, just done for you. And how good God's done for you. How he's forgive you of your sins. How he's raised you up off your sick bed and how he's put the words in your mouth to speak to somebody else when they ask you a question. But a minister's word is to reveal what the word of God reads and then interpret the meaning of it" (Marvin M., May 4, 1981).

The concept of testifying is closely aligned with the notion of witnessing. Through witnessing, members encourage outsiders to come to church or seek the Holy Ghost by telling them stories about their own conversion and the miraculous things God has done for them since.

Within the context of the closely knit church community at Johnson's Creek, however, the idealized notion of what constitutes a testimony and what, in fact, the women say when they testify are two different things. Analysis of many testimonies delivered in the context of this one church community reveals patterns of speaking, patterns of delivery, and a consistency of content that are quite unlike the man's testimony given above. Seldom do the women at Johnson's Creek testify about what God has done for them in terms of a specific healing or a deliverance from danger or pain. Theirs is a shared testimony that confirms their role and status in the community and homes and calls for mutual support from the other women for the continued ability to maintain community expectations. At the same time, testifying provides a forum for creative speaking and a temporary lapse of the normal impotency of the women. Each woman at Johnson's Creek can create for herself a space as the center of attention, and, if her delivery is convincing and effective, she may, in fact, take control of the situation, causing things "to happen," altering the social situation, or inverting the status quo, but only as long as the allotted prescribed time. Richard Bauman has addressed the potential power of performance to redefine social relations: "It is part of the essence of performance that it offers to the participants a special enhancement of experience, bringing with it a heightened intensity of communicative interaction which binds the audience to the performer in a way that is specific to performance as a mode of communication. Through his [*sic*] performance, the performer elicits the participative attention and energy of his audience, and to the extent that they value his performance, they will allow themselves to be caught up in it. When this happens, the performer gains a measure of prestige and control over the audience" (Bauman 1977, 43–44).

As a testifier, a woman performer in the religious service does not threaten male authority; by speaking from her place within the congregation, she reaffirms her position and confirms everyone's expectations. Yet she manages to manipulate the situation to her best advantage by communicating her concerns to her fellow sisters and asking for their unabated support for her own (and their) efforts to sustain the female role.

Testimony Structure

In describing Mexican *corridos* as a performance event, John McDowell draws on Roger Abrahams's use of the term "enactment" (McDowell 1981, 50). The same approach will aid in conceptualizing the testimonies performed in the context of a church service at Johnson's Creek. Abrahams defines enactment as "a cultural event in which community members come together to participate, employ the deepest and most complex multivocal and polyvalent signs and symbols of their repertoire of expression, thus entering into a potentially significant experience" (Abrahams 1978, 80).

Like the *corridos*, the testimonies embody a "powerful statement of community values and orientations" (McDowell 1981, 50). To show how this is so, I will examine testimonies of the women at Johnson's Creek to illustrate how structurally, thematically, and stylistically these testimonies comment upon community values and expectations and how in their performed context they become and elicit "significant experience."

The testimonies of the Johnson's Creek women are highly formulaic. They display standard beginnings and endings; enough formulaic statements are available that a testifier can give an entirely appropriate testimony without injecting a single novel phrase into the delivery. Testimonies may exhibit personal creativity in either content or style of delivery, if the structure of the testimony is maintained. Table 1.1 indicates the various traditional phrases that occur and recur in the testimonies at Johnson's Creek. The following actual testimonies illustrate how these standard, formulaic lines are rendered in performances in the church context. I have rendered my transcriptions of testimonies into lines based on where natural and dramatic breath pauses occur during actual performances.[2]

Testimony 1

I'm so glad to be here tonight.
I'm so glad for Jesus,
for his many blessings.
I praise him tonight

because he's kept his hands upon us
during this hot weather.
No doubt there's many people
left this earth
because of the heat.
I'm thankful tonight that Jesus
showed his mercy toward us.
I love him tonight.
And I have a desire
to go all the way with him.
(Paloma A., May 17, 1980, Johnson's Creek Church)

Testimony 2

Tonight, I want to thank the Lord
for the privilege of being in his house.
I told my children tonight
I felt so bad,
but once I got here, I feel better.
Praise the Lord.
I'm glad to be here tonight.
I know he's real.
I praise him tonight
because I can be out to the house of the Lord.
He is able tonight to do all things.
I love him tonight.
I praise him for everything.
Tonight, it's my desire to be stronger
and grow closer to him.
I desire your prayers
so I can get his favors,
do what he'd have me to do.
(Betty P., July 12, 1980, Johnson's Creek)

Testimony 3

I want to thank the Lord tonight
for what he means to me.
I want to thank him
because I know that he's a great big God
and is here to take me through
if I will just put my hand in his.
(Patsy S., July 12, 1980, Johnson's Creek)

The three testimonies given here are obviously based almost entirely upon identifiable formulaic phrases and stanzas as illustrated in table 1.1.

Table 1.1. Formulaic Phrases Occurring in Testimonies

I want to thank the Lord for the privilege of being in his house tonight

_____ for the privilege of standing before him

_____ for the privilege of testifying here tonight.

Tonight, before I came, I felt so bad

_____ I felt so tired and worn out

_____ I thought I would just stay home,

but I'm so glad to be in his house.

I know he is Real.

_____ God is Real.

I want to praise him tonight for all the things he's done for me

_____ for his goodness

_____ for his spirit

_____ for his many blessings.

I love him tonight.

I know he is able to do all things tonight.

He's a great big God.

It's my desire (my heart's desire) to be stronger

_____ to walk closer to him

_____ to stand by him

_____ to get a blessing tonight

_____ to be in heaven with him.

I want to receive his blessing tonight

_____ feel his spirit

_____ get a blessing tonight.

I desire your prayers.

Pray for me that I will do what he'd have me do

_____ do what he'd want me to do

_____ do his will

_____ grow closer to him.

I don't want to be lost.

I don't know what tomorrow (next week) will bring.

He won't pull me down

_____ fail me.

(*Continued*)

Table 1.1. Continued

He will put his arms close around me

_____ is a mighty friend

_____ will stand close beside me

_____ will keep his hand upon me,

no matter what happens.

I want to be ready to meet him.

Without Jesus I am nothing

_____ there is no heaven.

I want to go all the way with him

_____ let him have his way.

Let go.

Get more by reaching out.

Obey.

Praise the Lord.

Amen.

Thank you, Jesus.

Hallelujah.

Truly tonight.

As simple examples of actual testimonies, they can serve to illustrate certain structural "positions" within the testimonies.[3] The first position is the introduction. Introductory formulas are fairly standard and generally fall into what I shall designate as Position 1, where they are recognized as constituting the introduction of a testimony; some of the phrases characteristic of the introduction, however, may appear also in the body of a testimony as fillers or stalls. Position 1 usually takes a variation of the following form and carries what Roman Jakobson (1960, 354) has designated an "emotive function," serving as it does to focus on the addresser's "attitude toward what he is speaking about."

> Position 1 (introduction)   I want to thank the Lord tonight
> for the privilege of being in his house tonight.
> [or]
> I'm glad to be here tonight.
> [or]
> I want to stand up tonight and praise the Lord
> for letting me be here tonight.

The standardized, identifiable introduction (Position 1) may actually contain two or more parts, the second serving to reiterate the first. When positions are further segmented into identifiable subgroupings, I have designated these with a subscript number, Position 1_1. For example:

Position 1_1 I told my children tonight

I felt so bad,

but once I got here, I felt better.

[or]

There are a lot of things

I could be doing tonight.

And I'd probably enjoy a few of them.

But you know I enjoy coming to church.

Position 2, which serves to direct the focus from the addresser to the addressee, generally takes the form of a metanarrational device intended to introduce an upcoming narrative and serves a vocative or imperative function that instructs the addressee to "listen," as well as doubly serving a phatic or contact function intended to establish and maintain communication (Jakobson 1960, 355). We use metanarrational devices in both formal and informal speech to signal the listener: "Let me tell you a story about that" or "that happened to me once."

In the most variable position in a testimony, Position 3, a performer may employ a narrational mode of discourse. Forms of narration range from complete stories to reminiscences to fragmented narratives. Many of the stories embedded within testimonies given by women at Johnson's Creek take the form of *exempla*, or stories told with the intent to convey a moral or spiritual message; exempla have traditionally been associated with sermons (see Rosenberg 1970, 47). I have designated the explication of these stories within the testimonies as Position 4. The explication serves to justify the relating of the narrative within the context of the testimony and the religious service; it also serves to mark the end of one narration. Testimonies may, in fact, relate several reminiscences, personal experience stories, or anecdotes. The transition from one to another is generally recognized by the framing that the metanarrational device (Position 2) and the explication (Position 4) provide.

The following testimony is representative of the women's testimonies at Johnson's Creek. Note the use of formulaic phrases within easily discernable "positions," which have been separated by the use of broken lines. The performer's use of the narrative mode appears in two separate personal experience stories and reminiscences (Position 3).

Testimony 4

Position 1_1
(introduction)

I wouldn't want to come out to the
house of the Lord
without testifying.

***

Position 1_2

You know, I love the Lord with all my heart,
and I want to walk close to him
because I realize, like Martha said,
it's going to take a holy life, a pure, clean life,
and you got to have it down deep in our souls
if we're going to make it through
because we're not going to fool God anytime.
He knows everything we do
and everything we say,
and if we're not true to him, he knows all about it.

***

Position 2_1
(metanarrational device)

You know, I want to walk close to him.
I want to tell you about it.
You know, we sing that song about "Honey in the Rock."
You know, I love that song.

Position 3_1 (narrative)

But years and years and years ago,
when I was a little girl,
we still sung that "Honey in the Rock."
It was still just the same.
We can go to the Lord and the rock and the foundation,
and they say it tastes sweet and it tastes good.
There's Honey in the Rock.
You know, people that don't realize that God's word says these things,
unless you understand what's it's talking about,

you won't understand what you're saying.

Back then, when I was a child,

we'd play back of the church.

We'd get together as children and do the singing

and pray, of course, we were

trying to—we wasn't trying to make fun—

we was trying to follow what the old folks did.

And I had a cousin,

she had to sing "Honey in the Rock" every time we "had church."

I sang that song so much

I got tired of singing that song,

but she wouldn't have church if she didn't sing "Honey in the Rock" first.

But, you know, I love that song,

but back then I just didn't want to sing that song at all

because I got so tired of it.

But I didn't realize what we was a-singing about.

It was just so much singing,

it was just words.

In other words, to get the meaning out of it.

I wasn't seeing how good God was and how good the song was.

I don't know why she loved it so good,

but she always wanted to sing it.

But I'll always think about it.

It's been many, many years,

still every time we sing that song, I think of her.

Now, since I know what I'm singing about,

I really love to sing that song.

***

And truly I love the Lord.

***

Position 2$_2$

And I think about so many times,
so many times when we,
when things that have happened many years ago,
things come up like this.
They still bring memories back to you.

Position 3$_2$

The old times when we used to have such good services,
so many people would come out.
Of course, there wasn't nothing else to go to,
only church, back then.
There wasn't nothing around in the country here of the world to go to,
and we didn't have no cars
and no way of going anywhere,
only walk and go in the horse and buggy
or horses and wagons,
and everybody almost that was able went to church,
sinners and everybody, and the house would be full,
and outside the yard would be full
standing around.
And so many children, ah, yes,
and so many of them have gone on to meet the Lord,
and so many of them were faithful to God all these years
and all the goodness of the earth.

***

Position 4 (explication)

Thinking about it so many times,
you know, the good things of God,
how good he's been to us
and how he's kept us all these years,
brought us through so many hard places,
so many heartaches and so many trials,
so many tests that God has put us, us, brought us through.
He's always brought us out victorious.

***

Position 5 (conclusion)   Truly tonight, I love him with all my heart.

I want to walk closer to him

and do the things that he'd be pleased with

and do just what he'd have me to do.

Pray for me.

The first eleven lines of this testimony illustrate the creative manipulation of standard formulaic lines rendered by a seasoned testifier, especially in her multifaceted introduction (Position 1). In the body of her testimony, this performer inserts two personal experience narratives introduced by standard metanarrational devices that alert the listener to the impending story. Position 2_1 (metanarrational device) in the first half of the testimony takes the form of "I want to tell you about it." The story proper, Position 3, begins "but years and years and years ago, when I was a little girl." Position 2_2 designates the second metanarrational device in this testimony, which introduces a narrative closer in style to a reminiscence: "And I think about so many times . . . things come up like this. They still bring back memories to you." In the first narrative, the testifier tells about a young cousin who would not play church without first singing "Honey in the Rock." To justify telling that story in the church context, the performer clearly intends the story to contain a message for the group. This is made clear in the explication of her story (Position 4): "But back then I just didn't realize what we was a-singing about . . . people don't realize. Unless you understand what it's talking about, you won't understand what you're saying." Her story is meant to direct church members to pay attention to what they are singing about in order to understand the song's meaning and to have the song mean something to them. Structurally, the lines further serve to signal the end of the narrative. This patterning follows the text-context-application pattern of Puritan sermons that Rosenberg (1970, 32) documents as appearing in contemporary folk sermons. Her first personal experience narrative leads her naturally into reminiscing about what going to church used to be like (Position 2z): "They still bring memories back to you," which introduces another narrative that is, in turn, followed by its own explication (Position 4).

Position 5, or the closing, is usually as standard and formulaic as Position 1, the introduction. In the testimony above, it is clear to the listener when the performer is "winding down," and the testifier relies more completely on formulas. Both the formulaic patterns of these lines and the delivery style serve to signal the termination of the testimony.

Position 5 (closing)   Truly tonight, I love him with all my heart.

I want to walk closer to him

and do the things that he'd be pleased with

and do just what he'd have me to do.

Pray for me.

The following testimony also illustrates the "positions" of a testimony:

Testimony 5

Position 1   Hallelujah, thank you, Lord. Hallelujah, the Lord is wonderful tonight.

Position 2   I'm going to tell this little ol' story for the benefit of those who need a blessing.

Position 3   You know, I had a window in the kitchen that was broke out.

So Brother Willie put a piece of tin in there.

And he had a little hole in there,

he was going to put a stove in there,

but that didn't work out too good.

But he left the tin there, and, you know,

that just bothered me and bothered me and bothered me,

and I wanted that tin out of there so bad.

But I couldn't find any glass to put in it,

so, finally, it bothered me so much that I got up,

and I went through all the junk and everything around,

and I hunted for some glass until I fixed it.

***

Position 4   You know what? It's so much better to have light than it is to have darkness.

It's so much better to have Jesus living within you

than to have these old burdens deep down in here

just pressing down, you know.

And you know what?

It was worth every minute of the effort I put forth

to get that glass in there.

Tonight, I want you to reach up to Jesus.

Oh, Hallelujah, I believe he's worth every effort

that we put forth.

The things that he can give us

can take us through another week,

another month.

Whatever we need,

the Lord will be there

to give it to us.

Position 5   I desire your prayers.

I love the Lord tonight,

and I know he's an answering God.

Note that the most popular "connectors" in the testimonies of the women at Johnson's Creek are "you know" and "tonight"; these phrases are used consistently and provide continuity from testimony to testimony. The "you know" serves a stylistic function as well, maintaining the phatic (contact) function of communication (Jakobson 1960, 355). The "tonight" serves to place the testimony in the immediate context, attempting, actually, to destandardize the testimony but in the process becomes one of the most standard features of the deliveries.

Testimony Style

Women at Johnson's Creek deliver their testimonies in a wide range of styles. A woman may stand abruptly, deliver a standardized, completely formulaic testimony, and sit down. In general, women who perform in this manner do so consistently. On the other hand, other women in the group become recognized as the performers of creative, personalized testimonies. Still others may rely on standard formulas but expend their creative energies on the style of delivery rather than content. From service to service, the individual testifiers have identifiable styles of testimony delivery.

It is a sacred duty to give a testimony in each church service. The women at Johnson's Creek Church take this obligation seriously, and most deliver a testimony at each service they attend. While a hastily delivered formulaic testimony fulfills the requirement to testify, there is no question that the most important aspect of a woman's testimony performance is its effect on the audience. In fact, audience reaction to a testimony, like audience reaction to a folk sermon, is the manifestation of the audience evaluation of the competency of the performer. Testimonies delivered in a rushed, self-conscious manner rarely merit more than a quiet "Amen" at their termination. The women who deliver them are not capitalizing on the potential for power that lies with an effective delivery, even though they are meeting the requirements for giving their testimony. Effective delivery may rely on structure, style of delivery, content, or combinations thereof. The following is a transcription of a testimony that relies almost entirely upon formulaic "stanzas" delivered one after another. The transcription may suggest a rather staid testimony as the performer does not allow herself to interject personal statements, nor does she utilize a narrative mode within her testimony. However, this particular performer has a unique testimony delivery style. Her performances are always long and seem to ramble, but her style of delivery is sincere, tearful, high-pitched, fast, nearly breathless, and very close to a chant, complete with the gasp at the end of the line as punctuation (cf. Rosenberg 1970, 43).

Testimony 6

Position 1 (introduction)

I praise the Lord tonight
for what he is to me and for another privilege
of being in the house of God,
because he's kept us safe for yet another day.

***

If you love the Lord,
you wouldn't want to do anything
to disgrace his name, uh,

***

I've found him a true friend
in time of trouble.

***

You know God is always near
if we just call upon him, uh,

***

there's so many times
we grumble and complain,
and we don't always understand
the things that God's taking us through, uh,
but then someone will come along
and will say something
that will touch our hearts
and bring us back
into the avenues of truth, uh,

***

You know God is always there.
I was sitting there thinking
about that song that said
"Just go and tell Jesus on me," uh,
"whatever our weakness may be," uh,
"if you are my brother,
then don't tell another,
. just go and tell Jesus on me," uh.

***

You know, so many times
we go to others with our trials and our tasks
and the things that are brought our way
and talk about one another
in ways that are not Christian-like.

Position 2   This was brought home so forcefully
(metanarrational device)

Position 3 (aborted   the other day when Lana came home,
narrative)   and she said when she got in trouble,
she just went to God with it.

***

Position 4 (explication)   you know, and I thought, my,
how much better our lives would be
if we'd all follow that policy.
When we're in trouble,
and we see our loved ones in trouble,

if we'd just go to God;

he has the answer to every problem.

***

Position 5 (conclusion)   Pray for me

that I may walk the straight and narrow way.

(Mrs. E. D., May 17, 1980, Johnson's Creek Church)

The introduction to this testimony is standard (lines 1–4) and is followed by a series of formulaic subparts strung together, an aborted narrative, and a standard, formulaic conclusion. However, it is the style of delivery of this testimony that is of concern here.

The introduction was delivered in a low-key tone in recitation style. However, by the fifth, sixth, and seventh lines, the delivery had accelerated considerably, the pitch of the voice had risen, and the delivery became akin to the folk preacher's style with an "uh" punctuating the ends of lines 7, 11, 15, 20, 24, 25, and 28. As might be expected, the most personal lines in this testimony, lines 34–37, deviate from the chanted style, but they were, nevertheless, delivered in a high-pitched, breathless manner. This testimony was delivered in the same service as Testimony 5 given above. Although radically different in structural composition, both testimonies elicited intense audience response as a result of their deliveries.

The following is another testimony by the same woman who delivered Testimony 5 above; both are typical testimony performances for this woman. It is common for her to be enthusiastic in her performance; she frequently utilizes narration and interjects personal elements into her testimonies. She is extremely adept at gaining empathy with her audience by relying on phatic questions such as "and you know what?" and "you know what I mean?"; she makes direct pleas to her audience, too, such as "I want you to reach up to Jesus." It is important to note that this is the same woman who was allowed to preach on the night described above.

Testimony 7

Blessed Jesus. Thank you, Jesus.
Tonight I love the Lord.
I thank him tonight,
and I praise him
because I know he's real in my heart
this night.

***

As we sang that song "Jesus on the Main Line,"
it just made me think, you know,
when you dig around sometimes,
you get down there,
and you get these little streams.
You know, these little streams,
they're just not enough,
there's just not enough water there.
But when we hit that main line,
Hallelujah,
you've got plenty of water,
you've got plenty,
when you get Jesus on the main line.
Hallelujah.
You've got just what you need.
You know, those little trinkles
they don't do much for me,
Thank you, Jesus,
for I've been under the Holy Spout.
Hallelujah.
It does a whole lot more for me,
thank you, Jesus.
Hallelujah.
You know I might make you stay up for a while
because, praise the Lord,
Hallelujah,
I know he is real.
Whoooooooo,
Glory,
I know he is real tonight.
You know when I sing
and when I testify,
everybody looks at me,
and they think I'm kind of
peculiar.
But you know tonight we are peculiar people.
But you know something?
I'm not ashamed of Jesus,
Hallelujah.
Because this is the *Lord*
that I sing
that I testify for
that I stomp my feet for

that I clap my hands for
it's Jesus Christ,
and I love him tonight, Lord,
and he is worthy
of all praises,
everything,
everything
that we can possibly do for him,
he is worthy of it
this night.
Hallelujah,
Whooooooooooooo.
(Connie S., May 17, 1980, Johnson's Creek Church)

This woman's performance of a testimony is much closer to a "preaching" style than her preaching; furthermore, this particular testimony is much closer to a sermon than it is to a testimony. Like the folk sermons discussed by Rosenberg, this woman's testimony suggests a smoothness of content and delivery that might only come through repeated performances, even though the testifier, like the folk preacher, would insist that testimonies are a gift of the Holy Ghost and are spontaneously inspired by God. The notion of a "prepared testimony" would be just as abhorrent to the testifier as the "memorized" or "practiced" sermon would be to a folk preacher (Rosenberg 1970, 30–33). The themes elaborated by the female testifier are more closely aligned to the manipulation of theme available to the preacher than to the testifiers. This testifier is able to leave the text-context-application rigidity and spontaneously create a "sermon" built on the images of trickles, streams, and the Holy Spout. As with sermons, single lines or thoughts are expanded, but the reliance on narrative themes can be bypassed if just enough logic holds the sermon together.

In the mode of the sermons, this testimony is chanted (although she is at all times intelligible) and the delivery of individual lines quite metrical:

Because this is the Lord that I sing
that I testify for
that I stomp my feet for
that I clap my hands for

As with the other testimonies, this performance has been transcribed to indicate the testifier's own breath punctuation. Notice that this testimony has shorter lines, indicative of a chanted delivery (Rosenberg 1970, 36).

The delivery style of this woman testifier would be significant to the group, indicating that the woman was filled with the spirit during this testimony, as the folk preacher is "fed by God" (Lawless 1981). Meter, rhyme, rhythm, and timing are all in evidence in this testimony performance.

Both the testimonies of this woman transcribed for this paper emulate preaching styles set firmly within a testimony "frame," especially through the use of introductions that mark them as testimony and by the delivery from a pew in the congregation. But the preaching style of delivery as well as the audience response and enthusiastic reaction to these testimonies suggest the capacity of the "testifying" to serve the same function as preaching. In fact, in the testimony given above, the performer is unable to utilize a standardized, formulaic closing because of the overwhelming, emotional response of the audience. The significant point is, of course, that women can speak like preachers within the framework of a testimony, but they cannot do so within the frame of the sermon. It is interesting to note as well that when this same woman was at the pulpit, she set her "preaching" within an identifiable *testimony* "frame" by inserting the following formula into the first part of her sermon:

I praise the Lord tonight
because truly he is so good to me.

This may have been an attempt on her part to assure her male counterparts that she knows her place even though she is, at the present time, in a man's place in the pulpit.

Testimony 7 supports the contention that this artful performer knows the potential for control of the service through her verbal skills. This testimony was delivered rapidly and was close in style to a preacher's chant. By the time the woman had finished her performance, the entire congregation of women was marching around the church, dancing, and swooning "in the spirit." The audience response to her testimony was unanimous. The performer gained complete control of the situation as she and the other women began to "feel something" and identified it as God in the room. The shouting in response to this testimony lasted a full nine and a half minutes. The entire group became one in its complete surrender to the ecstatic experience; it is at such times that tongue speaking is likely to appear within the testimony service and did occur immediately following the testimony. Throughout the shouting period, the testifying woman could be heard speaking in tongues. At seven and a half minutes into the shouting time, she was permitted to dominate the floor again and speak loudly in tongues. She then interpreted her own tongue speaking.

Testimony Content

Not only is the testimony discussed above poetic and the delivery powerful, the content of the message is loaded with importance for the performer and her audience. The esoteric message gives her words their impetus: we are peculiar, and we're not ashamed of it. She outlines what behavior will prove the women's pride in themselves and in their religion: singing, testifying, stomping, clapping. The response to this testimony attests to its success as a performance. The content of the testimony reflects and reinforces the shared beliefs, attitudes, and values of the women. Style of delivery and content work together to lend emotional power to the performance. All the testimonies in a given testimony service contribute to the creation of a complex entity, a rich mixture of communal knowledge, signs, and symbols interplayed against a backdrop of religious significance.

The testimonies of the women at Johnson's Creek reflect a deep sense of the women's own place in a "natural" scheme that positions them under the men in their lives and subjects them to the will and domination of all men as well as the will and domination of their male religious figure, Jesus Christ. According to their worldview, their place is in the home and in the church. If a meeting is scheduled, it is their duty to be there. The frequent apology for wanting to stay at home instead of coming to church is a confession of weakness and is a submission to the demands of God to be "in his house." The assertions that God's house is where a woman wants to be and that now that she's here, she's so glad she came are gestures of appeasement to a potentially unhappy God. She nearly always thanks God, in fact, for the "privilege" of being in his house, thanks him for allowing her the physical ability to come. Her presence is a tribute to his benevolence.

The formulaic phrases in the testimonies of these women reflect a remarkable sense of faith in God for their daily lives. The women admit to being weak, to failing God, to doubting, to not following his directives. Openly, publicly, the women profess the desire to "be stronger, walk closer, stand by him, do his will, do what he wants" in order that Jesus will not "fail me" or "pull me down" but will keep his "arms around me, be a mighty friend, stand close, keep his hand on me." The general tone in the testimonies is that life will be hard, and the only hope for dealing with a bleak unknown is to believe that there is a cause/effect factor existing between their compliance to the wishes of an unseen God and his protection from hardship and pain. Many of the testimonies attest to the "trials and tasks of life," the "cross of life," the "burden that we have to bear," the expectation that "next week is going to be tough," and that "life is full of problems and troubles." But the testimonies also reflect the hope for something better. Here on earth, life becomes bearable because Jesus will be a friend and protect the believer *if* she obeys his every demand, and heaven is the promise of the ultimate "better place," also available only to those who "walk the straight and narrow path." By and large, the testimonies serve to let the women speak to one another about how difficult their plight in life is, how they are attempting to cope, and to request that their sister group members pray for their ability to continue to do what is expected of them.

Like the folk preacher, the testifier relies on her skill in manipulating and recreating formulas as well as on her knowledge of and sensitivity to the powerful emotional effect of theme and content on her audience. When she gains control over the service context, structure, style, and theme are intrinsically intertwined to create the "significant experience"—the enactment of the testimony. The women identify this moment as the experience of a "blessing"; any or all of them may leave the testimony frame and begin to shout, dance, cry, march, and speak in tongues. The blessing that is associated in the women's minds with an ecstatic, uninhibited service is the assurance from God that he is real, that there is hope for next week, and no matter what happens, He will be there to help them—if they are good Pentecostal women. The reaffirmation of God as real and as present in the room is identified with the tongue speaking, as well as the interpretation of what God "said" through the tongue speaker. The tongues themselves are a sign to the group that God is present and has "shown" himself through the speech of a woman (Lawless 1981, 23–39). The interpretation of the tongues given in the above service is closely aligned with the tenor of the testimonies and serves to answer the requests of the women that God will not fail them, will not forsake them, will keep them safe. The lines of the interpretation come from the Bible and are given as the words spoken by God to Joshua following the death of Moses:

> As I was with Moses, so I will be with thee.
> I will not fail thee, nor forsake thee. (Joshua 1:5)

When the testimony enactment occurs, the performer and the members of her community become one, in sentiment and in purpose. For a brief time in most Pentecostal testimony services, the power of the speaking women threatens male authority. Of course, it never gets out of hand. The authority of the male pastor to reestablish the structural components of the service is not lost, only obscured. It is precisely at the moment of communal "blessing" that the women create a situation in which they exhibit their own natural powers, a space in which to be free to communicate with each other and experience in that moment ecstatic joy. And as long as the moment is recognized by the group as the manifestation of God's spirit rather than the women's spirit, their moment is secure.

Women have developed a forum for a traditional expressive verbal art within the Pentecostal religious service. That forum is not, however, easily discernible or readily extrapolated from the service as a whole. Women can preach, but the restrictions upon their verbal and kinesic behavior in a position behind the pulpit are so constricting that expressive preaching is difficult. However, from her pew, the Pentecostal woman can stand and speak; from that position, she and the members of her sister group are able to transform the service through their verbal powers. They gain control through verbal art—short-lived control, to be sure, but a masterful illustration of the power of words.

Notes

1. To protect the privacy of the congregations, all participants' names have been changed, as well as the name of the churches. This article constitutes a good portion of the final chapter of my dissertation on women's speech in the Pentecostal church (1982). I especially thank Mary Ellen Brown at Indiana University for her incredible support and helpful criticisms of this material.

2. Dennis Tedlock uses line breaks to indicate pauses as well (1972, 122). For other approaches to performance transcriptions, compare Lord (1976, 30–67) and Hymes (1981, 309–341).

3. As far as I am aware, no other scholar has employed this term to designate structural elements in oral texts. Hymes (1981) does use "narrative sequences," "stanzas," "segments," "actions," and "episodes."

References Cited

Abrahams, Roger. 1978. "Toward an Enactment-Centered Theory of Folklore." In *Frontiers of Folklore*, edited by William R. Bascom, 79–120. Boulder: Westview Press.

Bauman, Richard. 1977. *Verbal Art as Performance*. Rowley, MA: Newbury House.

Ben-Amos, Dan, and Kenneth S. Goldstein, eds. 1975. *Folklore: Performance and Communication* [Approaches to Semiotics 40]. The Hague: Mouton.

Hymes, Dell. 1981. *"In Vain I Tried to Tell You": Essays in Native American Ethnopoetics*. Philadelphia: University of Pennsylvania Press.

Jakobson, Roman. 1960. "Closing Statement: Linguistics and Poetics." In *Style in Language*, edited by Thomas A. Sebeok, 350–377. Cambridge: MIT Press.

Lakoff, Robin. 1975. *Language and Woman's Place*. New York: Harper & Row.

Lawless, Elaine J. 1981. " 'What Did She Say?' An Application of Pierce's General Theory of Signs to Glossolalia in the Pentecostal Religion." *Folklore Forum* 3:23–39.

Lewis, I. M. 1971. *Ecstatic Religion*. Middlesex, England: Penguin Books Ltd.

Lord, Albert B. 1976. *The Singer of Tales*. New York: Atheneum.

McDowell, John Holmes. 1981. "The Corrido of Greater Mexico as Discourse, Music and Event." In *"And Other Neighborly Names": Social Process and Cultural Image in Texas Folklore*, edited by Richard Bauman and Roger D. Abrahams, 44–75. Austin: University of Texas Press.

Rosenberg, Bruce. 1970. *The Art of the American Folk Preacher*. New York: Oxford University Press.

Tedlock, Dennis. 1972. "On the Translation of Style in Oral Narrative." In *Toward New Perspectives in Folklore*, edited by America Paredes and Richard Bauman, 114–133. Austin: University of Texas Press.

2

RESCRIPTING THEIR LIVES
AND NARRATIVES

Spiritual Life Stories of Pentecostal Women Preachers

P ENTECOSTALISM IS A TWENTIETH-CENTURY, FUNDAMENTALIST, CHAR-
ISMATIC RELIGION THAT draws on the Holiness tradition of early Meth-
odism, especially religious injunctions concerning Christian behavior and
dress, one that stresses the importance of spirit-led and spirit-filled religious services (see Synan; Dieter; Nils Block-Hoell; Hollenweger; Anderson; Lawless, 1983, 1986, 1988a; and Bruce). Personal salvific encounters with
the Holy Spirit include public testimonies and experiences of glossolalia, or
speaking in tongues, as evidence of possession by the spirit (Lawless 1988;
1994; 2007). Since 1978, I have been researching and writing about the role
of women in this staunchly patriarchal religion as it is practiced in southern Indiana and southern Missouri in white, rural congregations. In this
rural, regional context, in the home and in the church, Pentecostal males
claim complete power, control, and authority over women and children;

Author's note: This article is perhaps most significant because it was published, in 1991, in
a non-folklore journal. Early in my career, I was concerned that much of the work folklorists do remains an isolated conversation in our own journals, particularly in the realm of
narrative. I still believe this is true; it seems folklorists read widely in affiliated fields and
utilize the work of scholars outside folklore, but too often I still read articles on narrative that
fail to notice the important work folklorists contribute. This article, published in a journal
devoted to the feminist study of religion, attempted to bring my knowledge of narrative work
in literature, religious studies, and feminism to bear on the narratives I was recording from
the women ministers I was studying at the time. My ethnographic approach offers something
new to many religion scholars, as does my attention to the oral narratives of religious women.
First published in *Journal for the Feminist Study of Religion* 7, no. 1 (Spring 1991): 53–71.

this dominant position for men is supported by a Pentecostal interpretation of Paul's writing in the New Testament, especially passages (always cited from the King James Version) that explicitly deny women authority and a religious voice: "But I suffer not a woman to teach, nor to usurp authority over the man, but to be in silence" (1 Tim. 2:12) and "Let your women keep silence in the churches: for it is not permitted unto them to speak" (1 Cor. 12:34).

Within this religious context, women who have become preachers and those who seek access to the pulpit or seek to maintain that access as pastors tell stories about their calling. In long testimonies, sometimes in prayers, in "witnessing" to others, in private conversations, and in their sermons, women tell their life stories. And, in the course of my research, they told their stories to me. This article, then, is an examination of the stories Pentecostal women preachers tell, illustrating how limiting our notions of "life stories" have been, and offering an examination of how life stories can become strategies for female liberation in sociocultural/religious contexts that openly work toward female subjection and submission to males. It will, finally, point to the fact that while the rescripted lives liberate in one sense, they can deny women the right to their own stories at the same time.

Field Research and Methodology

My fieldwork with Pentecostal women began while I was a graduate student in folklore studies at Indiana University.[1] I lived five miles south of Bloomington, Indiana, in the limestone quarry region. Nearby Bedford claims to be "The Limestone Capitol of the World," yet a drive through the countryside provides evidence of an industry that no longer thrives and has left the land looking used and abandoned. Strip mining has rendered the hills stark, with no vegetation replanted to cover the scars of years of abuse. Pieces of heavy machinery quietly stand rusting next to deep and mysterious quarries now filled with clear, blue water. In truth, the limestone industry provides little work for the people in this region these days. Work is predominately seasonal, for the limestone cannot be cut in the cold winter months. In the winter, quarry workers must seek government assistance to feed their families and heat their homes. Most of the small towns in this area suggest great poverty and need. In the rural areas, many families live in older, poorly heated houses or in weather-beaten mobile homes. The school system is poor, and many children quit school at the age of sixteen.

Women generally do not work outside the home, although some have been forced by the economic situation to seek part-time work to bring in additional funds for the family. Some of them babysit for other women in the area. Others have found work in Bedford at fast-food places or discount stores, but these jobs offer them minimum wage only and do little to better their financial situations.

My fieldwork in this region focused primarily on the rural-based Pentecostal churches that dot the landscape. Often, I would meet my neighbors at the collection of mailboxes at the end of our road, and they would urge me to visit their services. I saw this as an opportunity to learn more about this religion and the women who eagerly told me about their "wonderful" services. Most Pentecostals in this area prefer to remain independent and autonomous and have not associated themselves with the larger United Pentecostal Church or the Assemblies of God organizations. Sometimes two, three, or even four different churches can be found on one single country road; splinter groups are common when congregation members disagree on biblical interpretations or on proper decorum and/or dress. Ministers in these independent Pentecostal churches are rarely, if ever, seminary trained. In fact, it is a point of pride that if one is "called by God," seminary training is unnecessary, for the minister can always count on God giving the "message" to the people through the minister, who serves only as a mouthpiece for the divine. Occasionally, a minister will take a correspondence course in order to be licensed. To marry and bury people, most of them must be registered with the county as licensed ministers, but this is not difficult to do. None of the ministers here are paid for their services. They hold regular jobs in addition to their duties as pastor. Only occasionally is a house provided for them.

The services in these small churches are lively and loud and, to the newcomer, may appear to be unstructured. The notion that God will spontaneously provide a sermon for the minister while she/he is in the pulpit guides the services, which have no set schedule. Members in these churches decry the use of a printed bulletin, claiming that mere humans should not determine "where a service will go," preferring to go to church unprepared and "see where the spirit leads." In keeping with my training as a folklorist, my focus has generally been on the oral genres that are still a vibrant part of this Pentecostal religious tradition: prayers, testimonies, sermons, healings, songs and choruses, and speaking in tongues, all of which are delivered in a spontaneous, extemporaneous style, which marks the Pentecostal service as an arena for oral tradition and expression (Lawless 1983a, b). The oral genres found in the services are firmly framed in traditional patterns formed, protected, and performed in ways appropriate in terms of structure, content, style, language, and delivery; that is, prayers must always sound like prayers, testimonies like testimonies, tongues like tongues—at least in terms of the expectations of each particular group. My understanding of these as oral "performances," delivered in group-recognized and group-condoned patterns and styles and presented to a critical audience for recognition and approval, stems in large part from Richard Bauman's argument in *Verbal Art as Performance* (1977). Visitors to Pentecostal services often comment on what appears to be chaos and lack of structure in the spirit-led services, yet an understanding of the oral, traditional constructs and the confidence that God will lead, frame, and inform the service make it clear how the members of the group shape religious experience, practice, and ritual.

My field research from 1978 until 1982 consisted of regularly attending services in several of these rural churches. Over time, I gained permission to record all services, and I was allowed to take photographs. I was also able to interview several of the women I came to know in their homes. My in-depth interviews with the women in these congregations focused on my questions about their testimonies, their religious experiences, and the role of religion in their lives. I also interviewed some of the men in the congregations, primarily the male pastors. These interviews were all recorded. When folklorist Elizabeth Peterson and I wanted to make a film on the Pentecostal religious experience in southern Indiana, however, we were met with strict and unmoving opposition. Following an injunction against television and movies, these rural congregations never consented to our filming or videotaping their services, even though a congregation in Bloomington eventually did allow us to make the film *Joy Unspeakable* in 1981.

Field research, which resulted in my dissertation and first book, *God's Peculiar People* (1988a), revealed that, surprisingly, given the patriarchal foundations of the religion, the Pentecostal religious services I was observing provided a lively forum for women's verbal expression: women sang, prayed, testified, "shouted," and spoke in tongues more than we had expected (Lawless 1980; 1983a; 1983b; 1988a). The Pentecostal perception of women as more spiritual and more in tune with the supernatural set the stage for their active spiritual involvement, even leadership, in the various religious genres available in a religious service. Testifying, the act of standing in the pew and declaring, in a rather ritualized presentation, what God has done for the speaker most recently, was an especially fruitful arena for female verbal expression. Testimonies often became long, elaborate narratives set within the appropriate "testimony frame." If skillfully delivered, these testimonies could, in fact, become so long that if several women testified at length in one particular service, the male preacher would not have time to give his sermon. Of course, this power to disrupt the service and usurp the authority of the males was never openly acknowledged by the women, although they often matter-of-factly recounted stories about services where the women just "testified and testified" deep into the night. The men I interviewed were clearly disturbed by this pattern and were frustrated when their time in the pulpit was cut short or eliminated. I have argued elsewhere that the women understood their subtle power within this religious context and exploited it to their benefit (Lawless 1983a).

Occasionally, during my field research in Indiana, I would hear a Pentecostal woman preach. Given Paul's injunction against women speaking in church and the Pentecostal affinity for Paul's directives, I was surprised to find women actually gaining access to the pulpit in these small, extremely conservative churches. In the early 1980s, determined to learn more about how these women claimed the pulpit, I turned my field research to Pentecostal women preachers in central and southern Missouri, work that appeared in my book *Handmaidens of the Lord* (1988b). The women I encountered during this time were either itinerant ministers, traveling from town to town conducting revivals and camp meetings, or pastors in very small, rural-based Pentecostal churches.

The small towns and rural areas where I conducted fieldwork in Missouri have been hit hard by the farm crisis. Portions of central and southwestern Missouri kiss the foothills of the Ozarks and continue to evidence the kind of rural existence that has been the hallmark, and the stereotype, of hill folk in this region. Similarly, folks in central and southern Missouri are quite poor, salaries are extremely low, and the standard of living ranks far below that of northern Missouri and certainly of the fertile fields of Iowa. Fundamentalist religion thrives in a region still proud to claim the likes of Jimmy Bakker and other sometimes flashy television ministers who occasionally have some difficulties connecting with their more traditional rural populations. Ministers here, as in Indiana, are not seminary trained; both male and female ministers' right to the pulpit hinges upon a call from God to preach the word. As I intend to illustrate here, the legitimacy and authenticity of that call from God, as evidenced in the calculated construction

of their personal "call to preach" narratives, take on an exaggerated importance when it is women claiming the pulpit.

Personal Experience and Life Stories as Folklore

As early as 1977, folklorist Sandra Stahl argued for the traditional roots of
personal experience narratives, suggesting they were appropriate to the
study of folklore because the actual, personal experience narrative and the
shared, group tradition of such narratives (that is, in terms of form, content,
structure, and language) fuse in these stories, which, if closely examined,
often sound remarkably similar from one narrator to another (1977). Jeff
Titon's important article "The Life Story," published three years later, examined life stories and life histories as traditional "fictions," understood
as constructed stories told within the context in which they exist (1980).
Similarly, the study of life histories and life stories has come to the attention
of sociologists, anthropologists, literary scholars and theorists, feminist
scholars, and historians. The literary connections between autobiography
and life stories, particularly in terms of women's stories, inform the recent
works of Joy Barbre and the women in the Personal Narrative Group at the
University of Minnesota in their book *Interpreting Women's Lives* (1989),
Bella Brodzky and Celeste Schenck's *Life/Lines: Theorizing Women's Autobiography* (1988), and includes what Germaine Bree termed *autogynography*
in James Olney's new collection, *Studies in Autobiography* (1988).

Spiritual Life Stories of Pentecostal Women Preachers

Examples of what I have chosen to label *spiritual life stories* are representative of the kinds of stories Pentecostal women preachers tell about their
lives. There has been a fairly longstanding concern among anthropologists
and folklorists about the differentiations that ought to be made among *life
story, personal history, (oral) autobiography, and life history.* I am calling the
accounts given to me by women preachers *spiritual life stories,* for I hear
their recollections to a very large degree as "fictions" that draw on an understanding of *facio,* as suggested by Titon, not as a lie, but a "making." The
stories are creations; they cannot be viewed as *pure history* (although that
term itself is suspect). I prefer the term *life stories* (plural) because I am skep-
tical of the notion of the existence of a perfectly constructed oral life story
or life history (singular) that is formulated and delivered in chronological
order and somehow fits our etic notions of (oral) autobiography. The term

spiritual life stories enables us to assume that these very specific life stories about religious women are, in fact, not perfected entities, but rather each is a collection, a pastiche of stories, many of them based on both personal experience and traditional expectations at the same time. Like epic songs, the life story is, in fact, a series of smaller components, vignettes, each developed into a concrete story that follows the rules of traditional religious folk narrative. Most important to this present study is Titon's suggestion that "the life story's singular achievement is that it affirms the identity of the storyteller in the act of telling. The life story tells who one thinks one is and how one thinks one came to be that way" (Titon, 290).

The narratives of the Pentecostal women in this study clearly embody both unique life experiences and folk (shared, group traditions) narrative elements. While the stories are certainly related as personal experience stories, their archetypal structure cannot be ignored. Joseph Campbell's monomythic heroic pattern begins, in fact, with a call and a refusal to obey (1971). First, the women relate that they believe they have been called by God to preach. Then they relate their horror at such a fantastic notion—their discomfort, of course, reflects their awareness of the general opinion of their religious group about such an idea. The testing of God to validate the calling is a standard motif, and the style of narrating such an incident remains identifiable from one corpus of stories to another. Sister Anna's story illustrates such a "testing" of God and presents the preferred dialogic style of storytelling, which further authenticates the incident as "real." She told me: "I didn't know if this was of God or of the devil or of myself, so I said, 'God, if this is of you, then tomorrow morning at exactly eight, Brother Simmons is going to call me, and he's going to say, 'Anna, would you consider coming to be our pastor?' And, Elaine, the very next morning at exactly eight, Brother Simmons called me, and he said the very words that I told God. He said, 'Anna, would you consider coming to be our pastor?' And it nearly knocked the breath out of me."

Sister Walters loves to tell this story, and she has recounted it on many occasions and in many different contexts, including my interview with her. It has the flavor of a story told often and with conviction. Her account has analogues in nearly every interview I have conducted. Similarly, Sister Mabel Adams recounts how she felt the call and then resisted: "I felt like, no, I can't do that. So I began to pray, 'Now, Lord, if you really have called me to preach and you want me to preach, you have her call on me tomorrow in church to preach.' That was my point of contact, you know, for certainty.

And every time the Lord would give me a dream the night before, and in the dream he would give me the message, the scriptures and everything, and then the very next morning, on Sunday, she would call on me to preach, see, and then I knew." This motif—the testing of God for validation—is typical in the women's narratives and illustrates how so much of what they are doing is, of necessity, couched in terms of what *God* has called them to do. The stories always validate the calling and illustrate for the listener the woman's initial reluctance to accept the call; the "test" embedded in the story dramatizes for both the woman and her audience the authenticity of the call.

That many of the vignettes embedded within these women's life stories are identifiable, either in structure or in content, as traditional ones (belonging to the group) can be illustrated with examples taken from different states. The explanation for clear analogues collected in places over five hundred miles apart depends on understanding the role of oral tradition in these religious contexts. Although the Pentecostal women in Missouri may never have sat in the same church as the women from Indiana, their experiences have been similar, and women who have visited in one area attend meetings where women from another area speak, and then they bring those narratives home with them. Large camp meetings and revivals, where women testify and tell their stories, provide a forum for exchange not only of performance structure and style but content as well. Both in the pan-Pentecostal religious arena as well as in the local churches, there is clearly community collaboration on the "authentic" story, its structure, its components, and its performed delivery.

The spiritual life stories of women preachers illustrate the collaborative aspects of community-shared narrative. Early in my interviews with many different preachers, I became aware that their life stories certainly followed a pattern. Pivotal points of their narratives included the experiences of being saved, being baptized in water, being baptized in the Spirit, and getting the call to preach. At first, it seemed remarkable that the women I interviewed so often structured the story of their personal life in this sequence with little or no attention to their home life, their family, or any female adolescent concerns they might have had. While fully acknowledging that my presence as an interviewer collecting the life stories of women preachers biased the material from the start, I was, nevertheless, unprepared for the consistency of the narratives. I have come to understand that this patterning has shaped their identities—these events, these experiences do make sense of their lives, individually and within the religious community. These patterns further confirm the woman's identity, first, as a good Christian woman and, second, as a woman preacher. The women both hear these stories and tell them within a common community and before a "critical" audience that serves to authenticate and validate the experience as "from God." If it proves not from God, then the woman will not gain access to the pulpit.

Women who wish to become ministers must rescript their lives to fit the acceptable "woman preacher" life script. These acceptable narratives follow some of the same inclinations most personal-experience stories share and which Stahl and others argue place them in the world of "folklore"—that is, the components of a "good" or expected story come to replace or accompany "pure truth," while specifics, especially dialogue, often become formularized or crystalized so that the story comes to "say" what the narrator wants it to say. It is, after all, a story delivered to make some point or to entertain a certain audience. It will, therefore, have a focus. History will be modified, melded, pushed, and molded to create a story that is based on truth but is, in fact, a created story; there is a pact between the narrator and the listener that disallows scrutiny and allows a measure of embellishment, within mutually agreed bounds. The context determines the flexibility of the boundaries. Religion happens to be one area in which the range for creativity in personal-experience fictions is quite broad, largely because the narrator takes refuge in the world of the supernatural and/or the divine. Here we find a strong pact that allows for stories of visions, possessions, and healings that, delivered in any other context, might be met with scorn, disbelief, or hilarity.

In the religious woman's construction of her life stories, selection is critical. Which events, what themes, will emerge as most important? What will be developed? What excluded? The key appears to be just how concisely the narratives affirm the identity of the storyteller in the act of the storytelling. I would argue that the degree to which a life story has been formulated, honed, and developed will be in direct proportion to how secure the narrator's sense of identity actually is. In the case of Pentecostal women preachers, there is a clear relationship between the elaborated life story, complete with its crystalized, most important components (specific vignettes that are utilized in various contexts), and the degree of positive self-identification. Women who have "made it" as preachers—as pastors, especially—have much better-developed stories than those who have not.

When we read/hear the orally delivered stories of women preachers, then we need to listen for what identifies the narrators as individuals and what identifies them as traditional storytellers.

In the patriarchal world of conservative Pentecostalism, women are expected to be submissive to the men in their lives—their fathers, brothers, husbands, and male pastors. In the home, in the community, and in the church, they are denied their independence and most rights over their own bodies. While the women of this study must decry the feminist movement and deny that they have chosen a strong, feminist stance against the dictums of their world, it is undeniable that they have clearly chosen for themselves an alternative lifestyle, even against the wishes of husbands, family, and friends. Feminist scholarship that deals with narrative strategies in literature can aid us in understanding how these Midwestern women have had to rescript their lives. I am interested, then, in how these new scripts become available to women as acceptable scripts and how the scripts then become the models for lived lives. Carolyn Heilbrun, in *Writing a Woman's Life*, offers this provocative statement: "What matters is that lives do not serve as models: only stories do that. And it is a hard thing to make up stories to live by. We can only retell and live by the stories we have read or heard. We live our lives thorough text" (1988, 37).

Rescripting as Narrative Strategy

In her discussion of twentieth-century women writers, Rachael Blau DuPlessis has suggested that, unlike nineteenth-century women writers whose characters basically could choose only between marriage and death (because that was the reality of women's lives at the time as well), contemporary women writers are "writing beyond" those restrictive endings for women's stories (1985). DuPlessis has suggested that the mythic quest (or *Bildung*) was unavailable to women characters (and women) in nineteenth-century fiction (and reality), that the only acceptable social script available to them was that of the "helpmeet." To become a "heroine," the woman character had to embrace the roles of wife and mother or die, largely because the nineteenth-century novel had to obey the "structuring dialectics" of the social and economic limits of middle-class women as a group. But DuPlessis sees twentieth-century women writers as inventing alternate resolutions for the lives of women characters, a new set of choices. These alternative narrative patterns help to locate ways to "neutralize the power of the standard sociocultural script." Simply by virtue of rescripting, the author is commenting upon the status quo, calling it into question, dissenting from it.

In my attempt to understand both the lives of women preachers and their narrated life stories, I rely on such an understanding of narrative strategies. It is constructive for us to view the reconstructions, or rescriptions, of women's lives in the form of life stories, as narrative strategies that reinforce and validate the identity sought in the living script. The ability to create elaborations of reality may stem from what Patricia Spacks has termed the "female imagination," or the "power that penetrates the inner meaning of reality but also a power that creates substitutes for reality (1972, 4). The task of the folklorist here is not to determine where truth leaves off in these autobiographies and where imagination begins; rather, it is most productive for us to view the narratives as we do other oral, traditional genres—as stories with identifiable characteristics, structure, and content; stories that are dynamic and change with the context and the audience; stories that embody a shared understanding of the world and transmit that worldview to others within the group. The life accounts may or may not actually reflect historical fact, but for the women who develop and recount them, they become very real indeed. As real, in fact, as the alternative lifestyle they have chosen.

Like nineteenth-century women, women in this regional context know that their prescribed role is in the home. The only totally appropriate script is that of housewife and mother. To be an unmarried woman, an "old maid," is to live a sad and pitied life, cared for by no one. What better example, then, of the woman rescripting her life and refusing to accept the stance of female as muted than the woman preacher? Yet the woman who chooses this vocation—and she does choose it, all refutation aside—must work to make certain her independence and outspokenness do not appear as a denial of the traditional female role of good wife and mother. Most especially, her credibility must not be shaken by any suggestion that she is a feminist making a statement of women's rights or that she is in any way a threat to the status quo. Within the conservative, Pentecostal religious context, the only acceptable premise for her behavior is the assertion that God has called her to preach; luckily, this claim helps to keep resistance from others at bay, although it certainly will not eliminate criticism. Since no one can be quite certain how God works, it remains dangerous to question his motives, although a certain amount of grumbling about the woman in question is inevitable. If we follow DuPlessis's thinking, these women are feminists, in fact, simply by the act of rescripting—both in life and in the narrative reconstructions of their life. The rescripting itself is an implied comment upon the status quo. Ritual disclaimers such as "I'm not for ERA" or "Don't get me wrong; I'm not a women's libber (or a bra burner)" insulate the speakers from acknowledging the sagacity of their life strategies, while their narrative reconstructions reinvent the strategies and validate them for others.

The stories embody some of what the women actually did in their lives, which alone represents an astounding feat given the circumstances; they illustrate what the women perhaps wished they had done and said; and they present the women's interpretation of what has happened to them in their lives. Both the women's lives and their fictive reconstructions of their lives serve as alternative narrative strategies for women in this region.

The Women's Stories

The identifiable components of these traditional narratives of life experiences remain surprisingly consistent from narrator to narrator. The elements that nearly always figure in the narratives, in addition to those structural markers already mentioned, include a clear perception of difference from other young people, an often severe conviction of a sinful nature, an attraction for the religious revival and/or missionary work, a concrete recounting of the conversion and the call to preach, and a construction of an alternative life strategy.

Virtually every one of the Pentecostal women who has related her story to me has remarked that she was born into a very poor family. Almost all were raised in rural counties and grew up on farms or in very small towns in rural areas. Nearly all of them belonged to large fundamentalist families, usually of Baptist or Holiness background. Indiana and Missouri are largely Bible-belt states of rural thinking, staunch conservatism, and traditional values. Notions of the importance of the nuclear family, monogamy, female/male sex roles, and the importance of religion prevail and direct the daily lives of the people who live here. I stress this traditional milieu and value system because it bears directly upon the single most unusual aspect of these women's perceptions of themselves, supported by their lives and reinforced in their narratives, and that is their perception of themselves as *different* and their strength to act upon that perception in such a way as to reinforce and validate that difference. Most of these women were born into ordinary farming families with several, often many, children. The accepted roles of girls in this region were and continue to be clearly defined and inherently restricting.

Yet the life stories of women preachers hinge upon the fact that even as very young girls, they *felt* different or knew that they were different from other girls, from the other children in the family. Most tell that the most visible mark of their difference was their inclination toward the church, toward God, toward things religious. Importantly, this point in a reconstructed life story must be recognized as part of the narrative structure and strategy; that is, whether or not this is an actual historical point, it has become an important ingredient of the script that is created to validate the woman as different, different enough to become a preacher. And the women find dynamic ways to illustrate their difference. One woman tells an elaborate story of how she was ridiculed in primary school for her conservative clothing and her long, unadorned hair, which are required dress for Pentecostal girls and women. Her response to her difference was to ask the principal of the school if she could conduct prayer meetings in the cafeteria during recess. "And, you know," she said with pride, "they allowed it. And we had prayer meeting during our recess. And I led those services." This story embodies much that Sister Mary wishes to convey about herself. It is a crafted story, told as true and intended to convince. The incident occurred nearly fifty years ago, yet details in the story, such as precisely remembered dialogue, will surprise us unless we understand that it is a crafted fiction—a re-creation of an event. The girl speaks with authority, conviction; we have to applaud her strength, and, of course, that is the point of this story. It is one of the important vignettes in her life story; it sets the stage for the subsequent acts of pure impudence she will commit. The stories of other women preachers strongly parallel this woman's story, in effect if not always in content. Sister Anna loves to recall that even while still in her mother's womb, she was "marked" when her mother was frightened by a snake and stumbled. Anna's family folklore supports her belief that she is different, that she was "marked." A favorite uncle started a story when she was only two that her insistent babbling was actually her premature inclination toward speaking in tongues and the world of the spiritual.

Many of the women emphasize their family's poverty and lack of worldly amenities; most tell of walking great distances alone to attend church services, more inclined toward things religious than even their religious families. The women speak of being fascinated with the church and the religious services, acutely tuned to the spiritual aspects. Almost all, too, associate their gravitation to the church with their own conviction of their sinful nature. Many relate tearful experiences when they feared they might not make it into heaven, or as Sister Anna expressed it as a response to a song that suggested some would make it into heaven and others would have the door closed in their face, "I'll never forget; they sang a song, and here I was, just small, but I have used this as an illustration many times in my messages, that they sang this old song 'Standing Outside the Door—Oh, what an awful picture, left standing outside.' That made such an imprint upon my mind that I think that's why I can preach with vividness heaven as a real place."

Nearly all of the women interviewed stated that their first stirrings toward a religious life began in revivals. I think there is a good reason for this. Revivals were like carnivals come to town. In isolated rural areas, the church was and still is often the focal point of activity, at least of activity that could include all members of the family. Men and boys could certainly visit and hang around the local granges, the grain elevators, cotton gins, and even the taverns. The children went to school as much as possible, but the church was recognized as an arena for all members of the family to participate. The strict religious standards did not allow for exploring new places or possibilities, with the exception of the revival and camp-meeting circuit. For young girls in this context, there were all too few role models: their mothers, female schoolteachers, and the occasional woman preacher. Clearly, women preachers and religious leaders made an impression on many young women. Importantly, religious life provided the opportunity for young girls to leave home and travel. No doubt the life of a missionary or an itinerant preacher was an appealing one for girls who doubted that they would, in any other way, be able to be independent and actually leave home before marriage.

Missionaries brought excitement and glamour from faraway places, but the revivals held in the local areas certainly provided a more tangible kind of lure for young girls. Weeks, sometimes months, before a revival was scheduled to begin, flyers would be posted on fences, at the grain elevator, on the church and grocery doors. The face of a traveling evangelist would smile down on the readers' eager faces, promising exciting meetings, singing fests, and religious fervor. Just like the carnival, the revivals and camp meetings were often set up on the edge of town; men wielding huge hammers set up enormous tents that would put a circus to shame. In some areas, they constructed temporary "brush arbors," large, open-air constructions with roofs made of brush and tree limbs (cf. Bruce). Benches, logs, and chairs were lined up inside, a makeshift altar prepared, a pulpit tacked together; sawdust was dumped on the floor, and sometimes a piano was brought out. Services could last anywhere from three days to three weeks. Many women relate their religious conversions to these religious extravaganzas, and most of them can recall a most significant revival when a woman came to preach.

Like Dinah in George Eliot's *Adam Bede*, the traveling woman preacher was a sight to behold—bold in her independence, calm in her assurance of herself, captivating with her religious message (Lawless 1990). It was so easy to become enthralled, to respond to the calls to repent, to dedicate, to exhibit the zeal of the Lord. And respond they did. Historical accounts of revivalism always note the enthusiastic female participation in these meetings, and my own work attests to the consistency of women's religious enthusiasm. The messages took on a very personal appeal for these girls: they wept; they saw themselves as blatant, stained sinners; they went to the altar and prayed fervently; and some of them promised God they would live in his service—and that promise meant the possibility of an alternate life, a new life script. To be a revival preacher meant daily doses of new faces, travel, independence, and status. In fact, it just may have represented the most outrageous break with tradition available without castigation— offering much more mobility than school teaching, for example. And to make it even more appealing, if the call could be authenticated as from God and not of the girl herself, then the decision gained divine validation. But none of this is to suggest that just because there were women preachers, preaching was a condoned activity for women. It was not, and still is not, in most Pentecostal contexts; at best it is tolerated only because of the respect for and belief in divine intercession. God's call, then, becomes the single most important component in the rescripting. The girl's story must relate the moment when she believes she is being called to do and to be something special.

Because of the inherent danger of announcing this belief that God has called them, most of the women's stories have embedded in them a ritual disclaimer of sorts—a message that either clearly states or implies, "Look, I didn't ask for this. God called me. What could I do but obey? I tried to resist, but you really ought not try to resist God." Implied is the message that the young women did not actually wish to be called. Importantly, in the oral re-creation of the life story, a degree of hesitancy must be in evidence; no greediness, no rushing toward this life in the center stage is allowable. Mabel Adams, a minister from Hooperton, Missouri, told me, ". . . the Lord just spoke to me, you know, let me know that he had called me and wanted me to preach. And I just rebelled, I really did. I didn't feel like, you know, that I could. I just felt like, well, Lord, surely you could find somebody that could do a better job than I can. But he said, you know, 'You!' "

Resistance is important, for personal intent would discredit the woman's legitimate claim to the pulpit. While the woman must disclaim any personal desires, her stories must prove that she has, in fact, been selected by God and that she will be effective in the capacity of preacher. I heard words similar to these more than once from different women: "I've had to prove all of these years that a woman can be called into the ministry. And I've kept loving the people even when they've criticized me, and I tell them, 'Look, this wasn't my choice.' I've stood in front of the mirror lots of times and said, 'God, are you sure you know what you're doing? I'm a wife; I'm a mother.' I didn't come into this on my own."

Compare this narrative with the following story, which exemplifies the hesitancy, the reluctance, and the power of God in one woman's call-to-preach narrative. Leah Moberly, a young woman seeking a place in the pulpit, put it this way:

> Well, the call of God first come into my life when I was seventeen years of age; it like to scared me to death, and I said, "Lord, I'll do what I can to help others, but leave me alone." And which he did for a while. I would try to get away from it you know. I would rather not have went to preach. I would rather have set in the pews. But God slayed me under his power, and I saw a vision. I saw it seemed like the earth opened and a big river of water come pouring in, and in this I saw a bunch of sheep coming out through that water, and I said, "Lord, what does this mean?" And he said, "This river of water is the river of life that I'm willing to give unto the people that is ready and needing it." Then I saw a big field of people in this same vision. A large field and my brother who was a minister running back and forth, trying to preach to all them people. And I said, "God, what does this mean?" And he said, "That he has got more to reach than he can possibly reach, and I have called you to go and help him, and my calling is without repentance."

Compare Sister Mary's concern when she felt in the woods that God had given her, a mere sixteen-year-old girl, the sermon for that evening's revival service:

> And I never will forget that place because there was a big old grapevine, it was just about this big around. And when I—it just seemed like God just almost

slew me, 'cause I got down on my back, flat on that ground, and I couldn't get up. And I started praying, and God started dealing with my heart, and the Lord started saying, it just seemed like—not in an audible voice—but I could just hear the Lord speaking in a still, small voice, saying, "Will you go where I want you to go? And will you do what I want you to do?" And, you know, it was hard for me because I thought, now, is this *me*? Because I had admired this other girl that preaches *so much*. I'd always all my life, you know, I'd always thought, oh, I would like to be an evangelist, but the thoughts came to me, how can I preach? How can I do anything? But the Lord just kept dealing with me, and I couldn't get up, and finally I said, "Lord, whatever you want me to do, even though I within myself, I'm not, I know I'm not worthy of this calling, but I'll do anything you want me to do because I know that it's in your power to speak through me." And then I could get up.

The biblical nature of the language of these narratives further serves to authenticate them. These young, rural women adopt a stilted prose style in their stories, one that is generally incongruent with their everyday language, as they talk of "God slaying them in the spirit" and "dealing with their heart" and "speaking in a still, small voice." They tell their audience that they have agreed to serve God against their own desires and better judgment, openly acknowledging they are not "worthy of this call." God speaks to them as he spoke to his disciples, "Will you go where I want you to go? Will you do what I want you to do?" And the women finally acquiesce and answer, "I'll go where you want me to go; I'll do what you want me to do." Mary cinches the argument by recounting that she agreed to follow God's directive because, she says, "I know that it's in your power to speak through me." No person in this religious context is able to argue with that definitive statement. They would *all* have to agree that God has the ability, the power, to speak through *anyone*, even a woman.

A striking number of these young women called to preach actually did have female models to follow, usually within the context of the tent revival or the religious camp meeting. And that is where they heard other women recount their stories. In many cases, in fact, the pivotal point of their decision to undertake the ministry revolves around an important encounter with a woman preacher. Over and over, the turning point in the story is a reference to how a woman preacher helped her to make the decision to follow God's call. By this female association and perhaps, even more importantly, through the stories of other women's lives, the call to preach was received in a context of possibility, if not probability, that what they sought to do was not totally absurd, for other women had done it. Sometimes these influences came from total strangers or from the stories of total strangers, but sometimes the influences were very close to home. Experiences in their own families were the ones that would assure the young girl that she could act on her calling, that a rescripting of the "normal" female life strategy did not necessitate a rejection of home and family, but it would require the adoption of new life strategies for both women and men. Anna Walters echoed back to other women who had preceded her in the ministry.

> My grandmother was a minister for many, many years. She was Church of God—Holiness—and so she wasn't pastoring, but she was an evangelist for many years, and she had five children. And my grandmother was holding a revival down at a little old schoolhouse way down south, and my mother was about middle ways in the family, and I've heard my mother say, course she had long hair, and that Grandpa's hands were so rough, so she always hated it when Grandma was gone to revivals because Grandpa had to braid her hair. But, then, when Grandma'd come home, and instead of money about all they could give her were squirrels and rabbits or deer meat, because that's all they could give her, but she'd be so thrilled because she could bring that home—course that wasn't what she was in it for. But this is really where I got my background.

Sister Anna is speaking about the early years of this century in central and southern Missouri, and, given the cultural milieu, it is an instructive narrative. The force of the narrative is not so much the discomfort the girl experiences when her mother is gone as it is the matter-of-fact way in which the mother's occupation and traveling, her leaving five children in the care of the father, is depicted—her leaving to preach is a given. Religion makes women brave; God's business is not to be scoffed at by any person. Yet neither is the woman's place in the family and in the home to be neglected or ignored. Many stories clearly embed images of home and children, making the rescripting more palatable. Sister Anna, when offered the pastorship of a small church two hundred miles from her husband and family, tells how she begged God for answers as she "agonized, slumped over a basket of clothes." The women are careful not to suggest that theirs is a life in the public eye, that they seek the world over the home.

After a Pentecostal woman has entered the world of the ministry and either taken the position of itinerant preacher or church pastor, her life does not necessarily get any easier. She continues to encounter opposition to her right to the pulpit. People stop her in the grocery store or in the parking lot to quote scripture that "proves" women should not be preachers. Some women preachers say they receive threats and harassing letters and books that damn women preachers. Their stories about life in the ministry, then, accentuate their position, its inherent dangers, and their strategies for dealing with opposition. As one woman so aptly put it, "I've been told folks don't believe in women preachers. I've told them they didn't hire me and they sure couldn't fire me. *God* called me, and I'll be here!"

Conclusion

The oral narratives, the spiritual life stories, of Pentecostal women preachers serve as model life scripts for women entering the ministry; the scripts of women who have come before them in this strange and demanding world serve as scripts not only for their lives but for their own narratives; and, in turn, the narratives serve to dictate the structure of other women's lives, as much as texts are able to influence life experiences. Life experiences are interpreted within the constructs recognized as the appropriate components of a narrative life script, a text that serves as a rescripting for an actual life.

This delicate interweaving of text and life experience, script and rescripting, serves, on the one hand, to illustrate the power of language and narrative to validate and authenticate the lived life. It suggests how women's stories serve to cautiously disrupt the status quo, call it into question, and provide the means to weaken male power and authority and deflect religious injunctions intended to silence women's voices. It is indicative of the ways that women take control of their lives and their voices, subvert the dictates of a male hierarchy, and violate manmade codes that restrict them. The story of the Pentecostal woman preacher can be read as a validating statement about strong women who defy restrictions that dictate what they can do and say; it can be interpreted as a story they tell about themselves—a story of liberation.

On the other hand, a critical feminist reading of these texts and their utility for the women who tell them suggests that the stories may not, in fact, authenticate, validate, or honor the actual "lived life." The life lived by the individual woman may be subverted in the telling of these rescriptings prescribed by the group. The narrator may feel, in fact, that she must abandon her *actual* story in favor of the *acceptable* story. The "rescripting" DuPlessis has suggested for female characters in literature constitutes an actual move toward liberation for women, while these new scripts for women preachers may not always have the same liberating effect. DuPlessis speaks of new and better choices for women, alternatives to the "marry or die" constructs that restrict their narratives and their lives. We see some of the characters in the literary stories *and* some real women actually altering the status quo, changing the rules of the game, and, we hope, eventually coming to enjoy a variety of life choices without castigation, repression, or reprisals.

A feminist reading of the women preachers' rescripting of their lives suggests also a level of denial, however. On the one hand, rescripting one's life to fit the expectations of the group and "authenticate" the call from God to preach is certainly a calculated narrative strategy that ought to be applauded, for it certainly works to provide a way for women to gain access to the pulpit.

On the other hand, we must acknowledge the discomforting effect of having to structure one's life narrative to fit an acceptable pattern (and in the process perhaps abandon the reality of what actually happened). Furthermore, in the oral, community-based context in which these stories are related, heard, and retold, they come to serve not only as acceptable scripts for life narratives but also as scripts for lived lives. That is, the power of the structure of the narrative comes to be superimposed upon the lives of young women who believe they should be preachers. The rescripting, then, may become the blueprint for experience, or how experience will be interpreted and articulated to others. Is this construction, then, liberating for women? Yes and no.

Within the Pentecostal context, rescripting does afford a modicum of independence, a space in which to move as a female minister. It does not allow women, however, the truth and vibrance of their own stories; it may not validate and authenticate a woman's own, individual, unique narrative. In some ways it perpetuates the status quo and molds itself to the constraints of the religious context in which the women live. But in other equally important ways, it provides the means for new and different life scripts—and the women are, in fact, involved in the process of the rescripting, of both their stories and their lives. That in itself is liberating.

Note

1. All the names of persons, churches, and towns have been changed to protect the privacy of those involved in this study. My use of "Sister" for the women in this study reflects how most women, particularly ministers, are addressed in their community. Although I have done some field research in African American Pentecostal churches, most of my work has focused on white Pentecostal traditions. I can see both similarities and differences between the black and white Pentecostal traditions, yet none of these should be

assumed in this article. All of the members of the churches mentioned in this article are white and belong to small, rather idiosyncratic congregations. Thus, I am suggesting no conclusions for Pentecostalism in general.

References Cited

Anderson, Robert Mapes. 1979. *Vision of the Disinherited*. New York: Oxford University Press.

Barbre, Joy Webster et. al, eds. 1989. *Interpreting Women's Lives: Feminist Theory and Personal Narratives*. Bloomington: Indiana University Press.

Bauman, Richard. 1977. *Verbal Art as Performance*. Rowley, MA: Newbury House.

Block-Hoell, Nils. 1964. *The Pentecostal Movement*. Oslo, Norway: Universitetsforlaget.

Brodzki, Bella, and Celeste Schenck, eds. 1988. *Life/Lines: Theorizing Women's Autobiography*. Ithaca: Cornell University Press.

Bruce, Dickson. 1974. *And They All Sang Hallelujah: PlainFolk Camp-Meeting Religion, 1800–1845*. Knoxville: University of Tennessee Press.

Campbell, Joseph. 1971. *Hero with a Thousand Faces*. New York: World Publishing Co.

Dieter, Melvin. 1980. *The Holiness Revival of the Nineteenth Century*. Metuchen, NJ: Scarecrow Press.

DuPlessis, Rachel Blau. 1985. *Writing beyond the Ending: Narrative Strategies of Twentieth Century Women Writers*. Bloomington: Indiana University Press.

Heilbrun, Carolyn G. 1988. *Writing a Woman's Life*. New York: W. W. Norton and Co.

Hollenweger, W. J. 1972. *The Pentecostals*. Minneapolis: Augsberg.

Lawless, Elaine J. 1980. "Make a Joyful Noise: An Ethnography of Communication in the Pentecostal Service." *Southern Folklore Quarterly* 44:1–32.

———. 1983a. "Shouting for the Lord: The Power of Women's Speech in the Pentecostal Service." *Journal of American Folklore* 96:433–457.

———. 1983b. "Brothers and Sisters: Pentecostals as a Folk Group." *Western Folklore* 43:85–104.

———. 1986. "'Your Hair is Your Glory': Public and Private Symbology for Pentecostal Women." *New York Folklore* 12:33–49.

———. 1988a. *God's Peculiar People: Women's Voices and Folk Tradition in a Pentecostal Church*. Lexington: University Press of Kentucky.

———. 1988b. *Handmaidens of the Lord: Pentecostal Women Preachers and Traditional Religion*. Philadelphia: The University of Pennsylvania Press and the American Folklore Society.

———. 1990. "The Silencing of the Preacher Woman: The Muted Message of George Eliot's *Adam Bede*." *Women's Studies* 18:116–136.

Lawless, Elaine J., and Elizabeth Peterson, co-producers. 1981 film. *Joy Unspeakable*. Bloomington: Indiana University Radio and Television.

Olney, James. 1988. *Studies in Autobiography*. New York: Oxford University Press.

Ortner, Sherry. 1974. "Is Female to Male as Nature Is to Culture?" In *Woman, Culture and Society*, edited by Michelle Z. Rosaldo and Louise Lamphere, 67–89. Stanford: Stanford University Press.

Spacks, Patricia Meyer. 1972. *The Female Imagination*. New York: Alfred A. Knopf.
Stahl, Sandra K. D. 1977. "The Personal Narrative as Folklore." *Journal of the Folklore Institute* 14:9–30.
Synan, Vinson. 1971. *The Holiness-Pentecostal Movement in the United States*. Grand Rapids, MI: Wm. Eerdmans.
Titon, Jeff Todd. 1980. "The Life Story." *Journal of American Folklore* 93:176–192.

3

ACCESS TO THE PULPIT

Reproductive Images and Maternal Strategies of the Pentecostal Female Pastor

I N HER INTRODUCTION TO A SPECIAL ISSUE OF *American Quarterly* devoted to women and religion, Janet Wilson James argues that "an exploration of women's part in the history of religion soon encounters two constants: women usually outnumber men; men exercise the authority" (1978, 579). James goes on to point out, however, that the "shock waves of the sixties" have weakened the "familiar authority structures," and women are flooding the religious scene, searching out the "liberating promises of scripture to revise theologies," contending for the "right to be ordained and to exercise sacerdotal authority" (1978, 579; cf. Behnke 1982). Intrigued by the significant number of Pentecostal female preachers I had located in both southern Indiana and central Missouri in 1983–1986, a phenomenon that seemed to fly in the face of the tenets of this male-dominated religion, I set out to examine James's contention in terms of Pentecostalism.[1] My study of female preachers in the Pentecostal faith does not illustrate how women

Author's note: Following several years of field research with Pentecostal women in southern Indiana in the late 1970s, concentrating on the various verbal genres they performed within the context of the religious service, I began researching Pentecostal women preachers in southern Missouri in 1983. Before my book *Handmaidens of the Lord* appeared in 1988, I published several articles in journals about women's sermons, including examinations of the structure of their sermons, images of God that prevailed in their sermons, the poetics of their sermons, and the women's spiritual life stories. An aside in footnote 7 is indicative of my first struggles with the conflict between my interpretation of the various images and themes in the women's sermons and their own insistence that I might be wrong. This article was originally published in Susan Hollis, Linda Pershing, and M. Jane Young, eds., *Feminist Theory and the Study of Folklore* (University of Illinois Press, 1993), 258–276.

have weakened authority structures or sought the "liberating promises of scripture to revise theologies." This study challenges the contention that men always exercise the authority, but ironically, it in no way demonstrates that many women consciously or overtly strive for "liberating promises" or support efforts toward a "new theology" or a "new ethics." Rather, it is the strong connection these women maintain with conservative religion and patriarchal constructs that enables them to acquire the position of power and authority in a church as pastor and provides the means for them to maintain that position.

Firmly entrenched in Pentecostalism, as practiced by whites in southern Indiana,[2] is the tension between the religiously inscribed inferiority of women, who are expected to be submissive to men, and the belief in individual equality before God in terms of salvation. The traditional belief in the inferiority of women is based on an interpretation of the biblical story of the Garden of Eden, an interpretation that insists on Eve's transgression and her subsequent seduction of Adam to join in her disobedience to God's direct orders. Pauline directives to the Christian Church have remained the clear directives of God for this denomination, stemming from "the fall": "Let your women keep silence in the church: for it is not permitted for them to speak: but they ought to be subject, as also the Law saith. And if they will learn anything, let them ask their husbands at home: for it is a shame for a woman to speak in the church" (1 Cor. 14:34–35). And later, Paul writes to Timothy, "Let the women learn in silence with all subjection: I permit not a woman to teach, neither to usurp authority over the man, but to be in silence" (1 Tim. 2:11–12).

While it certainly seems clear enough in the verses quoted above that Paul insists on silence for women, he also confuses the issue when he says, "But every woman that prayeth or prophecieth bareheaded, dishonoreth her head" (1 Cor. 11:3–5).[3] Given the scriptural foundation for the muted subjection of women in Christian religions, how is it, then, that women in the strictly conservative Pentecostal religion come to be selected for the chief post of church pastor, and images are most salient in their attempts to authenticate both their religious power and their church authority? By firmly basing their role as preacher and pastor within the frameworks that support a traditional and spiritual religiosity, one closely aligned with nineteenth-century notions of religion as part of the woman's sphere and maintained close to hearth and home, these female pastors are able to gain power and authority through already established female attributes (Welter 1976). The maternal and reproductive images they convey as religious strategies serve to strip their presence behind the pulpit of its most threatening aspects.

Most important to the congregations that have a female as pastor is the perception of that woman as "mother" to the congregation. When group members are asked to say why they think a particular woman is a good pastor, they often answer, "She takes good care of us," or "She's just like a mother; she cares for everybody." Female pastors themselves recognize the importance of acting out the role of symbolic mother to their congregations:

> Women have a special gift of compassion, don't you think? A real caring, loving compassion. Maybe it's because God made us mothers, you know. We know how to comfort our babies, you know, when they're little, and they need attention.
>
> And I think it's a special love God puts into the heart of a mother and gives her such tender love for her family, and then, naturally, why couldn't he use that tender love that he put there to begin with, you know; he made the mamas. He made the mamas, you know, and he put that love in their hearts to be mamas, and so it is a special love, so why can't he use that love out of a woman to relate to the people that need encouragement from him? I believe it's that motherly quality of love that God puts in a mother to bring up that baby . . . a motherly love. And I believe the people can feel that—that goes along with this guy I worked for, even though he didn't believe in women preachers, he did say to me, "I believe that ladies can have more compassion to minister than the men do."[4] (Sister Pat Roberts, Centerville, Missouri)

> I think a woman has more of a tendency to mother the people than lead them as a shepherd. And it's hard [for a man] to follow a woman pastor [i.e., be the next pastor] because they don't take a firm stand on things. It's more or less "Yes, honey, I understand," you know, like that. (Sister Alma Cotton, Smithville, Missouri)

> God told me, "I've chosen you. I've put you in the furnace of affliction that others can identify with you." Because I had prayed, "Lord, give me compassion.
> Like you feel compassion for people." And you can't feel that with people unless you've gone through what they have. Unless you can walk in their shoes.
> But I'll tell you one thing, here's one preacher that will sit and listen when somebody is read to, needs somebody to listen. I've been told a number of times, "Sister, I believe it's because you're a mother. I feel a compassion that I don't feel in men." (Sister Anna Walters, Centerville, Missouri)

These statements are filled with the implications of what a "mother" is likely to do for her "children." Several of these female pastors speak of their congregation members as their "babes in Christ," especially new converts who have just joined their churches. Traditional "motherly" images include caring, compassion, empathy, the ability to be a good listener, cheerfulness, understanding, loving, and comforting; most of these capabilities are offered as positive attributes of the female pastor and are often offered in contradistinction to the attributes of many male pastors, who are more often characterized as fine leaders or strict disciplinarians who "lead them as a shepherd." This characterization of female pastors certainly reflects Carol Gilligan's suggestions that women are more inclined toward care and community (1982; cf. Ortner 1974).

To complement the image of the female pastor as the "mother" of the church, the women know that in addition to mothering the congregation, they must be biological mothers as well. The sermons of the women in this study are filled with references to their own children, to the raising of their children, to the family as a unifying image. Adrienne Rich, in her examination of motherhood, focuses upon society's need for women to be mothers: "Women who refuse to become mothers are not merely emotionally suspect, but are dangerous. Not only do they refuse to continue the species; they also deprive society of its emotional leaven—the suffering of the mother" (1977, 164). An unmarried woman, rejecting the life of wife and mother, would pose a serious threat to the equilibrium of a socially conservative congregation. A female pastor's own maternal experience becomes weighted and must be foregrounded to minimize the danger that her elevated position in the church be perceived as a rejection of (what is perceived to be) her "natural" role as wife and mother. The following remarks from female pastors reflect the importance of this image of them first as wives, mothers, and caretakers and only secondarily as pastors. These quotes are equally full of disclaimers about their own ambitions for the pulpit; the tradition of women placing the responsibility with God for calling them into the ministry can be traced back to medieval female visionaries whose instructions to write down their spiritual experiences came directly from God and were often met with resistance from the women themselves.[5]

> When my own kids were little, I'd hold two kids and preach, you know. They'd be crying without me, you know, so I'd hold them and preach. I've always said I've got more sermons over the ironing board and the dishpan than I ever did on my knees. (Sister Ruth Hatley, Murray, Missouri)

> I've had to prove all of these years that a woman can be called into the ministry. And I've kept loving the people even when they criticized me and telling them, "Look, this wasn't my choice." I've stood in front of the mirror lots of times and said, "God, are you sure you know what you're doing?" I'm a wife. I'm a mother. I didn't ask for this. (Sister Anna Walters, Centerville, Missouri)

> Two or three months [after being saved], that's when I began to feel it [the call to preach], but I didn't let on, you know, I didn't know what it was. Really, the most I felt it was, like, when I was home alone, just me and the Lord. Like when I'd be at home with, just reading my Bible, and you know, maybe the babies playing or something at my feet. I enjoy what I'm doing. I enjoy just what God's made me do. I enjoy being a lady. I enjoy being a wife, a mother, a grandma. I just love it. (Sister Pat Roberts, Centerville, Missouri)

In light of the mothering capacities of female pastors, it seems no coincidence that almost every woman I interviewed had an invalid mother of her own.[6] In nearly every case, these women had to take on the duty of mothering their siblings at a very young age, often forfeiting their own education and aspirations to care for an ailing mother and carry the responsibilities of the household. Sister Mary did not finish high school until she was an adult: "See, when I was a sophomore, right before I was called to preach, when I was fifteen, my mother got real sick, and she miscarried, had a stillborn baby. And I had to quit school because I was the oldest." Anna's story of how she had to quit school and care for her family similarly illustrates how she developed her virtuous maternal inclinations at such an early age. Her success as a young "mother" to her siblings served as a test, perhaps, of her strength and stamina, one that prepared her well for another extraordinary "test," the call to preach.

> When I was nine years old, my mother's health began to fail, and when I was almost ten, my mother gave birth to my youngest brother, Danny Joe, and she later had pneumonia and took strong medicine, and her heart began to bother her. So more and more responsibility fell upon my shoulders. I had to learn to cook, and Mama would tell me to put a dash of this, a pinch of that, and this is how I cooked for the family when Mama was bedfast. My responsibilities grew, and it was very difficult to care for a bedfast mother and five younger brothers and sisters. And I helped my dad and two older brothers milk and do usual chores on the farm. There was water to carry, and I would heat it on the wood cookstove to wash clothes for the family. The night before, I would pick up chips and bring in dry corncobs. They made it easy to start a good, hot fire in the morning. My dad felt he didn't have a good start for his day if he didn't have biscuits and gravy along with his ham or bacon and eggs. At night I would light the coal oil lamp and turn out the electric lights, and while everybody else slept, many times I've rubbed my mother's back; she never had a bedsore in all of her time of being bedfast. This was a nervous strain upon young shoulders. She was in and out of the hospital so much before she died at the age of thirty-seven years.

Sister Anna does not remind us, in this portion of her narrative, that she was born with severe scoliosis of the spine. Doctors tried to get her family to take her to St. Louis for surgery and remedial treatment, but the family's finances and their unfamiliarity with urban centers prevented them from seeking the help that young Anna needed. A local doctor warned her family that she would never be able to carry or deliver children of her own. Yet Anna sensed the importance of her own maternity and denied the doctors the last word on that matter.

> I prayed and prayed to get pregnant. I just pleaded with the Lord. And I lost my first one. But—I don't know, maybe it's stubbornness, God has given me a lot of something—God has given me a lot of determination and willpower. I have three now. They fixed a support, and I would go, and they would adjust that support every month, then, for me to carry my children. But God was so good to me during the time that I carried them. I was suffering so bad during the time I was carrying my children, and each time, of course, it spread the spine more and crippled me a little more—but God was so good to me [by allowing her to become pregnant and carry the children].

The female pastor is expected to be tough. She must possess stamina and display the fierce, tenacious tendencies of a mother likely to protect her young. Many of the women speak of the determination God gave them to survive the hardships of being a female preacher. They speak of the criticism, heartaches, and ostracism they have encountered both in their families and in the community. The accounts they give of their experiences sound very much alike. When asked about women as preachers, Sister Mabel Adams answered, "I've thought all right, then, I thought he could make a woman preach if she wanted to, if he wanted her to. I've told them they didn't hire me, and they sure couldn't fire me.[7] God called me, God sent me, and I'm here!" Similarly, Sister Ruth Hatley recalls that there have been moves to oust her from her post, but she says, "They did not hire me, and they can't fire me. So I got God to answer to. I've got a determination that I am not going to give up. When God has something for us to do, he means for us to do it." This image of the women as tough and hardy, able to withstand the threats of both men and devils, can be readily reconciled if considered within the imagery of ferocity of the "natural" mother, strong enough to protect her own children and her position.

Within the religious community, female pastors have clear directives: they must be compassionate, caring, loving mothers for their congregations, and it will be most beneficial if they are biological mothers as well. As pastor of a church, a woman's strength in that capacity will lie in her ability to apply all the maternal aspects of her female being to the care and guidance of her symbolic family, her "babes in Christ." Much of what the women preach about is, I believe, firmly entrenched in this same maternal imagery. Gilligan's thesis that women's perspective is more inclined toward connection and community is also reflected in the rhetoric of women preachers (1982). The most common foci of women's sermons are variations on the themes of "total sacrifice" and a sharpened concern with "making it into heaven," no matter how godly a life one has lived; for women, anyway, the concern seems to hang in the air.[8] The reunion of the family—both biological and religious—in the community of heaven as an extension of this latter theme seems to be an excellent illustration of Gilligan's hypothesis. Sister Anna, for example, in an interpretation of a Bible verse, uses a particularly striking image of heaven as a low-slung balcony, just out of sight of earthlings, where our families who have gone on before us watch us and wait for us to join them:

> [Reading] "Likewise, I say unto you,
> There is joy in the presence of the angels of God
> Over one sinner that repenteth."
> I believe that that simply means this: All those people in heaven
> There in the presence of angels and the presence of God
> They rejoice.
> I believe that a precious Mom and Dad who have prayed long and fervent and hard
> For unsaved children, I tell you, I believe,
> Even though they went on home to their reward, and they didn't see those children saved,
> I want to tell you something,
> I believe when that one, that child, bows on their knees to God
> That that Mom and Dad rejoice in heaven.
> I believe over the balcony of heaven this morning, if one soul in this congregation this morning repents of sin
> They know it, and they rejoice in the presence of angels.[9]

These women must be loving and tough, but they must deny that they have or seek equal footing with men. The "mother" of the church must not be confused with or made the equivalent of what the "father" of a church might be. This is due largely to the maintenance of a strict hierarchical power structure in the home and in the community, a hierarchy that is expected to prevail in the religious context as well, even with a female at the helm. The forceful role of men in the homes, recognized by the believers as God-given and prescribed by the Bible, is mirrored in the context of the religion: even when a woman is the pastor, much of the organization of the service is determined by males, and the governing body of the church is made up of male deacons. The women know that their position must not suggest an attempt to usurp the divinely authorized authority of men: "It's been a real barrier of criticism, because they've used the scripture that the women keep silent in the church and so on. But I usually tell them, it's usually a man, I've never found a woman being critical—they've never spoken to me, now, they might have, in their hearts, but never said anything—but it's usually a man, and I'll tell them, 'If you men will do what God wants you to do, we women won't have to.' And that usually hushes them" (Sister Alma Cotton, Smithville, Missouri).

The scriptural directives that insist on female silence in the churches are not taken lightly by either the women or the men in the congregation. Pentecostals take the Bible to be literal truth (although interpretation is, of course, evident at times even to them), and Paul is quite clear on the issue of women speaking out in church. Most men would, in both theory and practice, agree with the following clergyman's assessment: "They [female ministers] are handmaidens. They should wait upon the [male] ministers of the church—[as] a handmaiden to Christ. A woman's got no right. She is over the house. She is not over a man. A man is over the woman, and Christ is over the man, over the church. Now, she's got a place in the church as a Sunday school teacher or maybe as advising to the women. But she can't stand up in that pulpit and tell people what to do because that makes her over the man, and that's not according to God's word."

Women most often justify their position behind the pulpit by agreeing that they are merely "handmaidens of the Lord" going about the business of saving souls in these "last days." They point to Joel's prophecy in the Old Testament, which is repeated by Paul in Acts 9:16 and 17, after a group of both men and women experienced speaking in tongues together. The scriptures read, "And it shall come to pass afterward, that I will pour out my spirit upon all flesh; and your sons and your daughters shall Prophesy, your old men shall dream dreams, your young men shall see visions; And also upon the servants and upon the handmaids in those days will I pour out my spirit" (Joel 2:28, 29). The implied authority given in these verses to women to "prophesy" is repeated by female preachers as evidence of their own right to speak in church. Yet the women know their use of ritual disclaimers will act to remove from the situation some of its threatening potential. The women are most accommodating.

The following was spoken from the pulpit by the female co-pastor of a fairly large congregation: "I always present myself as a handmaiden of the Lord. Let the men take the part of the ministry and the government of the church because they are the head. The Bible clearly says we are the weaker vessel. Relax, I don't call myself a preacher. Let the men do that; it's all right. But you have got to give me the right to be a handmaiden of the Lord, and he has poured out his spirit unto me, and he has called me into his work, and I'm here" (Sister Wanda Nelson, Taft, Indiana). While male ministers may offer similar disclaimers such as "I'm only a mouthpiece of the Lord" or "The sermon you are about to hear comes to you directly from God and not from me," such disclaimers do not have to justify his presence in the pulpit; they only have to serve to indicate his meekness. Like the disclaimers of the women, his speech acts to place responsibility for the message on God rather than on the person speaking.

Interestingly, the Bible verses that are being interpreted to allow women to speak in the religious arena are verses that give voice to "your daughters" and to "servants and handmaidens." It is understandable, I think, that the women focus on the term *handmaiden* rather than on the term *daughter* to justify their role as pastors. Referring to themselves as "handmaidens of the Lord" acknowledges both their servant status and their subservience to God and men. Most of their ritual disclaimers downplay their own abilities and acknowledge that some people may be more comfortable if they distinguish between women "preaching" and women "teaching": "Well, I kinda hope you all aren't expecting too much. Now, I want you to know that I never thought about these things on my own. I prayed, and the Lord revealed these things to me. I have not got that much sense in my head. I'm not intelligent. Now, this may be kinda like teaching, I don't know. You know, sometimes it's kinda hard to preach, but maybe a mixture of both, preaching and teaching" (Sister Connie Morton, Johnson's Creek, Indiana).

The pressure to acquiesce to societal notions of propriety for women is stronger on a female pastor than it is on a female itinerant preacher, who does not have her own home congregation but travels from church to church. This is evidenced by the different preaching styles of women pastors and women preachers: women pastors are more subdued in their presentation style and much more vocal about their personal concern for the individual members of their congregations (see Lawless 1988b). Traveling female evangelists, on the other hand, are much more likely to be energetic behind the pulpit and adopt a preaching style that is more like that of a male preacher, largely because they will not have to answer to the concerns of the congregation the next day. A traveling female preacher does not have a position of power and authority in a church; thus, she does not have to be so careful to protect that position. While the women applaud their own tenacity and determination to survive all criticism, males in the congregation might agree with this man: "I don't believe in women preachers. God didn't have any. He told the men to go out and preach the gospel. He never told a woman to do that. Lord told his disciples, 'I send you amongst wolves.' Now, do you think I'd send my wife out amongst a bunch of heathens? Sinners don't care what they do. They'll string you out. They don't care" (Brother William Bird, Bedford, Indiana). Yet Sister Anna denies this point of view and sees herself as fearless and paints that image of herself in her narratives. She believes the "hard hearts" against her are a direct influence of Satan; yet she illustrates her bravado against a Satan who might approach her directly:

> I've felt it right in this room with me. Some time ago when I was in bed, it woke me up. His presence was so strong that it woke me. And I knew—I felt that same eerie, cold darkness there that I recognized as Satan. And so I said, "Devil, in the name of Jesus, get out of here! Leave me alone." And I literally felt him go. I went back to sleep. He woke me up for the third time.
>
> Finally, the third time, I said, "All right, devil, I am tired of you. I need my rest. You get out of here, leave me alone. I am going to put this Bible under my arm. And I'm going to sleep on the promises of God, and you're not coming back in here to bother me anymore."
>
> And with that, I reached over and got the Bible and laid it under my arm. And I went back to sleep.

Strong maternal and reproductive images help us to understand how a woman functions within the role of pastor more than they aid us in understanding how she got there in the first place. To understand that, we must probe much deeper into the various levels of human mythology—both the mythology of male/female characteristics and the prevailing religious mythology as well. In addition, we must ground our analysis in an understanding of southern Pentecostalism (see Lawless 1988a).

Barbara Welter has argued that during the nineteenth century, a "feminization" of American religion developed because the conceptions of sex-role divisions of labor stipulated that men were out doing the "important business," and religion became categorized as an "expendable institution," one that eventually became the property of the "weaker members of society which . . . generally meant women." This reallocation of religion to the women's sphere determined that it became "more domesticated, more emotional, softer and accommodating—in a word, more 'feminine'" (1976, 84). Welter notes, of course, that the authority of religion did not become "feminized" at all; rather, the churches were filled with women who were subject to male control. With the rise of camp-meeting and revival religions, she found the language to be "sexual in its imagery," urging the (largely female) penitents to "stop struggling and allow yourself to be swept up in his love." She suggests this language was familiar to women: "Whether in the divine or human order, woman was constantly urged to be swept away by a torrent of energy, not to rely on her own strength which was useless, to sink into the arms of Jesus, to become absorbed and assimilated by the Divine Will—the kind of physical sensations which a woman expected to receive and did receive in the course of conversion. 'A trembling of the limbs,' 'a thrill from my toes to my head,' 'wave after wave of feeling' are examples of female reaction to the experience of 'divine penetration'" (1976, 93).

The father/husband who generated this experience through the male pastor or preacher was a jealous God and a demanding one. He expected full submission and obedience to his will. Should he be angered, he would "cast out" his "children" without relent. In time, however, camp-meeting religion's emphasis on religious emotionalism, spirit possession, and a personal relationship with Jesus for all participants, female or male, eventually led to the emergence of twentieth-century Pentecostalism. From camp-meeting religion to Pentecostalism, the large number of women involved saw Jesus as friend and helper, mediator between not only the religious women and their earthly life and problems but, to some degree, the mediator between the women and an awesome, fearful Father God. Jesus was the husband their own husbands could never be: kind, loving, sympathetic, empathetic, and merciful; furthermore, he was available to them through the Holy Ghost and spirit possession. And it was in the enthusiastic revival and camp-meeting services that women came to realize and execute their own spiritual power.

Dickson Bruce, in his examination of camp-meeting religion from 1800 to 1845, tells us, "The major operations of the churches were dominated by men, who had all the ecclesiastical authority. Only at the height of excitement in a camp meeting could women come to share in the leadership of frontier religious activities" (1974, 76). That this was unusual and potentially disruptive is borne out by Bruce's continued comments: "Given the usual position of women in the religious organizations and in plain-folk society, their behavior here [the conversion 'pen,' analogous to a spirit-filled altar call in Pentecostal services] constituted a significant reversal of status, for those who were normally expected to take a subordinate role in life were here enabled to take control of a situation. Not only were the structures of the meeting—which replicated the social structure—purposefully negated, but for a time they were turned upside down" (1974, 86–87).

To help us understand how religious fervor, spirit possession, and emotionalism have been closely aligned with the female religious experience, it may be helpful to note the perceived differences between male and female characteristics and tendencies prevalent in the nineteenth century, as outlined by such scholars as Barbara Welter and Sherry Ortner. The dichotomous model offered by these and other scholars suggests that the female arena came to be associated closely with the home, hearth, and religion—spheres connected in the thinking of the time with woman's "natural" reproductive and mothering capacities. In contrast, the male was associated with an arena defined as more "cultural," one associated with work and politics and centered outside the home. According to this point of view, perceptions of men and women, their affinities, and their roles in society may arise from distinctions based on broad stereotypes that identify man as the hunter/provider and woman as the procreator/nurturer. The various aspects of these polarities in terms of male/female spheres and attributes include culture/nature, public/private, active/passive, dominant/submissive, producers/reproducers, and rational/spiritual.

Certainly, in the years since the publication of Rosaldo and Lamphere's groundbreaking work, *Women, Culture, and Society*, which included Ortner's essay outlining this nature/culture duality, the dichotomous model has been challenged, with arguments suggesting it is too simplistic and overgeneralized and suggests a cross-cultural homogeneity that simply does not exist. Janet Sharistanian specifically addresses the evolution of thinking about the public/domestic dichotomy and reports that arguments against the model—or reinterpretations of it—usually focus on its cross-cultural limitations, its inability to account for transhistorical variation and change, and its insensitivity to considerations of race and class (1986, 4; also 1987). Yet Sharistanian asserts that the "domestic/public paradigm continues to be of value, when it is given precise definition and tested by a specific context" (1986, 7). It is in this spirit that we can find the public/ private dichotomy applicable to the specific lives of Pentecostals in the Upland South, as well as in other sociocultural arenas where patriarchy reigns and where thinking and behavior clearly delineate specific roles and spheres for women and men based on what is "proper" for a woman (domestic) and what is "proper" for a man (public). In the areas where I have done my fieldwork, in southern Indiana and in Missouri, specifically, the male-dominated hierarchy in homes and religion persists, and these rural people are suspicious of and stand rigidly against change. Here it is appropriate for men to "go out" and get jobs (usually employment done in conjunction with farming) and work in the public arena, while the women are expected to stay at home with the children. It is a matter of intense pride that a man can say his wife "doesn't have to work." If she finds she must work to help lighten the financial burdens, this is often perceived as sad and unfortunate, perhaps even pointing to the failure of the husband to provide for his family. As Bruce suggests, the social hierarchy is replicated in the structural composition of the religious beliefs and services. Not only is the pulpit generally reserved for men, who are in a direct line from God to Jesus to man, but many staunch believers still quote the Pauline directives that instruct women to be silent in the churches.

The maternal and reproductive imagery discussed in this essay derives from a culturally based perception of the woman's "natural" role as mother and nurturer. Because of the various fluid emissions that naturally flow from the woman's body (such as blood and milk), her cycle of menses, her ability to carry a child until she bears it, childbirth itself, and her perceived maternal instincts to nurture and protect the child, the female is both consciously and unconsciously seen to exist in a state that is closer to nature than to the world of men (see Douglas, 1966). This "natural" world in which the woman operates has been relegated by men to the domestic sphere because the home is assumed to be the seat of the family, the reproductive lair, the safe haven for the rearing of the children, the escape for the husband. Mother and children are safely ensconced in the private sphere of the home, while the male goes out into the cultural and political arena. While we may not appreciate this picture, it does accurately reflect a way of life for most of the Pentecostals in this study.

How, then, did women during and following the camp-meeting era find ways for spiritual and religious expression within the services? In religious terms, woman's "closer-to-nature" nature was closely aligned with her spiritual nature, which gave her easier access to spirits and religious ecstasy (of course, in other eras, this perceived feminine nature allowed her to consort with devils and demons). While it was easy to say women were simpler, less complicated, more childlike, and therefore more likely to succumb to emotionalism and interactions with spirits, their spiritual powers were, nonetheless, respected and even encouraged. As Bruce points out, it was a woman's access to spiritual power that could lead to "control of a situation," as is the case in women's testimonies that are so long and elaborate that they actually serve to dominate the church services (see Lawless 1983b).

While it is true that males have argued that their arena is the more important and sophisticated, they have, nevertheless, never lost sight of the importance of female spiritual power and reproductive capacity. In an insightful article on the roots of patriarchy, Azizah al-Hibri has further suggested an important connection between reproduction and immortality, positing that the awe men feel about women's ability to reproduce themselves is intensified by the notion that her progeny actually serve to immortalize her. Males, on the other hand, suffer a bit of a crisis when they realize that they cannot bear their own progeny. Certainly men have claimed the seed of the life force and attempted to hyperbolize their reproductive participation, but in the end, they can only call their ideas, their books, and their technological products the "babies" they have "labored" over. The bottom line, according to al-Hibri, is that they can only produce, not reproduce (1983).

Man's inability to come to grips with the seat of female power, in sexual, spiritual, and reproductive terms, underlies the seemingly contradictory stance males have taken toward the hearth and home and toward women and religion. The image of woman as a dangerous temptress, powerful and capable of controlling men, has its counterpart, of course, in woman as mother and faithful wife, protector of the family, the hearth, and home, the upright advocate of Christian morals and ethics. This is not a new nor unique notion, of course. Writing about the Puritans, Mary Dunn comments that "feminine virtue became a family affair. Indeed, it is through the family that the Christian community would be preserved. To be a good woman is to be a good Christian" (1978, 594). By relegating woman to the domestic sphere and by claiming dominance over that sphere, men have attempted to render it, and the women in it, ineffectual and unimportant, yet relegating morality and even salvation to the sphere of women enhances women's status. Welter, examining the attitudes of males toward wife and mother, found that women came to embody all the values men profess to hold so dear—family, home, purity, and piety. She proposes that as the world became more and more unstable, "true womanhood" became the one stable element (1976).

Spiritual power, as opposed to church authority, is permitted the woman because it does not detract from her natural feminine delicacy; it makes her, in fact, even lovelier by stressing her attributes of holiness and encouraging her to maintain her position in the home and remain submissive to her husband. Woman is held to be stronger only in her defense against the evils of the world and in her ability to give birth and raise children; she was often held up as perfect. Woman, dressed in holiness garments, told she was pure and selfless, was given the responsibility of rearing the children and maintaining piety. She ran the risk of becoming a self-fulfilling prophecy. Of course, this image of woman also denies, ignores, and defeats woman's sexual powers while still allowing for the deep-seated notion of woman as sin incarnate but under control.

During the great revivals of the eighteenth and nineteenth centuries, spiritual fervor swept the country, and women were noted to have participated in great swelling numbers (Bruce 1974). Mary Ryan makes a connection between women's religious roles and the rise of American revivalism and enthusiastic religion: "At the time of the first [documented] revival [in New York, 1814], women constituted 70% of the church population. The mother, in other words, firmly planted the families' religious root on the frontier" (1978, 602–624). Even today, women dominate in numbers in Pentecostal churches and persist in their conviction that the secular and the sacred are to remain separate worlds.

My own fieldwork has consistently indicated that the moral and spiritual aspects, which may be recognized as religious concerns, remain within the women's sphere, closely associated with home and hearth and with the rearing of offspring. In southern Indiana, for example, very few men attended the churches I observed with the exception of a male pastor (if that was the case) and older men.[10] When I asked men why there were more women attending the services, they were often embarrassed and contended that religion was a bit "sissy," especially in the small churches where emotionalism, tongue-speaking, and shouting was the norm. The men perceived this to be female behavior. Women, on the other hand, expressed great love for the church services and the opportunity to see the other women in their immediate geographical community. They often hugged and kissed one another in greeting and departure, talked at length both before and after service, and claimed the women in the church were their "sisters." Their strong devotion and dedication to things religious directly affected the perception of women as the protectors of the spiritual realm. On the other hand, it was noticeable that male religious leaders were often more inclined to move the church into a more public, political, and secular arena. As religious leaders seek to become community powers, their authority often crosses various public and political boundaries. This move into the public, secularized arena is a move that is resisted by many staunchly conservative Pentecostals in this country, both women and men.

How does all of this help us to understand how women might come to have the power and authority of the pastorate of a Pentecostal congregation? The answer lies in the recognition that Pentecostalism has resisted secularization largely because its constituents are more comfortable within the spiritual world of traditional religion than they are in the secular world (see Clements 1974). The central concerns of Pentecostalism rest firmly in the sacred, spiritual realm, one that rejects outright the secular world and all the evil it is perceived to hold. All aspects of "the world," as they refer to any arena not connected with the spiritual/religious world, are shunned and perceived as sinful, evil, uncontrolled, and inspired by Satan (see Lawless 1983a). Humans are safe, they believe, only within the confines of the religious world. Ironically, the power a woman is able to utilize in her quest for the pulpit and in her procurement of religious authority stems from the most conservative, traditional roots of this twentieth-century American denomination. If a woman can assure her conservative congregation that she will keep the religion closely connected to the spiritual realm and the family-based community, as far away from the secular as is realistically possible, then she has a better chance of gaining the pastorate than a man who may be perceived as more likely to take the church toward undesired intersections with the secular world. The female pastor's disregard for the public arena and her inclination toward the home and family represent the aspects of life her congregation holds most dear. By making a clear commitment to the sacred/religious realm and by pronouncing her intention and ability to keep the church within the domestic/spiritual sphere, she can win their confidence. And, further, if she "mothers" the congregation members, cares for them, nurtures them, empathizes with them, counsels them, and can pray their souls into heaven, then they are all that much more likely to allow her to serve as their pastor. It is, after all, her ability to confer with God's spirit that has made her a spiritual being; therefore, she must utilize this perception of her natural/spiritual powers to assume a position of authority within the church. She is, they recognize, a spiritual being who can reproduce herself; she is close to nature and close to God and his spirits. Unleashed, her power becomes contradictory, even dangerous, but employed for the guidance and nurturance of men and women's souls, it might prove beneficial. At least for this conservative religion, the risk is worth taking. Her guidance in the spiritual world becomes a reality, especially as opposed to a dreaded move toward secularization and the evils the world has to offer.

Anna Walters and her sister Pentecostal pastors do not represent "a flood of women searching out the liberating promises of scripture to revise theologies," nor are they taking great strides toward a "new theology" or a "new ethics." Within the context of their lives, such a stance would be counterproductive. These women are not liberated from the prejudices and restrictions that hamper other women in this conservative milieu, but they are liberated from the standard script of cloistered wife and mother. The penalties can be high, however, for they must also be "superwomen." The young woman who contemplates being a pastor must also be a wife and mother, and she must extol the virtues of those capacities at every opportunity. She must demonstrate her "motherly" nature and exclaim her delight in being a wife and mother, her joy in her children and her home. She must deny her sexuality, and she must acknowledge her inferior status as woman and submit herself to all men. Yet she can extol her spiritual power and utilize her reproductive and maternal capacities as strategies to strengthen her position. The role is complex, full of pitfalls and possible infractions. The female pastor must balance her life carefully—a move too far in any direction could alter the balance of sacred and domestic power.

Notes

1. My work from 1983–1985 was generously supported by research grants from the University of Missouri and by a National Endowment Humanities Research Fellowship. Bible citations are from the King James Version, the only standard version accepted by the Pentecostal churches included in this study. All names of people and places have been changed to protect the privacy of the participants. A shorter version of this essay was delivered at the American Folklore Society meeting in 1987 and subsequently appeared in 1987 in the *Journal of American Folklore* (Vol. 100, Issue 398: 469–479) as "Piety and Motherhood: Reproductive Images and Maternal Strategies of the Woman Preacher." A longer version of this material was also developed in my book *Handmaidens of the Lord*

(Illinois, 1988), as well as several articles, including "Tradition and Poetics," in *A Memorial for Milman Parry* (1986) and "Traditional Women Preachers in mid-Missouri," *Missouri Folklore Journal* (1984).

2. I am aware that scholars familiar with traditional African American religion in this country and the role of women often note significant differences with this Anglo-American religious tradition and female pastors.

3. Bible citations are from the King James Version, the only version accepted by all of the Pentecostal churches included in this study.

4. Most of the interviews with the women in this study were conducted in 1983 and 1985. The tapes are housed in my personal archive. All names of people and places have been changed to protect their privacy.

5. See, for example, Petroff (1986), especially her introduction (3–59).

6. I am particularly intrigued with the notion of these mothers being "in-valid" for their daughters, noting the historical correlation of femaleness, illness, and "invalidity" in the early years of this century.

7. Both of these women claim that their churches "did not hire me" and cannot fire me." In truth, some of these small rural congregations do not actually hire a pastor. The process is rather loose at times. Ministers do not have to attend seminary or gain official documentation of their status except from the state in order to marry and bury people. Persons who feel a call from God to preach may make the rounds from church to church, preaching only when the opportunity arises for several years before becoming established as the pastor of a church. They must be selected, in essence, by the congregation, but often there is no money involved, so the women may be technically correct in asserting the congregation "didn't hire" them and "cannot fire" them. I suspect these strong statements also reflect a shared opinion by the congregations and the pastors that *God* calls one to preach and that, in reality, God hires and God fires, and that is not the prerogative of the congregation members.

8. While the women in this study have seen my descriptions and interpretations of their lives and their preaching and, in general, approve of my conclusions, they do not agree with my interpretation of this particular point. Even though I can point out to them (and they, of course, already know this) that a considerable number of their sermons come back to a concern with "making it into heaven," they do not agree that this is an indication that they are, in fact, fearful of getting into the gates of heaven themselves. My own interpretation suggests that the predominance of this image stems from their own ambivalence about their role in religion and their public role in the church. I do not make this suggestion lightly or without attention to their point of view; rather, I think it is possible that the concern may be there in an unconscious way and is revealed in their religious rhetoric and the language they use. Neither of these foci of sermons is gender-specific; that is, one would find sermons on total sacrifice and making it into heaven in male sermons as well. The particular ways these topics are developed in the sermons of women, however, do suggest a female perspective. The themes of Pentecostal women's sermons have been examined in more detail in my book *Handmaidens of the Lord*. I have also continued my thinking on this issue in two other published articles (1991; 1992).

9. This sermon by Sister Anna Brock Walters can be found in its entirety in the appendix of *Handmaidens of the Lord*, 171–188.

10. It is my observation that the men come back to church later in life because they have agreed all along with the tenets of the faith and believe it is important to "get right with God"

before it is too late. Most often during their middle-aged years, however, they were more likely to drop off their wives and children at church and wait until the time to pick them up; I have even known men who will sit in the car and wait for their family through the entire church service.

References Cited

al-Hibri, Azizah. 1983. "Reproduction, Mothering, and the Origins of Patriarchy." In *Mothering: Essays in Feminist Theory*, edited by Joyce Trebilcot, 81–93. Totowa, NJ: Rowman and Allanheld.

Behnke, Donna. 1982. *Religious Issues in Nineteenth Century Feminism*. New York: Whitsom.

Bruce, Dickson. 1974. *And They All Sang Hallelujah: Plain-Folk Camp-Meeting Religion, 1800–1845*. Knoxville: University of Tennessee Press.

Clements, William. 1974. "The American Folk Church." PhD diss., Indiana.

Douglas, Mary. 1966. *Purity and Danger: An Analysis of the Concepts of Pollution and Taboo*. London: Routledge and Kegan Paul.

Dunn, Mary M. 1978. "Saints and Sisters: Congregational and Quaker Women in the Early Colonial Period." *American Quarterly* 30:582–602.

Gilligan, Carol. 1982. *In a Different Voice: Psychological Theory and Women's Development*. Cambridge: Harvard University Press.

James, Janet Wilson. 1978. "Women and Religion: An Introduction." *American Quarterly* 30:579–581.

Lawless, Elaine J. 1983a. "Brothers and Sisters: Pentecostals as a Folk Group." *Western Folklore* 43:85–104.

———. 1983b. "Shouting for the Lord: The Power of Women's Speech in the Pentecostal Service." *Journal of American Folklore* 96 (382): 434–459.

———. 1988a. *God's Peculiar People: Women's Voices and Folk Tradition in a Pentecostal Church*. Lexington: University Press of Kentucky.

———. 1988b. *Handmaidens of the Lord: Pentecostal Women Preachers and Traditional Religion*. Publications of the American Folklore Society, n.s., no. 9. Philadelphia: University of Pennsylvania Press.

———. 1991. "Women's Life Stories and Reciprocal Ethnography as Feminist and Emergent." *Journal of Folklore Research* 28, no. 1 (Fall): 35–61.

———. 1992. "'I Was Afraid Someone like You . . . an Outsider . . . Would Misunderstand': Negotiating Interpretive Differences between Ethnographers and Subjects." *Journal of American Folklore* 105 (417): 302–315.

Ortner, Sherry. 1974. "Is Female to Male as Nature Is to Culture?" In *Woman, Culture, and Society*, edited by Michelle Zimbalist Rosaldo and Louise Lamphere, 67–87. Stanford: Stanford University Press.

Petroff, Elizabeth Alvilda. 1986. *Medieval Women's Visionary Literature*. New York: Oxford University Press.

Rich, Adrienne. 1977. *Of Woman Born: Motherhood as Experience and Institution*. New York: Bantam Books.

Rosaldo, Michelle Zimbalist, and Louise Lamphere, eds. 1974. *Woman, Culture, and Society.* Stanford: Stanford University Press.

Ryan, Mary. 1978. "A Women's Awakening: Evangelical Religion and the Families of Utica, N.Y., 1800–1840." *American Quarterly* 30:602–624.

Sharistanian, Janet, ed. 1986. *Gender, Ideology, and Action: Historical Perspectives on Women's Public Lives.* Westport, CO: Greenwood Press.

———. 1987. *Beyond the Public/Domestic Dichotomy: Contemporary Perspectives on Women's Public Lives.* New York: Greenwood Press.

Welter, Barbara. 1976. *Dimity Convictions: The American Woman in the Nineteenth Century.* Athens: Ohio University Press.

4

"I WAS AFRAID SOMEONE LIKE YOU . . . AN OUTSIDER . . . WOULD MISUNDERSTAND"

Negotiating Interpretive Differences between Ethnographers and Subjects

This article is about reflexivity, about the role of the ethnographer in the wave of thinking about a "new ethnography"; it is about acknowledging who we are as we do ethnography and where we are as we write up these ethnographies and as we offer our interpretations of the materials we study. To be reflexive, I must talk about my work and about myself *in* my work. That is what this article is about: *where we are in our work*. As ethnographers striving to be conscious of our own ideologies, we are obligated to present ourselves in our texts as we are in our work: humans seeking understanding, engaged in dialogue and interpretation

Author's note: This article represents a reflexive look at the role of the folklore ethnographer in field research and in writing. Here I address the ethical and scholarly dimensions of a continued dialogue between ethnographers and subjects. This article was a turning point in my ethnographic life. My new work with mainline congregational pastors in mid-Missouri helped me identify what was inadequate in the ways I interpreted the Pentecostal women's sermons and life stories and enabled me to move forward toward a more collaborative, dialogic ethnography that I am calling "reciprocal ethnography." I presented a shorter version of this article at the 1989 American Folklore Society Annual Meeting in Philadelphia on a panel entitled "Reflexivity and the Role of the Ethnographer in Religious Folklife Studies," sponsored by the Religious Folklore and Folklife Section of AFS. The panel included Don Yoder, Diane Goldstein, David Hufford, William Wilson, Leonard Norman Primiano, and me; the discussant was Jeff Todd Titon. This article appeared in the *Journal of American Folklore* 105 (Summer 1992): 302–315.

with other people who are engaged in dialogue and interpretation, seeking meaning. My concern with reflexivity and my position in my fieldwork and in my writing does not, I think, constitute the kind of self-aggrandizement suggested by Mascia-Lees et al. in their critique of the "new ethnography" (1989); by making myself (the ethnographer) into a character in the ethnography, I do not intend to commit, once again, the error of reinforcing the status of the researcher as the more authoritative speaker. My intention is, in fact, to remedy such a situation. A reflexive stance should illuminate the biases and preconceptions that inform our interpretations (where *we* are) and move us forward, then, in the direction of collectivity in interpretation and a new authentication of a multivocal kind of ethnography, which includes, as well, where *others* are but which does not privilege one interpretation over another.

As anthropologists, folklorists, historians, feminist scholars, narratologists, sociologists, and critical theorists openly move away from a positivist approach and toward interpreting case studies, we find a common language in this new interdisciplinary movement: we hear of authenticity, thick description, verisimilitude, negotiation, reciprocity, and empowerment. According to James Clifford and George Marcus, this movement is consciously ideological, postpositivist, and postmodern in that we are currently in a "crisis of representation" that "arises from uncertainty about adequate means of describing social reality. It is an expression of the failure of post-World War II paradigms . . . to account for conditions within American society, which seem to be in a state of profound transition" (as quoted in McCall and Wittner 1991, 7). The new "corrective sociology," which, according to Ken Plummer, calls for (1) paying tribute to human subjectivity and creativity, (2) paying attention to concrete human experience—talk, feelings, action, (3) developing an "intimate familiarity" with such experiences through fieldwork, and, finally, (4) a self-awareness of the ultimate moral and political role of the ethnographer (as in McCall and Wittner 1991, 4–5), sounds surprisingly similar to what folklorists have known and stressed for some time—but without the proper attention to and respect for (4) above. Much of my thinking for this article comes in response to the works of James Clifford, George Marcus, and Michael M. J. Fischer, particularly *Anthropology as Cultural Critique* (Marcus and Fischer 1986) and *Writing Culture* (Clifford and Marcus 1986); from Jay Ruby's *A Crack in the Mirror* (1982); and most recently from the work of sociologists Howard Becker and Michael McCall, as developed in their collaborative book,

Symbolic Interaction and Cultural Studies (1991), a book that is written as a dialogue between disciplines. Finally, my thinking has been sharpened by the thoughtful critique of the "new ethnography" by feminists Frances Mascia-Lees, Patricia Sharpe, and Colleen Cohen (1989).

In 1983, I began fieldwork in Missouri for a book on Pentecostal women preachers, eventually published in 1988 as *Handmaidens of the Lord*. In those five years, I came to know several women preachers quite well and one in particular very well. I would like to say, and I believe, that this woman (identified in my book as Sister Anna) has become my friend. I know that, on some level, she considers me her friend—she sends me cards and letters, and sometimes, when her problems become quite unbearable, she calls me on the phone late at night to talk, and mostly I just listen. I am, I am certain, a "safe" listener, far from her home and her congregation. She still writes to me and I to her.

For my part, I have come to love this woman in a very special way. Mostly, I admire her. She exemplifies everything I find to be admirable. She has discovered a way to be a real force in her (very male-defined, male-dominated) community; she is energetic, independent, strong, her own boss, creative, and powerful. Recognizing her small-town, rural milieu as so very close to the one I grew up in myself, I know why I admire her so much. Without ever leaving, Anna has managed to defy all the typical expectations for women in her world and to be her own person. I admire women with energy and enthusiasm who learn how to direct their own lives. Anna is, in fact, everything my mother is not. She has found her voice in a world that tries to tell her she has no right to speak.

My admiration for Sister Anna and her sister preachers is evident in my book. In many ways I do feel that Sister Anna is an extraordinary woman. She is diminutive, weighing only about ninety-two pounds. She is in constant pain with scoliosis of the spine, she endured a bout with cancer several years ago, and she works night and day. She runs the church where she has served as pastor for nearly twenty years. She drives the bus to Sunday school, teaches Sunday school, runs the youth camp, bakes the cakes for the weddings, and then performs the weddings. I actually cannot see where she gets her stamina, the strength to do three to five services per week, preach at the county nursing homes, visit the sick at home and in hospitals, counsel those who need it, *and* be a loving wife, mother, and grandmother. How does she do it? The fact that she does evokes my greatest admiration, although I must also admit my frustration that she is required to perform all of these duties well and in eternal cheerfulness. *She says* God does it. *She says* he gives her the strength. *She says* it is all the joy of her life, not work, because he makes it so. But I tend to ignore what she is saying to me. From my viewpoint, *she* is her own strength. Self-denial seems appropriate to the picture. This tension between her view and mine is the focus of this article.

My fieldwork on Pentecostal women preachers took basically three angles: I collected the life stories of many women preachers and pastors; I interviewed them about their calling and about their ministry; and I recorded their sermons, typing them verbatim with some regard for performance style and identifying patterns (repeated images, words, language, stories). The book includes, first, a brief description of the fieldwork context; it then offers four verbatim life stories of women preachers, and it also includes several interpretive chapters in which I (1) analyze the importance of the similarities of the women's life stories, postulating that women who feel they have been "called" to preach mold and "recreate" an acceptable story about their calling and testing of God's intentions to validate their position behind the pulpit; (2) describe the differences I perceived between the way women preachers and women pastors preach—and offer some reasons why this might be so; (3) discuss the themes I felt were most prevalent in the sermons I collected and examined in detail—and offer reasons why these women gravitated toward these particular themes; and (4) discuss the maternal and reproductive images that I felt factored in women's sermons, suggesting how these images serve as strategies to ensure women access to the pulpit (Lawless 1987).

The women I was working with in central and southern Missouri seemed comfortable with my presence in their homes and churches—to a degree. They seemed to get used to me being there, and several, especially Sister Anna, professed that they had begun to look forward to my visits. Although many were openly flattered by my attention, and by my intention to include them in a book, as many were also very nervous about my attentions because within their community they had to strive always to keep a low profile—at least low enough to avoid eliciting criticism—as women preachers and pastors, as independent women, as counselors to both men and women, and as the authority figures in their churches. Most walked a tightrope of nervous tension within their communities—trying to do and be all they wanted and needed to and to remain a bit invisible at the same time. This tension was especially apparent when I went into private homes to interview the women, and their husbands became noticeably agitated—and was even more apparent if the man was also a minister and felt I really ought to be there to interview him.

I tried to tell the women what I was going to write and why. They seemed comfortable with the notion of a book on women preachers in Missouri and, although most asked me not to use real names, privately delighted to be included. Many gave me tape recordings of sermons they had given in the past. They signed releases indicating that they knew what I was doing and were comfortable with the book's concept, and they freely gave me permission to use any and all material accumulated largely through taped recordings.

Each of the women was given a copy of her own life story. I asked them to tell me if anything should be changed or deleted, if names should be changed, and if they had included anything they really didn't (now) want in the book. I felt somewhat reticent about this last part because it seemed too much like informant censorship, and I recalled how uncomfortable Betsy Peterson and I were when church members showed up in the television studio at Indiana University as we edited *Joy Unspeakable* (1981) and offered their own views about how that film ought to be put together. Most of the women ministers, however, changed very little except a few names of people, towns, and church supervisors. One woman kept insisting that she had not said certain things, so I went back and listened to the recordings and, although the comments were clearly on the tape, I eventually omitted the questionable sections. I also gave each woman at least one transcribed sermon of her own. Many expressed amazement that they had "said that!"

What I did not do was to take all my ideas, my interpretations, and my conclusions about their lives, their ministry, and their sermons back to them and ask for their interpretations of my interpretations. Now, certainly, we as ethnographers do this all the time, at least on one level. We wonder about something; we find a tactful way to ask a question of our informants; we put it to them casually—"do you think . . ." or "what do you think is meant by . . ." But I did not give refined versions of my interpretive chapters to these women and seek their opinions about my opinions. And now, in retrospect, I have to ask why I didn't. Do you? Was it fear that they might disagree with me and throw me off guard? Was it the belief that since these were largely uneducated "folk," they would have difficulties understanding sophisticated academic interpretations and probably would never read my book anyway? Was I afraid I might possibly be wrong? Did I just not think about doing it?

Or is it possible, as Becker has suggested, that I was responding to what I know to be a bias about bias that exists within my own academic community? Becker argues that "an accusation [of bias] arises when the research gives credence, in any serious way, to the perspective of the subordinate group in some hierarchical relationship. In other words, we provoke the charge of bias, in ourselves and others, by refusing to give credence and deference to an established status order, in which knowledge and truth and the right to be heard are not equally distributed. 'Everyone knows' that responsible professionals know more about things than lay people" (Becker 1970, 125–127).

My research and thinking about a new book I am working on have helped me to be reflexive about this finished work, a process I shall elaborate on later in this article.

Jeff Titon, in his book on religious folklife, *Powerhouse for God* (1988), has suggested that hermeneutic phenomenology seems to be the best available framework for folklorists contemplating the affective performances of folklore within a community (13). Relying on Dennis Tedlock's insistence that we develop a "dialogical method of interpretation in which the dialogue is carried from the field to the scholar's published account," Titon guides us toward formulating reinterpretations that are based on our informant's interpretations of our interpretations (1988, 13). Such a dialogue, argues Tedlock, "creates a world or an understanding of the *differences between* two worlds, that exists between persons who were indeterminately far apart, in all sorts of different ways, when they started out on their conversation" (as quoted in Titon 1988, 13). Although Titon suggests that, as far as he knows, no folklorist or ethnomusicologist has attempted an interpretive work from this standpoint, he has some ideas about how such a work ought to be approached:

> In these published accounts, the "folk" will be allowed to speak for themselves, and they will speak—as they do—to each other and to the folklorist. The "folk" texts and the folk interpretations of texts will be presented as one part of the dialogue. The folklorist takes up the other side of the dialogue, and will be presented in dialogue with the folk: that is, his or her questions and responses and interpretations in performance will be presented as well. . . . The folklorist continues to return to the "folk" where they are to continue the dialogue . . . not to do "follow-up" fieldwork or verify conclusions, but to continue the dialogue, knowing that the conclusions will never be conclusive. And then . . . there is yet another dialogue, and this is between the scholar and his or her colleagues, students, and the interested public. (1988, 13)

What Titon implies but does not explore here, but which is *critical* for us to examine, is the natural (but very difficult) extension of his methodology—that is, to carry this dialogue past the scholar's interpretations, back to the people involved, and into the published work so that the dialogue is actually visible for the reading audience. Of course, such a "dialogue" is implicitly involved with any readers and the works they are reading; that is, they may agree, or disagree, or be left pondering, or not caring, and so on. But to ensure an actual dialogue, with different viewpoints being offered to the (imaginary) reader, the dialogue between the scholar and the people being studied must somehow be foregrounded for the reader as well. If the dialogue is left implicit, or masked, or subsumed, then the reader can only guess at what the scholar's first interpretations were and how the dialogue with the people involved might have altered or expanded the scholar's viewpoint(s).

Allow me to diverge a bit here and tell you how this *did not* happen with *Handmaidens of the Lord*—although now I desperately wish it had—and how I want to try to make certain that it can happen in my future work. As mentioned earlier, the women ministers in my book saw portions of the work before it was published—but not the interpretive sections. When the book came out, I proudly carted free copies of it around to all the women who featured most prominently, told them I hoped they liked it, and then left town. Perhaps many of you have done exactly the same thing—I guess I hope so!

Before proceeding, I do want to share the final paragraph of the epilogue of my book because I think it is germane to my discussion. You should know that Sister Anna's husband had left her some weeks earlier and had threatened to divorce her.[1] He was jealous of her church time and knew this was a way to get her in line—if he divorced her, she would lose her pastorship. In the epilogue, I wrote:

> Several weeks later I was not surprised to get a call from Anna telling me that her husband was back; she had taken him back in. I still do not know fully what the terms of the reconciliation are, but I do know that taking her husband back was the only way Sister Anna could maintain the position of pastor of her church and hold onto the power and authority she had worked so hard to acquire. I also suspect that by taking him back, she had to relinquish some of her freedom. She had to trade her independence for the right to retain her role. She was reined in by this man. From the privacy of the home, his home, came the message loud and clear: we have a "monster" on our hands. This woman has clearly overstepped her bounds. You must support my effort to

put her back in her "place." She must submit, first, to my will—then God's. In my house, I am Lord, and I will not be subject to my wife. She must obey me. I will allow her to be your pastor, and you can love and respect her. But you can keep her only if she first heeds my will. If she does not bend, then I will divorce her. And you will throw her out, because you know you agree with me. (Lawless 1988, 170)

Most of the women really never responded to the book—other than to say it was nice. I am really not certain they even read it. Sister Anna, however, whom I had come to know and love and who is featured very prominently in the book, with her photo on the cover, did read every word, and she did respond—most vociferously. I have in my possession several letters I received from her during this time. She was flat on her back with an injury and had plenty of time to reflect on what I had said and to tell me what she thought.

If I quote portions of these letters—even if you've never read the book—I believe you can understand just how different our perceptions of her role were or are. Anna wrote to me (letter to the author, September 30, 1988),

Thanks very much for the book. I have found a few mistakes, a few places of misquotes—but I know it would be very difficult to be writing about others and get every detail correct. For the most part I feel it is a great book and I am almost afraid to share what I felt coming through it—perhaps I am too judgmental about my own preaching. The part that really scares me is the part about [my husband]. He is still very much opposed to me. . . . Also, the place where you said I "bundled up my husband and children and moved from Kansas City." This makes it look like I was "boss" and my children *know* this was far, far from the way our house was. Their dad was certainly the head of our home in every way, and I was the submissive wife as the Bible commands, but *he, he* is the one who saw in me the gifts and talents that I didn't even give myself credit for and pushed me to use what abilities God gave me. So he loved it when we left K.C.

I have been afraid [underlined twice] people (outsider's like yourself) would see me as trying to be a "Superwoman" by doing all I do, but the real truth is, it's the *joy of my life to do for others*! I really have *never* neglected my family or my house. My kids—esp. my boys have told me over and over, this. [My first husband] assured me of this! I've always cooked "home-made" bread, cakes, cookies, etc., kept a clean house and laundry always done up and only one time I was away from home one full week in ministry and my daughter was with me. . . . I never did this until my children were older. . . . I really wish the book had read with more of the real place I took—not the brash woman who led my family or ruled it! Really, I was a very timid person who stood back until I knew I was wanted and approved of. . . .

Anna's letters were painful for me to read. Somehow I think she read my epilogue as saying that I, too, saw her as "monstrous"—a superwoman on the one hand, an unfit wife and mother on the other. She is clearly uncomfortable with the superwoman image, knowing fully how such a characterization would affect her standing in the community and within her immediate and extended (church) family. My first very difficult task was to convince Anna that the final paragraphs of the epilogue did not in any way reflect my own thinking about her and what she had chosen to do but that I had merely hypothesized what her husband was thinking and saying as he tried to get her to do what he wanted her to do. Convincing her about my interpretation of her sermons was much more difficult.

In the sermon chapters of my book, I examined two major themes I found to be most in evidence in the women's sermons I studied: (1) the importance of "total sacrifice" for God and (2) the fear of not making it into heaven. About these two themes, I wrote that these were sermons of "passive submission." The preachers admonish their congregations not to "boast for their own accomplishments, for that is sure to provoke the wrath of God—and the ultimate consequence of disobeying God's plan and inciting his anger is to not make it into heaven" (Lawless 1988, 124). I argued that the women perceived themselves as "children" of a threatening and powerful "Father." I quote from my book:

> Embedded here is the message that life on this earth is not a particularly pleasant one; even compliance with "God's plan" does not guarantee a "bed of roses" she [Anna] says. The passive obedience outlined here strikes me as a female stance appropriate for women in this context; there is not much explanation, no real rationalization for this total submission to "God's plan" and the total denial of one's own capabilities and accomplishments, yet complete compliance is expected, even demanded. The only explanation given is that disobedience is bound to provoke the wrath of God and result in the loss of one's place in heaven. We shall see how this theme is duplicated in other sermons. (124)

> Most of the women who preached these sermons became quite emotional before their sermon was completed. Their fears are genuine, heartfelt; the urgency they preach is an urgency they truly believe. Their fear is for their own salvation; without a doubt Sister Anna has a dreadful fear of being left "standing outside" the door [of heaven] when it is shut. (139)

> Basically, it seems, they cannot rid themselves of their eternal state of transgression. They feel worthless, inept, full of sin, and no matter what kind of life they have led, they are certainly not convinced of their own salvation. They are afraid and it shows. (142)

Anna's response to my interpretations came in one of her long letters (letter to the author, September 30, 1988):

> I preach a lot about a loving Father, a caring Father and I serve him because I love him so very much, *never* because I am afraid of him. I'm afraid people will be left with the feeling I only fling out judgment—fear and that people must be perfect. No one can be, and God is a just, loving God as well as He can and will be an angry God when people reject his son Jesus Christ. "The joy of the Lord is my strength." Though flat on my back, I have joy and I'm not defeated or discouraged—God always turns around for our good what Satan means for evil against us. "Greater is He that is within me, than He that is in the world." I *know* I am a forgiven child of God and ready for heaven and I know I will go in the Rapture. I really wish this had been brought out in the book—really I don't fear God will shut the door on me, He will only close the door on those who reject His Son who gave Himself for us.

After several more pages of this, Anna closes with "Please don't feel I am upset with you. I am sorry I *came across* like I wanted to be a Superwoman or that I 'ruled' in my home and church . . . God is so good. I love you. Anna."

While I kept Anna's letters to me, I did not make or keep copies of the letters I sent to Anna during this dialogue. I wish I had. In my letters, I tried to make her understand that she certainly had not "come across" as someone who wanted attention because she was trying to be a "Super Woman." I tried to tell her that I admired her strength and that I knew she had done it all—kept her house clean and taken care of her home and children, the laundry, the cooking, even as she was serving as the pastor of her church. I pointed out that I never suggested that she didn't take care of these things. I had less to say about her interpretations of my interpretations of her sermons. I held fast to my belief that she and the other women harbored a very deep fear that somehow they had overstepped their bounds and feared repercussions at the Pearly Gates—that somehow someone was keeping tally of how things were going. Certainly Anna's crumbling second marriage was cause for concern. But I knew that Anna had misunderstood my admiration and feared it would paint a negative picture of her. I sensed also that even if we openly disagreed in our interpretations of the sermons, I had privileged my interpretation over hers. I had not, in fact, even included hers. I knew, too, from her letters that she believed that I felt she had overstepped her bounds. But the dialogue was difficult. Anna wrote back (letter to the author, November 2, 1988):

> I was so relieved and thrilled that it was me who misunderstood. I am proud of the book and always of you, and listen real, real love can't be turned on and off like a water faucet. So our friendship has been tested now and survived the test

and we will be stronger for having done so! Just as long as I know *you* didn't "mis-read" my actions is all that matters. . . . Honey, thank you very, very much, My daughter and sons want one of the books very much. I'll explain to them how I misunderstood so they won't make the same mistake I did.

Needless to say, somewhere long before this book went to the publishers, the "dialogue" had been disconnected. Now, as I review these letters, I wish my book had not ended where it did; this continued dialogue with Anna should have been included. I wish that her interpretation of my interpretation had been included—followed by the reinterpretations I would write after hearing her own. Most important is our understanding of the "folk hermeneutic," which may not appear so vividly unless it is in response to our own interpretations. Equally important is the reminder to us as scholars that our interpretations are not the "last word," that our interpretations are not necessarily the right or the insightful ones.

Whether or not I agree with everything Anna wrote to me in her letters, the fact remains that what she has said has made me rethink my methodology as well as my interpretations—especially the premises upon which those interpretations were based. Certainly, her responses to my interpretations have complicated the issue. It was easier, cleaner, and simpler for me to analyze the sermons and determine that they revealed fears she and the other women had about making it into heaven. It was easy for me, a female scholar in an arena that recognizes my rights and abilities (on occasion, and especially if I demand them and call attention to them), to compose a picture of Anna that reflected independence, creativity, strength, and power. My cultural lens, however, is very different from Anna's, and my flattering descriptions hurt and confused her. She is actually not supposed to be any of the things I said she was. She does not (cannot?) believe she is strong or powerful or independent. She has composed for herself a script that is in alignment with her sociocultural surroundings; my picture of her is skewed by my stance as "an outsider" (Anna's words).

Anna feared this would happen, she says; the perspective I took to her small, midwestern town did not fit her life and community. Her interpretative message should have been offered as well as my own in the chapter on themes in women's sermons. The scholar presents her interpretation; the native responds to that interpretation; the scholar, then, is required to (perhaps) adjust her lens and determine why the interpretations are so different and in what ways they are and are not compatible. In some ways, I may still believe the women who preach so often about not making it into heaven are fearful, yet I am morally obligated to listen and hear the words of my subject and offer them juxtaposed with my own. Anna emphatically states, "I know I am a forgiven child of God and ready for heaven and I know I will go in the Rapture. . . . really I don't fear God will shut the door on me" (letter to the author, September 30, 1988). This could not be any more straightforward or honest. My analysis might insist on probing Sister Anna's words and determine that, indeed, her protest does nothing to alleviate the reality of her fears. But I am not a psychoanalyst; thus, I find myself in the position of having to acknowledge that my interpretation was possibly naïve and presumptuous. Most certainly I should not have privileged my interpretation over Anna's.

Titon claims that hermeneutic phenomenology, as we attempt to write the rules for its application, is based on the principle of the hermeneutic circle—going back to the performance, or lived situation, and continuing the dialogue with the persons we are studying. We must fight the bias Becker has criticized and authenticate the voice of the participants.

So I had two ideas. First, I would write a critique of *Handmaidens of the Lord* and how it failed to continue the dialogue, and, second, I would include the dialogue that has taken place between me and the subjects of my new book, tentatively titled *(W)Holy Women: Invoking a Connected Theology of Wholeness and Well-Being* (1993) in the final published work. Perhaps this critique of *Handmaidens of the Lord* will appear in subsequent editions of the book as a second epilogue, or, perhaps, this article itself will serve as a second epilogue and, as such, acknowledge Anna's point of view.

As I have worked on my new book about clergywomen in many different mainline denominations, including ordained Episcopal priests, United Methodists, Baptists, and Disciples of Christ, I have involved the clergywomen featured in the study in interpretative ways. I have attempted to invoke the full hermeneutic circle.[2] I have come to call this new methodology and collective interpretation "reciprocal ethnography." Thus, after life stories were recorded, transcribed, and returned to their owners; after interviews were conducted with individual clergywomen and transcribed for my study; and after sermons were recorded and transcribed and shared, *then* the clergywomen and I met on a regular basis to discuss their stories, their lives, and their sermons *as well as to discuss* my thoughts, interpretations, and conclusions about how all of those aspects of their lives were integrated and what their importance might be.

Without hesitation, I can say that these sessions have dramatically influenced my interpretations and conclusions. At times they convinced me I was completely wrong or, at the least, off the mark. At other times, they enabled me to move beyond a fairly narrow interpretation to perspectives I would never have been able to achieve on my own. Sometimes we continue to disagree, and this group of women has been able to work with me toward a respect for all opinions, including my own. But I have to be reflective and reflexive; I am forced to support my interpretations if I intend to keep them. They, on the other hand, have always been generous about acknowledging their own expanded perspective when the other members of the group, including me, have presented persuasive arguments. The most difficult part of this process, however, was not doing it but writing about it in such a way that the reciprocal aspects of the ethnography are evident in the presentation of the material. Keeping the dialogue intact, allowing the reader to participate in the evolving nature of the inquiry, and projecting the hermeneutic circle onto the finished product have been extraordinarily difficult primarily because there are no models for this kind of presentation. How it will be received is yet another concern, I am certain, both for me and for the publisher. But the experience has been exhilarating. I would not have done it any other way. The results have been dramatic. The collective interpretations far surpass the individual, scholarly ones. This is not to say the group has written the book. Obviously, I have, and the scholarly voice is most definitely there, framing and shaping the material. Hopefully, my voice is still strong and my opinions legitimate. I have not relinquished my role as interpreter, as thinker, as objective observer. But I have given up the notion of scholar voice as privileged voice, the scholar's position as more legitimate because it is the more thoughtful or more credible one. I have felt it is important for me to write about how this hermeneutic circle affects my own thinking as I am forced to see the world of my collaborators through their eyes—rather than only through my own—and to invite them to see their world through mine.

This topic—the ordination of women—is an extremely complex one. I see it as an issue fraught with deep-seated, centuries-old misogyny and sexism in their most naked and insidious forms. To my mind, the struggle of women for equal rights in the pulpit and in the church hierarchy stands as the single most representative obstacle to equal rights for women on all fronts. As long as blatant sexism and the degradation of women can flourish because they are seen as sanctioned by God Almighty, then there is very little hope for women to win equality in other social, cultural, and political arenas. At times it may seem as though my stance, which may differ substantially from Sister Anna's, is merely a stubborn and unwarranted one. However, my view of what I see is colored by my own upbringing in southern Missouri in a strongly fundamentalist and patriarchal household and religion. It is from experience that I see Anna as different and strong and independent; I know it takes unusual strength of character and willpower to do what she is doing. And I know exactly why she gives God all the credit for her strengths and abilities; I am *not* denying that God may provide strength for her, but I insist that she has the right to also claim that strength as her own. My own painful experiences in breaking away from a cultural reality that nearly parallels Anna's strengthens my conviction that she is, indeed, daring to persist in her mission. My stance outside her experience, on the other hand, convinces me that the feminist scholar looking at an oppressive situation for women has both the right and the obligation to point out that the situation is oppressive and that the women involved may justifiably fear repercussions for their actions. Hence, my argument in this article is not that I have come to accept Sister Anna's interpretations over my own; rather, the argument is that it is critically important that I allow her to respond to my interpretations with her own, and simultaneously I insist on the credibility of my interpretations even when they are different from hers. The point is that both should be presented and that the dialogue between us should be part of the whole picture. No one gets "the last word"; we merely share the opportunity to speak directly to the reader. By looking long and hard at the lives and struggles, the sermons and stories, that clergywomen in contemporary America tell, and in listening to them interpret the belief systems that support them as people and as clergy, only then can we hope to gain a better understanding of this "intersubjective world," the intersubjective reality that the folklorist strives to know.

In an ideal world, we learn as we move through our lives, and our work evolves as we strive to make meaningful contributions to understanding and knowledge. I learned a great deal from my experiences with Sister Anna Walters, and I regret what did not happen in my interpretation and presentation of her life and ministry. Yet my belated dialogue with her about my book convinced me of the critical importance of a new ethnographic approach that will not only direct our methodology but also inform our interpretations and challenge the presentation of our conclusions. I would be the last to claim this approach is an easy one. It is not. However, if we insist upon interpreting other people's interpretations, at the very least, we are obligated to allow them space to respond. At the very most, we stand to learn far more than we ever bargained for.

In the end, although my presence certainly dominates this article, I am hoping that the reflexive stance exhibited here does not illustrate a case of scholar as "star" but rather illustrates how the role of this ethnographer affects and informs the work that she produces. That, in the end, becomes the critical question: How does our presence in a cultural context different from our own affect the context? And, by extension, how does our presence, and all the cultural baggage we bring with us, affect what we say about what we see and hear? The final phase of the hermeneutic circle, then, demands that we subject our interpretations to the interpretations of our subjects.

Notes

1. All names of individuals, churches, and towns have been changed to protect the anonymity of the participants.

2. If I may play Mary Daly for a moment, I would like to suggest an expanded interpretation of the word "hermeneutics" to include its Greek origins, which provide a way to see interpretation as a combination of male and female characteristics, invoking the notion of a holy or a whole, a connected theory of interpretation that includes all participants and all points of view.

References Cited

Becker, Howard S. 1970. *Sociological Work*. Chicago: Aldine.

Becker, Howard S., and Michael M. McCall, eds. 1991. *Symbolic Interaction and Cultural Studies*. Chicago: University of Chicago Press.

Clifford, James, and George E. Marcus. 1986. *Writing Culture: The Poetics and Politics of Ethnography*. Berkeley: University of California Press.

Joy Unspeakable. 1981. Color, ¾", 58 min. A videotape program produced by Elaine J. Lawless and Elizabeth Peterson; executive producer John Winninger. Indiana University Television Productions.

Lawless, Elaine. 1987. Piety and Motherhood: Reproductive Images and Maternal Strategies of the Woman Preacher. *Journal of American Folklore* 100:469–479.

———. 1988. *Handmaidens of the Lord: Pentecostal Women Preachers and Traditional Religion*. Philadelphia: University of Pennsylvania Press.

Marcus, George E., and Michael M. J. Fischer. 1986. *Anthropology as Cultural Critique: An Experimental Moment in the Human Sciences.* Chicago: University of Chicago Press.

Mascia-Lees, Frances E., Patricia Sharpe, and Colleen Ballerine Cohen. 1989. "The Postmodernist Turn in Anthropology: Cautions from a Feminist Perspective." *Signs* 15:7–33.

McCall, Michael M., and Judith Wittner. 1991. "The Good News about Life History." In *Symbolic Interaction and Cultural Studies,* edited by Howard S. Becker and Michael McCall, 1–35. Chicago: University of Chicago Press.

Ruby, Jay, ed. 1982. *A Crack in the Mirror: Reflexive Perspectives in Anthropology.* Philadelphia: University of Pennsylvania Press.

Titon, Jeff Todd. 1988. *Powerhouse for God: Speech, Chant, and Song in an Appalachian Baptist Church.* Austin: University of Texas Press.

5

WOMEN'S LIFE STORIES AND
RECIPROCAL ETHNOGRAPHY
AS FEMINIST AND EMERGENT

IN 1989, I PARTICIPATED IN A PANEL AT the American Folklore Society Meetings in Philadelphia that focused on the topic of reflexivity in the ethnographic study of religion and belief. The five presenters were concerned with the writing of ethnography, particularly in terms of the field research folklorists do in the area of religion.[1] In that presentation, I examined the ways in which I had been reflexive in acknowledging my role in the field research for my book *Handmaidens of the Lord: Women Preachers and Traditional Religion* (1988), but I admitted that I felt a disappointment in that I had not established an interpretive dialogue with the Pentecostal female ministers about whom the book was written. That is, while I established a close and friendly relationship with the women in the study and did fieldwork with them for over two years, I committed the scholar's crime of collecting my data and disappearing to "write it up." The women

Author's note: The details concerning this article's genesis are made clear in the first paragraphs below. Exposing myself the way I did at this AFS panel was a bit unnerving for me in that it exposed the errors I felt I had made in not discussing my arguments with the women about whom I was writing. Not only did this article call for a more dialogic and transparent fieldwork methodology, but it also addressed the important question of how we write our ethnographies after our field research and our conversations with our participants are completed. In many ways, this article continues my examination of the limitations of reflexive ethnography, as it was developed in the 1985 volume by James Clifford and George Marcus in *Writing Culture*, by offering, instead, the elements of reciprocal ethnography I was hoping would provide a more nuanced and balanced approach to both doing and writing ethnography. In many ways, this article anticipates the welcome work of Ruth Behar and Deborah Gordon in their 1996 volume, *Women Writing Culture*. This article first appeared in *Journal of Folklore Research* 28, no. 1 (Fall 1991): 35–61.

felt comfortable leaving the task of writing the book to me and trusted that I would represent them and their ministry fairly. In many ways, that trust was well founded, but as it turned out, many of the interpretations I made and conclusions I drew about their beliefs and their lives were clearly representative of my point of view as researcher writing about them and did not always or necessarily reflect their own interpretations or provide a way for them to respond to mine.

When the featured minister in *Handmaidens of the Lord*, Sister Anna Walters, read my book cover to cover, she was dismayed by the tone of some of the things I was saying and in some cases strongly disagreed with my analysis and interpretation. She wrote long letters to me explaining her perspective on the various topics. At that point, it was obviously too late to include her point of view along with mine—the book had already been published. While I certainly would never advocate that the subjects we study take on the role of "censor" of our work, in the AFS conference session, I argued that we need to establish a more collaborative methodology for fieldwork and a theoretical framework of knowledge-sharing that will allow for dialogue. This dialogue can be included in the ethnographic field research as well as in the presentation of that ethnographic work, as a part of the discussion, serving to privilege no one voice over any other. In many ways, I still disagree with some of Sister Walters's responses to my interpretations, or I see the issues in perhaps a larger and more complex arena of women, religion, society, and culture. Nevertheless, her point of view juxtaposed against mine would certainly have illustrated the polyphonic nature of belief, interpretation, and presentation. I believe scholars are fearful of such honesty; it makes us vulnerable to attack, questioning, and critique from our subjects as well as from our peers in a new and disconcerting way. The challenge must be met, however.

In the past decade, anthropological and folkloristic inquiry, at least from some perspectives, has addressed a critical question: how do we write ethnography, and how does the ethnographer acknowledge her/his role in the field situation? While several important works have emerged on this topic, some anthropologists calling for "reflexive anthropology" have been chided for talking about it more than actually doing it and in the process have managed to be so reflexive that they have successfully directed the spotlight onto themselves once again (see Mascia-Lees et. al. 1989). The fact of the matter is, however, that we must first be conscious of the issue before we can tackle it, and, certainly, James Clifford and George Marcus's

Writing Culture: The Poetics and Politics of Ethnography (1986), Clifford's *The Predicament of Culture* (1988), Jay Ruby's *A Crack in the Mirror* (1982), and other studies have called our attention to the concern for reflexivity. I see my own approach as a natural product of the evolution of ethnographic studies in this country in terms of the attention to reflexivity and the conceptualization of the ethnographic "other." Certainly, Charles Briggs, in his *Learning How to Ask*, has tackled the problematics of the interview; his work, however, remains in the mode and frame of the dynamics between interviewer and interviewee, although certainly his comments clearly address the problems I encountered when the women "heard" me ask different questions, problems which led to varying degrees of candidness from them. What I shall be proposing here only begins with the one-on-one interview and grows into a series of dialogic sessions with the flow of interactions taking on multiple forms and overlapping functions; the dialogues go beyond the ethnographer asking the informants if s/he "got it right," and the conclusions (if there are any) emerge from the discourse between and among all the participants, ethnographer included. Briggs correctly assumes that this dialogue session will represent a second speech event, and I fully acknowledge the necessity for that second event. I disagree that "what is needed is some means of rechecking one's perceptions against those of the participants *at the time*" (emphasis mine, 1986, 108). I sympathize with Stephen Tyler's assessment, in his work *The Unspeakable*, of where ethnographic thinking has gone awry. Tyler suggests that the ethnographer has "missed the true import of 'discourse,' which is 'the other as us,'" for the point of discourse is not, he suggests, how to make a better representation but how to avoid representation. "In their [the ethnographers'] textualization of pseudodiscourse they have accomplished a terrorist alienation more complete than that of the positivists. It may be that all textualization is alienation, but it is certainly true that non-participatory textualization is alienation—'not us'—and there is no therapy in alienation" (1987, 205).

The approach I am advocating, which I have termed reciprocal ethnography, seeks to humanize the ethnographic endeavor. It seeks true dialogue, both among the participants and between the participant and the ethnographer, and will emerge, hopefully, in the vein of what Tyler calls ethnography "in the right spirit," along with the work of, for example, Vincent Crapanzano (1980) or Kirin Narayan (1989). This past year, in doing the field research for a new book I am writing, *Wholy Women, Holy Women: Celebrating Wholeness in Connection*, I have attempted to put reciprocal ethnography into practice. This approach will, I hope, take ethnographic studies into a new and more multilayered, polyphonic dimension of dialogue and exchange. My current interest in women in mainline ministry is a natural evolution of my work in *Handmaidens of the Lord*, which focused entirely on Pentecostal women ministers (this study includes no Pentecostal ministers).

Initially, for this study, I tape recorded life stories,[2] interviews, and sermons in one fairly small region in the upper Mississippi Valley.[3] I should comment on my selection of contemporary women in ministry as a focus for study. The group I have been working with represents mostly white, female ministers from the Episcopal Church, the Methodist Church, Church of Christ-Disciples, Unity, Unitarian, and General Baptist. There were also two Catholic nuns and an African American AME minister in the lunch group who chose not to participate in the dialogue group. All of these women are highly educated—graduates of Yale, Harvard, Stanford, Brite Divinity School, Union, Texas Christian, and Yale Divinity School; they range in age from thirty to sixty-five; some are single, some married, some have children, and some are lesbian. They are reflective about their ministry, their lives, their beliefs every single day; the work for this book simply provided a different forum for a focused discussion of these concerns.

At first, it was fairly tedious trying to locate women ministers and conduct my fieldwork; eventually, however, my work took a significant turn when I found that a group of women in ministry (which included many of the same women I had been interviewing) met on a regular basis and had formed an informal but very close-knit lunch group—a group that did more than get together "just" for lunch. Most definitely, for a while, *I* was the topic of conversations at this lunch. I had asked if I could join them every first and third Tuesday for lunch. After no little pain and trepidation on my part, as I realized just how much my presence could potentially alter the lunches and possibly deprive the women of this much-needed "safe" arena for discussion and sharing, I was allowed to join this group for their lunches and other meetings. My fieldwork then began to focus exclusively on this already established group. After more than two years of working closely with these women and considerable intermittent fieldwork later, I believe I can say that my presence has not, in the end, hindered them from talking openly and honestly. I cannot, of course, say that my presence has not had an *effect* on the meetings and the women involved, because it has.[4]

In the most fortunate way, then, this naturally formed group afforded the opportunity and framework for me to begin a series of group discussion sessions during my leave year (about fifteen total) where I could bring my thoughts, ideas, questions, and writing to them as a group, seeking their response to what I was perceiving in their life stories, our interviews, and in their sermons. While I met with the group at both our meetings and their regularly scheduled lunch times, I never brought up our "book work" material at the lunches. I knew it was imperative to keep the two occasions for meeting separate while keeping the composition of the groups stable. In our dialogue sessions, we explored a range of areas including the content of their life stories, the structure of their stories, what they left out of their life stories and why, their concepts and images of God, the problems and issues for women in ministry, sermon-making, and sexuality and the ministry. These sessions were all tape recorded and transcribed verbatim. Along with the life stories, portions of this material form the basis for this particular article.

My work with female ministers is reflexive in that I readily acknowledge my presence in the research and the possible and very real effect my presence has on the field experience. And my work is reciprocal in that we, the women and I, have established a working dialogue about the material, a reciprocal give and take. This process is *not* to be understood as *reciprocity*, where obligation or payment is the motivating factor, but *reciprocal*, in the best sense of sharing and building knowledge based on dialogue and shared/examined/reexamined knowledge.[5] In this sense, I also perceive this ethnography to be a feminist ethnography, growing out of an understanding of how women come to know what they know (Belenky et.al. 1986); here I include myself, as a knower who is constantly learning new knowledge, as well as the women in the study, who were able to examine and articulate what they know in dialogue with each other and with me. Their knowledge and mine are presented as a collaborative multivoiced ethnography. While I fully acknowledge that I am the one writing this article and eventually the book, I am committed to presenting the work as collaborative, as dialogic, and as emergent, not fixed.

Given that my criticism of the "reflexive" anthropologists is that some of them are talking about ethnography more than they are doing it, and given that I have suggested an improvement upon, or at least an evolution from, reflexive anthropology with my reciprocal ethnography, I will attempt in this paper to present, from the transcripts of our dialogue sessions, what *exactly* has been the advantage of this approach. Is there an epistemology that emerges from the women talking *about* their lives, their ministry, their preaching? What have I, as a scholar, learned in the process? Have the dialogue sessions taken me further in my own knowledge and understanding, or have they actually served only to validate and authenticate what I already knew or suspected? My theory was, of course, that reciprocal ethnography would serve to deepen the hermeneutical epistemology, to improve what I had seen as dangerous flaws in my own earlier work and the work of others. In fact, this article will demonstrate how reciprocal ethnography served, in this case, to illuminate a new understanding of what life stories are for professional women who, in contemporary times, find that their lives and their ministries segment, and fragment, their narrated experiences. This collective examination will, in the end, further our understanding of *women's* life stories in that it demonstrates the importance of a multilayered story, one that balances text and interpretation. My work calls into question the efficacy of a developed, integrated "life history" (which I refer to as a "life story") as well as points to the critical nature of ethnographic inquiry.

The first thing I did in this field research was to record, on tape, the life stories of the women identified for this study. I have chosen to focus on these life stories and the group's responses to their stories as the basis of this article. The initial fieldwork included many more women than the number in the lunch group, and I examined all of the life stories I had collected, attempting to discern patterns, determine content, and look for structural frameworks, language, and other aspects of the life stories. I did not know the women well when I first met with them and basically asked only that they "tell me your life story." "Begin at the beginning," I said, "and tell me how you came to this point in your life as a woman minister." I explained that I was trained in folklore, anthropology, and literature and that I was committed to the efficacy of their story *as* story, that I felt the text of their life story as they delivered it to me would be valuable and provide insight into their individual life pattern and the collective patterns of other women in the group. I wanted them to talk without interruption, deciding solely on their own what would be included. I transcribed these life stories verbatim. Only later, in individual interviews with each of them, did I ask specific questions.

In the dialogue sessions when we met together, I chose to talk with the group about the structure, content, style, and form of women's life stories in general and about their life stories in particular. All of the women in the group had received printed copies of their own typed, verbatim life stories. They hated them. They came to the group session and slammed them down on the table with remarks such as "I hate this!" "This is ridiculous," "This makes me look very stupid; I don't like looking stupid," "I'm horrified; I cannot even read this." This article will explore some of the reasons for their responses to their own stories.

In our group sessions, I presented to them some of the current thinking about women's and men's life stories and autobiographies and sought to explore their responses to their own stories and to the scholarly opinions about women's life stories. My presentation to them included a discussion of the works of Sidonie Smith, who writes about a "poetics of women's autobiography" (1987); Carolyn Heilbrun, who poses how we approach "writing a woman's life" (1988); of Bella Brodzki and Celeste Schenck, who theorize about women's "life/lines" and who, in their collection of essays, include articles by Nancy Miller and Mary Mason (1988); of Domna Stanton's notion of "the female autograph" (1984); of Joy Barbre and the Minnesota Women's Group, who have been "interpreting women's lives" (1989); and of James Olney (1980; 1988), William Runyan (1984), and Lawrence and Maria Barbara Watson-Franke (1985), who write about both female and male life stories and life histories and autobiography (cf. Jelinek 1980; Langness and Frank 1981). The broad conclusions the reader can draw from these various approaches can be summarized with a comment by Sidonie Smith, drawing on the work of Wilhelm Dilthey, Georg Misch, and Karl Weintraub, that autobiographies (read "male autobiographies") are seen "as texts of 'individuality' and the pursuit of the typical and the model," while women's texts, in contrast, are seen (by Elaine Showalter and others) as "wild—they lie outside the dominant culture's boundaries in a spatial, experiential, and metaphysical 'no-man's-land'" (1987, 9). In general, male autobiographies have been characterized as logical, linear, objective, goal-oriented, fixed firmly in ideal notions of selfhood, and structured in accordance with the dominant order, while female autobiographies tend to be characterized as nonlinear, even chaotic, subjective, experiential, interpersonal/relationally oriented, connected to the world and its inhabitants, less individualistic, and more spontaneous.

Although I very much wanted us to discuss the content of the stories they gave to me, we did, first, agree that one of the difficulties with this kind of material is reading an orally delivered account that has been rendered into print. They knew, as I did, that their first response to the typed material was based on the linguistic markers—that is, the false starts, the "you knows" that dotted the page, the pauses and "uhs" that abounded. We agreed, however, that we all understood that these were a function of the oral style of story delivery and ought not to be the focus of our discussion about the oral life histories in general. It is a given that *written* autobiographies would have been quite different. This difference, of course, also points to the difficulty of utilizing the scholarship on autobiography as literary scholars approach the subject; working with oral texts is always different but not different enough for us to ignore the identifiable corollaries between these genres.

In response to the paradigm that suggests that men's stories will be linear and logical and women's fragmented and loosely formed, the women in the discussion group had some pointed objections. At the outset, Kathleen Miles-Wagner, a Unitarian minister, observed how value-laden those terms were and suggested that linear was, in fact, quite one-dimensional and that she preferred to think of women's stories, and lives, as multidimensional: "If there's anything that we are, that *we* are, that *I* am, it's multidimensional, or three-dimensional, or fully rounded out—and that's *not* formless.... The difference between linear and multidimensional is more acceptable than linear versus formless."

I pointed out to the women that I found *their* life stories to be, by and large, long and detailed, often lingering a long time on one segment of their life, and only after considerable attention to that would they move on to yet another lengthy segment. I offered to them the observation that rather than seeing their stories as *either* linear or fragmented (the binary opposition suggested by the scholarship), perhaps a better way to look at their stories would be to conceive of them as "blocks." I thought they were relating their stories to me in completed, deeply explored blocks of experience. At the end of each of these "blocks," it seemed, they would declare that whatever they had been exploring during that segment wasn't working for them, wasn't what they ought to be doing, and they moved on (after much pain and consideration) to a new segment. I saw the blocks as segments of searching, of trying things out, a "reading" of the stories that corresponds with Gillian Bennett's notion of "superblocks" in women's storytelling, blocks which she found created a "many-layered, multi-textured structure" (1989, 170). I quoted from one of the women, who put this metaphorically: Flannery Eilers, a Disciples of Christ minister, said she "just kept on trying on the clothes of first one thing and then another, but the clothes just never seemed to fit. Until finally, she put on the vestments of a minister, and they felt *right*."

In response to my theory about blocks, they agreed, but they took it further than I ever could/would have on my own. What emerged from the dialogue, however, was new knowledge for the women there, as well as for me. Kathleen continued to speak: "I really respond to your theory about blocks. I have often thought of my life as a series of doing something until I had sort of taken it to its limit. I had mined a segment of experience, taken it to its logical extreme, done it thoroughly, until I realized that it wasn't what I am looking for somehow. . . . But I've always thought nobody else's life is like that." They responded eagerly to the idea of women not having early in their lives one set goal from which they never wavered (a characteristic noted about men's lives and stories). But they reinterpreted my metaphor of "blocks" in challenging ways. Amy Seger, a young Disciples of Christ minister, responded:

> I was thinking when you were talking about blocks of time—I was trying to draw blocks. I was starting with building blocks, and that wasn't helpful because every time I kept thinking about building blocks, I kept thinking about pyramids and hierarchies, and I kept yanking them down. But as Kathleen started talking, I've seen more of a train. But I haven't decided whether the train is adding cars or taking them away. [laughter]

Flannery asked:

> Is this train coming or going? [laughter]

Amy responded:

> Well, actually, it's a sort of continuum.

Kathleen interjected:

> Yes, there's something that has to get done which I think represents "spiritual journey," which it seems like is being done with each of these blocks, and each one is taken to its conclusion, and then you start over, and it's always the same thing I'm trying to do.

Amy continued:

> And the block itself—because you have the edge, and then the turn, and then you have another direction, and it gives shape in a whole, and you have a wholeness there, but in the forming of that you are really going in *different* directions—taking different turns.

Carter Buchanan, an Episcopalian priest, said:

> Then, too, there's the multidimensional box—it's a cube, a kind of a puzzle, but it's a round puzzle that's made of rectangle pieces of wood that all fit together. And that's what happens: you get to the end of one block, and you look at what you thought it was—at least that's what happened to me—it was something quite different.

I offered to the group the suggestion that since they had too few real-life models or written life scripts to follow for their own stories, they were often making up their own script as they went along.[6] At this point in my work, I did not believe that the women in mainline denominations were participants in a strong oral tradition that included stories about becoming a female minister. As it turned out, this was not actually the case; there is an oral tradition of particular stories, such as the "called into the ministry" stories and the abbreviated life histories, which are often required at some point during the ordination process. However, it is important to note that when I asked the women in the group, they could not recall having heard many stories from other women. The truth seems to be that there is an *unperceived* (and perhaps unexpected) oral tradition, one that is verifiable only by looking at the style, content, and structure of the stories themselves and, in essence, working backward. The class, station, and context of the lives and ministries of these well-educated, sophisticated, professional women who seem to live every moment in the literate world deceive us into a static, class-oriented approach to folk/oral traditions—try as we may to avoid such thinking. Clearly, there is not, in this case, a strong oral tradition, and just as clearly the women who elect to become ministers do very much perceive of themselves as anomalies.

Brodzki and Schenck, I recalled, write about the female self being mediated, her invisibility resulting from her lack of a tradition. I remembered their characterization of a male autobiography that might be "an objective and disinterested occupation in a work of personal justification" and their caution that the decision to "go public" is particularly charged for a woman, especially one who has defied the culturally determined expectations for women: "To justify an unorthodox life by writing about it is to *reinscribe* the original violation, to reviolate masculine turf" (1988, 50). Because they *have* chosen a profession perceived by the culture as *male*, I felt their stories were often masking or justifying their choices, their positions. It seemed the long diversions in their stories might be serving as ritual disclaimers of sorts—saying, "Look, I tried all this other stuff I was expected to do, and it just didn't fit!" Carter, an Episcopal priest, responded to Flannery's metaphor of the clothes she kept trying on:

> I remember when I was talking, I went on and on and on [general laughter], but it was very much like that—like trying on clothes. But there *was* a role for that [school teaching]—there's an appropriate "teacher role," and you can tag it: a high school teacher does these things. And I did keep trying to do them, and I *couldn't* do them. Oddly, it was very much like: here *now* I'm doing something for which there are no particular models, and it feels so much more right than it did to try to do something for which there were generations of models, of a variety of which you would think that I could have fit, but I didn't.

But Kathleen questioned her:

> And it's the lack of models that makes the clothing feel so good? Well, I don't know. See, I'm not willing quite to say that, but it is a fact that here you can *do*. I've really felt that the ministry was a place where I could *do*, do what seemed to be the right thing to do. I could form myself . . . without having to conform to a lot of structures. But even that didn't work. It turns out that there are a lot of expectations and structures. The question was, was I going to fit into them or not?

Anne-Marie, a Methodist diaconal minister,[7] revealed that she had given this a good deal of thought:

> You know I am in a denomination where one of my real concerns is *about* the models of the ministry that I know are in place, and the hierarchical structures and which I am considered a part are rigid enough that I'm concerned about what it's going to do to *me*.

Amy interjected:

> There's not a model for a woman minister. Yes, there are similarities among us, but there is also a diversity among us, and that's something that I hope we will lift up as well. Because of the very fact that we *don't* have those models and we *don't* have those scripts, we are writing our own scripts, and they're coming out differently. There are some parallels, but there's also that openness and freedom and flexibility for something new.

Kathleen responded:

> And I don't sense that we are coercing each other to try to find the one "right" script.

This group session finally evolved into a discussion of just how vulnerable the women actually felt once they had determined that the clothes of the minister felt just right to them. They fully acknowledge and understand that not everyone else thinks the clothes fit them particularly well. Linda Stewart, a Methodist minister, talked at length about a radical newsletter she edits and how the group of women ministers who began it had wanted to title it *Naked in the Pulpit* because, she said, "in talking about how we felt—'naked in the pulpit' was the way we were saying that we were feeling very much of the time, but we needed it to be safe." So they named it, instead, *Notions 'n Pins* and laughed hysterically as they acknowledged the subliminal messages of this domestic image.[8] Linking this clothing image with Flannery's, Linda told a story about another woman minister she knew who was tiny and whose robe, purchased by the congregation, swallowed her and seemed to make her vanish: "Her pulpit robe is too big—she's very small. So she's getting a new robe that will reveal her more. She said, basically, that there was a difference between being too covered up, which is how she feels now, and being naked in the pulpit, which is how she felt before." Conversely, another young Hispanic Disciples of Christ minister, Maria Gonzales, talked about claiming the power and authority of the vestments: "I am beginning to take the liberties of the robe—sort of putting on the clothing."

Finally, in the group sessions, I presented to the women the scholarship on women's stories, including works by Carol Gilligan (1982) and others, which indicates that women will relate their life stories in terms of "relationships" with others—primarily fathers, mothers, siblings, husbands, companions, and children. I then shared with them my observation that in their life stories, they had *not*, in general, told what appeared to be at the outset recognizable "relational" stories—stories that pivoted around key figures in their lives and their relationships with those key figures. Gilligan has suggested that if there is *anything* we can note about women, it is that they are relational. Why, then, I asked the group, are your stories not particularly relational? In fact, as I further pointed out, most of the women in the group who were married and had children had definitely glossed over those aspects of their lives—made great leaps, in fact, over these relations. Others, particularly those who are lesbian, had left out all references to significant others in their lives. The responses from the women were varied, quite heated, and certainly illuminated further the ambivalence that makes the lives of female ministers often seem so disconnected.

At the beginning, Kathleen suggested that for ministers, the "community" becomes the "significant other" and that she would suppose that if I looked for relation in that perspective it would emerge in terms of the congregation as community. Interestingly, most of the other women rejected this notion outright. Even those who did feel comfortable calling their church an "extended family" did not want this to substitute for the *actual* relationships in their more private lives. The initial response of most of the women in the group seemed defensive to me at first. Several declared with vehemence their "right" to present themselves as women first and as wives and mothers later. At first, they seemed proud that they had "come through" as professionals. Amy, married and with a small child, spoke clearly:

> I have tried in the last few years to get away from identifying myself as Gary's wife, mother of Kevin, because this was the way I identified myself for so long. Even after I was a professional person, I still thought of myself that way and identified myself that way. So if I came through that way, that would be wonderful. I'm happy about that.

Linda, a young mother married to a minister, responded:

> You said you were writing a book about women in ministry. My guess is that I filtered that to say I'm going to deal with the professional stuff. I'm very conscious right now of how I am perceived—as the mother of a toddler, not a professional. If we see the bishop, he says, "Hi there, little momma. How's that big boy?" and to John he says, "Well, hello there, John, how are things down at the First Methodist?" [Linda serves two small rural churches, while her husband is downtown in one of the largest churches in the city.]

It became clear to me during this exchange that there is a basic *problem* with relationships—how to have them, what kind they can be, how questions of ministry and family get resolved—in the life of women in the ministry. If, in fact, the life stories related to me were not "relational," there had to be a good reason. Was it because the women were not "relational" in the way they connected with other humans in their lives? Brodzki and Schenck have proposed that "women tend to present their stories as a delineation of identity by alterity . . . self-definition in relation to significant others is the most pervasive characteristic of the female autobiography" (1988, 8). Did the lives of these female ministers *not* pivot around relations the way women's lives have been depicted? Or had the life stories become a negotiation, an alternate strategy for presentation of self? What would/could the life stories tell us, then, about this critical issue? Is there embedded in them what Brodzki and Schenck suggest is "a compelling subtext . . . which defies socially constructed definitions of appropriate female behavior?" (1988, 8)

The women themselves began to answer these important questions. Kathleen's response reminded me of Nancy Miller's comment that "to the extent that autobiography requires a shaping of the past, a making sense of a life, it tends to cast out the parts that don't add up" (1988, 56):

> Relationships have always been problematic along in my life. They are filled with pain, sometimes for good reasons, sometimes for bad reasons. The possibility is that the ministry is my way of trying to find solutions to the relational ambiguities and paradoxes and confusions of life. They're left out because they're too confusing. I'm unable to resolve them. What's put in there is what I could resolve about my life, which is the sort of intentional structure working with community or trying to work within the community.

Others agreed with her and went on to vent the frustrations that can actually wreck their relationships and do considerable damage to how they perceive themselves. Amy, who had defiantly told us at the beginning of this session that if she had presented only herself, then she was "happy about that," suddenly began to realize that she felt she had been cornered. She began to verbalize how limiting she felt the expectations and perceptions of others could be and began to reexamine her presentation of self and her dissatisfaction with that image. She also began to express her anger about the restrictions she felt were in place to prevent her from revealing her whole self in terms of her significant relations.

> Can I say one more thing on that "significant other" stuff? Because this is really on my mind. I think I may be the only one in this group [and, of course, she wasn't], but I feel that it's really—I don't know what it is—but that it's a real 'no, no' to talk about my husband, even in this group, but it's not the first time in a women's group. Even in seminary, somehow, I felt that you're *supposed* to be a person by yourself, and if you start talking about your husband, it sounds like you're not being real anymore. I find that I don't feel I'm *allowed*. I don't allow *myself* to claim that significant relationship and its worth and its value in terms of who I am. If I'm not at my best because the three-year-old has kept me up for the last three nights in a row, *that is then a part of who I am at that particular moment.* If a male colleague says the same thing, folks will ask, "Oh, is the wife out of town?" [laughter]

Brodzki and Schenck ask the critical question: how do women "find ways to challenge inscription into conventional feminine identity" and autobiographical representations of selfhood and at the same time "exploit the textual ambiguity of their partnership with significant others?" (1988, 11) The dialogue that emerged in this group session directly answers this question. The women revealed that being "relational" was, in fact, a terribly important part of the way they perceived themselves; they were also explaining that to be "relational" was obviously perceived by others as being "female" and carried, then, a less than serious value. They had learned, therefore, to couch their presentation, as well as their stories to me, in terms of this expected, isolated, professional image. As Gail Reimer has pointed out, mothers can write, but they cannot write as mothers—mothers must be absent and silent (1988, 208). Miller speaks of "the writer who gave birth to a child" (1988, 53). Here we have "the priest who gave birth to a child," and the impact is even greater.

Because the hierarchy devalues them as women and devalues the "wholeness" of their lives, women in ministry are forced to be ambivalent about and deny some of the most significant aspects of their lives. They had, in fact, shuttled between what Brodzki and Schenck suggest is an "objective representation of a Significant Other . . . and prescriptions for ideal femininity" (1988, 9). Women inhabit the space between these two poles; they posit, refusing inscription into either by employing deft evasions and purposive self-contradictions because a fixed/named identity is too dangerous. They make displacement work for them—a "double displacement" (1988, 9)—what Sedonie Smith calls a double helix of the imagination, a double dialogue between or among "two, three, or four stories. The female narrator gets caught in a duplicitous process: she exists in the text under circumstances of alienated communication because the text is the locus of her dialogue with a tradition she tacitly aims at subverting" (1987, 51).

Talking about these issues in the group context, and in direct relation to the life stories they had given to me, allowed many of the women to come to a new realization of the anger they felt about this yoke that they agreed came from outside sources but the wearing of which they had participated in. They revealed, in the process, that they had, in fact, been speaking from this space between poles, refusing inscription into either. Marsha Johnson, a Methodist minister married to a clergyman, and mother of two children, brought the margins back to the center:

> If, in my life story, I gave you the impression that that part wasn't at the heart of my life and that the professional side was everything, I misinformed you. I think I *was* responding like, what does it mean to be a professional minister. If you've got to leave out anything, for me, *don't* leave out my children. Leave out my professional church work. But I just get so angry . . . because, I told you, this first district supervisor I ever met in Iowa said to me, "Don't try to become ordained as a woman—you're a woman! Why should you be ordained? That's like bashing your head against a wall." Then the clincher was, he said,

"Have you even seen a pregnant bishop?" He just sat there and just laughed and laughed . . . and I'm sitting there thinking, *Why is this man laughing?* It just made me furious. So I'm still acting out my fury, I guess. I don't like people telling me what I can't have.

The juxtaposition here of this woman's intense feelings about the importance of her family and the anger she feels about the district supervisor's comments about women in ministry marks the nexus of relation and ministry for many of the women in this group. It also marks the derailment of what the women perceive to be their right to talk openly about the importance of their relationships and their lives—they feel "unrepresentable." Like Amy, Marsha feels cheated because she has not been *allowed* to speak about her family; clearly, she does not allow herself the luxury of revealing all the parts of her life. To do so would only feed the ugly misogyny of the supervisors in her denomination. But her denial of family is obviously not without cost. Ultimately, I heard the women articulate their own emerging theory about women's stories. Carter began:

Our worry about what we've done here is that they [our stories] don't sound like men's stories but that we are applying men's criteria, I guess, to how to tell our stories. So, then, if I turn it around and say, "Well, OK, I want to tell a woman's story," *then I don't know what that is.*

Anne-Marie picked up on Carter's train of thought:

If I think more the way men do, and then I try to make myself say, "Oh my goodness, I ought to be a woman," OK, but then the other part of that is that because these are the accepted categories, that's how we're supposed to do it. Then I must say, *I don't know what a woman's story sounds like,* and that does not have a great deal of validity. I'm sitting here saying I can't believe I told my story that way. On the other hand, I'm glad I was asked to.

And Carter continued:

I look at what I said, that's written down on paper, and at the categories that have been taught us by primarily male people—male methods of looking at the world—and I mean I'm embarrassed because I look so stupid. Because we have said that if you're intelligent, you think this way. And then if we turn around, and then we're saying also that our stories aren't as important as male-constructed stories would be because they're not coherent and they're not this and they're not that, *then we can't even tell them.*

What does this dialogue tell us about the life histories as collected from these female ministers? It tells us a great deal. Mostly, it tells us how, as

Miller suggests, to "overread" them—both in terms of what is there and what is missing: "How do we look for the 'unsaid things'? [Overreading] is a double reading—an intratextual practice of interpretation and a 'gendered overreading' which does not privilege either the autobiography or the fiction" (1988, 58). Such a reading suggests that the life histories are suspect in terms of what we can actually learn about certain aspects of women's lives from them. It warns about taking theoretical postulates and trying to apply them to raw data. The dialogue helps us to answer the question of why Gilligan's "relational" aspects were missing and leads us to understand that as women change their roles in society, they are learning how to change their public presentation to fit a prescribed and largely male image—yet realizing the futility of that effort early on but having no alternative as a substitute. Women have learned how necessary it is to cloak their relations, their inclinations, their values, their sexuality, themselves. Reading these stories, as Miller suggests, is "rather like shaking hands with one's gloves on"; their stories become "deliberate fictions of self representation, rearranged fragments of emotional life" (1988, 57). The pain and anger in these group exchanges revealed a level of negotiation not even hinted at in the life stories they gave to me.

Originally, I was stymied by the stories, by the ways in which they did not, in fact, follow the expected patterns and content I'd been led to believe would characterize the way women live their lives and tell stories about them—at least in terms of the relational aspects of them. On the other hand, I was uncomfortable calling the disjointed quality of many of the stories "chaotic" and "nonlinear." I was much happier with our collective assessment of the stories as experiential and emergent. In many ways, the life stories are not at all "accurate"; instead, they represent a working out of a woman's identity. But as Kathleen pointed out, "What's there is what I've been able to resolve," which leaves me dissatisfied, then, because the looming question is, of course, what have they *not* resolved? That seems to be the key to understanding where a woman in ministry finds herself today. What she has resolved and presents is significant on the one hand, but the cauldron that contains all the anger, fear, guilt, hurt, ambivalence, denial, joy, growth, and setbacks is a vital arena for our continued and emergent exploration. These autobiographies belong to what Miller calls "a defense and illustration, at once a treatise on overcoming received notions of femininity and a poetics calling for another, freer text." She quotes Elaine Showalter, who, in *A Literature of Their Own*, claims women's stories as feminist in that they represent a "protest against the standards of art and its views of social roles and as advocacy of minority rights and values, including a demand for autonomy" (1988, 50).

During the time we were dialoguing about life stories and discussing whether or not these life stories the women had given to me were legitimate texts that represented their lived lives, I heard Norman Denzin deliver a talk about postmodern approaches to sociology (see Denzin 1989). Denzin seemed to be saying that the postmodern obsession with representation and simulation had so invaded our existence that there were no longer pure lived experiences, only texts. This, of course, bothered many in the audience who clung to the notion that they had indeed had some "real" experiences, alone or with their most intimate friends, and were offended to think that Denzin questioned those as pure lived experiences. Denzin approach is illustrative of the postmodern point of view, suggesting that even our conversations are fed by the representations of what conversations in our society ought to sound like and be, that even the way our kitchens are set up or the way we cook our meals, talking all the while, is but a mirror image of television, movies, and advertising.

Like others in the audience that day, I admit that Denzin's thinking makes me uncomfortable. It seems to me a more reasonable approach, based squarely on an understanding of how the media world affects our lives, our very being, would first be to acknowledge that there *is* pure experience—we walk across the street, we have a conversation, we feel the rain. As long as that experience remains a phenomenological essence—a lived experience—it is not a text, but the moment that act, whatever it is, is framed in some way, it becomes a text. The moment we reflect on the event, reimagine a conversation, analyze how we crossed the street correctly or incorrectly, rewind the tape, so to speak (the essence of a postmodern metaphor!), and look at the event—then it is text. Now, Denzin and others may argue that our media-blitzed world is so reflexive, so representational, so oriented to intertextuality that the original text can never be retrieved for all the layers of super- and subtext; that is their privilege. It is more useful for me, however, to conceive of text as the *framed event*, framed in order to perceive it, comprehend it, analyze it, reflect on it. Certainly, Denzin would argue (probably correctly) that we are so tuned to what we are doing that we barely act before we are analyzing our actions, reflecting on what we just did or said; we rewind the tape and review our actions as quickly as we move toward the next act, the next event. It is this approach to experience and text that best informs how I have come to "overread" the women's life stories in this study.

What does this have to do with ethnography? Ethnography is the framing of cultural events. It is first, of course, a description of people's lives within a certain context. But once the events have been described, it is the ethnographer's task, along with the subjects themselves, to interpret, to analyze, to reflect, to conjecture about what makes that framed event meaningful to the persons involved and finally to the ethnographer and her audience. And what events are profitable for study? Folkloristics guides us to an understanding of the importance of events already framed by the participants as set-aside time, framed for a purpose other than every-day, ordinary life: festival, storytelling, ritual, dance, artful representations in material form, song. Even in a media-blitzed, overtextualized world, the oral and the traditional prevail. Denzin's work with the stories of alcoholics, his fascination with film, suggests that these forms are really no different than those recognized by the folklorist as the oral and traditional forms that persist in the face of literacy—the film becomes the myth and the folk tale; the drunk's story, told and retold, formularized, adapted, and accepted, is identical to other conversion stories held as appropriate by folk groups in many contexts, sacred and secular; commercials and advertising share the fanciful, other-worldly qualities of the fairytale, the *marchen*. We come to believe in the efficacy of the perceived genre, that is, the notion of a life history as an entity—a legitimate text.

With Clifford and Marcus we ask the question: how do we write culture? On what events and acts do we focus? Which framed texts will enrich our understanding? And how do we frame what is so elusive as lived experience? Of course, it is still beneficial to turn to the people we study to see, to ask, how they frame their experiences. This emic point of view must be the first step in understanding how they have conceptualized what they do. Beyond that, however, our etic configurations are difficult and always bear the responsibility of accuracy; that is, how true to the lived experiences are the frames that we, scholars and outsiders, place on them?

In my current research with contemporary female ministers in a postmodern context, it is more difficult to maintain the clarity of genres, the definitive approach, for the oral genres are not prevalent, the life story not developed. So simple a fieldwork question as "tell me your life story" suddenly becomes problematic. Often, to direct their reply, to urge them in their telling, I would modify this question to "tell me your life story—that is, tell me how you came to be a woman in ministry." Innocent differences on the surface of these questions, seemingly straightforward, not leading, geared to produce a text of a life—the life, in particular, of a woman who is a minister. But through the course of our dialogue sessions, it became increasingly clear to me just how loaded those simple first questions of mine actually were for women who are professional women trying to balance their separate, barely integrated, public and private lives. In fact, one woman became quite angry because she felt she had revealed far too much. She claimed the other women had understood the "rules," but she had not. Her concerns had arisen when she read the life histories of all the women in the group and realized that she had been much more candid in the telling of her story than most of the other women. We talked at length about the difference between the request for a "life story" and the request "tell me how you came to be a woman minister." When I listen to the recordings of the life stories, I often said both, but different women heard different requests and interpreted the requests in different ways. Most heard "tell me your life story *in terms of how you came to be a woman minister*," which colored the way they told their "life story" to me—which, of course, is defensible in some ways because I had come to collect their life stories *because* they are female ministers. *Not* framing my question in this manner seemed inappropriate because I did in fact want them to include that information within the context of their larger life story. The one woman who felt she had told far more than anyone else argued that she had only *heard* me say "tell me your life story"—and she did, revealing much more than the other women had.

Looking back, I probably sought both stories in my initial thinking about the fieldwork and the life stories I wanted to record. I wanted the women's life stories—the whole story (which is a misperception, I think, of this genre): where they were born, where and how they grew up, their family life, their schooling, the significant influences on their lives, their families, etc. I also very much sought to get their life story in terms of how they had come to be ministers; I hoped I would be able to discern parallel patterns in important professional decisions, the call to preach, the execution of the will to preach, and the integration of ministry and other life choices. What is apparent now, and certainly was not at the outset, is that we perceive our "life stories" (and here we need to begin to focus on discreet stories within the larger story) in different ways, from different angles, with different emphases depending upon the context of the telling. For these women, the critical part of this telling was determined by what they heard me say. Those who heard "tell me your life story" delivered one text; those who heard "tell me how you came to be a woman minister" delivered a different text. The separation of these texts reveals the segmentation of experience they live with every day. Because they cannot integrate these aspects of their lives, they cannot relate a text that integrates them. It was only as we explored these various aspects of their lives and their stories that the women and I were able to synthesize the various strains of their stories and their lives. This mutual exchange of information, of creativity, this moving back and forth that I am calling reciprocal ethnography, is clearly a cousin to symbolic interactionism, to Denzin's interpretive interactionism, but hopefully it will take us even further.

I determined to follow the natural extension of this exploration. Does a life story accurately portray a lived experience? The women first agreed that their stories did not represent a "life story" that had been told and re-told, honed over time, reflected upon, presented/performed for a critical audience. They did, however, agree that they told portions of their story to different audiences. In fact, further work with different segments of the life stories, in terms of looking at particular stories (e.g., "called into the ministry" stories), demonstrates much more congruity in both style and content than the larger, unwieldy "life stories" that have been discussed here. I think it *can* be argued that certain kinds of stories do exist within an oral tradition of exchange among women in mainline denominations. Anne-Marie perceived that one problem was telling the life story for the researcher—who may pose a difficulty for the performer. There cannot be a life story in a vacuum; a life story requires an audience:

> I think that most of the telling of a life story is one of those textual, aesthetic things that you tell with an audience in mind. We have stories we tell to different audiences. I have one I tell my family, one I tell to my personnel committee, the staff parish committee. Our problem with this one was we didn't know who our audience was. And that's why the story is so chaotic, so sort of "unformed." All of our aesthetic principles couldn't be brought to bear on this, and we didn't know who the audience was.

Carter agreed with this and continued:

> We just had one question—which is, tell your life story. I think what I was doing anyway, and maybe the rest of us, too, I was telling a story to you and interpreting it at the same time, which is partly why the diversions are there. I was thinking about experience—I think we do have experiences, and then we

begin immediately to interpret them. What I was doing was hearing myself tell a story and then interpreting it at the same time and saying, "Well, this is important because of this and this and this." But I still have a very hard time reading it. See, I had to do a piece of this [life story], anyone who has gone through a seminary process had to do a piece of this, over and over again. But the main thing was there were two questions: in my case, "How did you arrive at the assumption you have a call for the ordained ministry?" and "What can you do as a priest that you cannot do as a layperson?"

Some of the women wanted to go back to the previous notion of men's constructs and women's constructs as different. Kathleen wanted to present the notion that the life stories they gave me were closer to "truth" than goal-oriented, linear constructs might be:

The stories we gave you were not constructs. They're sort of selections from reality that focus around some point real clearly. We're giving you the chaotic nature of reality. That's what you're getting. And I think that's a plus. It may make your work more difficult, but . . .

Anne-Marie felt it was important not to focus too much on the notion of the life story as "the" truth. She preferred to think in terms of "multiple" truths:

I would still want to talk about *truths*. Because I told it, this is true. This is all true. But there's a lot of other stories I could tell that would also be true, which would also trace all the way through my life. I could take people, for instance, and just talk about people and how relationships have led me through my life. I think that's one of the things that bothers me more than the grammar and the fragmentation is that reading back through mine, I'd say these things, and there was all this other stuff under them. It's like an iceberg, and I'm only giving you the tip here, and I could have, and I wish that I had, on important issues, said, "And then this means this, and this is important because of this"—*I wish I had said more what they mean*.

Conclusion

When a woman dares to put on the robes of the ministry and take on the role and the authority invested in those robes, she is consciously calling into question all the standard stereotypes of both females and males. When her story is so clearly a redefinition of, a questioning of, a reconstructing of female rights and roles, then her story cannot any longer be unselfconscious. Because these women are *not* men, the male constructs of "life story" do not work. Yet because they have been raised and trained in a culture that privileges male constructs, they are aware that they have internalized them and have accepted male notions of what is a good, intelligent, respectable story. When asked to relate their own life stories, they tried to maintain the perimeters of this notion of "good story" as they told theirs, but because they are not men, they often diverged from the "appropriate script" and, in the end, found the result frustrating and unacceptable.

The women in this study recognized that their rejection of their stories went beyond their failure to adhere to the male construct of a "good story." They rejected their stories because they recognized them as only skeletal representations of their actual lives. They regretted that they deleted important figures in their lives from them; they were frustrated that they did not communicate what they believed to be the meaning of what they did relate; they were dismayed by the "professional image" that prevailed, one that, in the end, they felt did not capture them as the women they actually were. Most importantly, our group discussions revealed what Carter articulated so well: "We don't know what a woman's story sounds like because we've never heard them." And because we've never been asked to tell our stories, and because we don't know what they sound like, women can become paralyzed; as Carter says, "We can't even tell them."

In our dialogue sessions, the female ministers have called into question the application of male constructs (or female constructs, for that matter) to their own stories. They have pointed to the difficulties inherent in telling a "woman's story" when the expectations for them, as women in ministry, are different. They explored the critical need for models and scripts that would provide a construct for their stories, one that would allow for validation and respect from others but would remain true to the "truth" of the wholeness and the complexity of their lives as they see and experience them. And, perhaps most importantly, they have articulated a theory about women's life histories that suggests that, for women, textual constructs alone are ultimately too confining—that texts without interpretation are invalid, that a linear progression without digression and reflection fails to tell their stories. They rejected the stories they had given to me as *their* life stories because they perceive their lives, and their narratives about those lives, as a multilayered text with interpretation. When their stories fail to balance both, they feel estranged from them.

The stories of these women in ministry are, indeed, raw. They are what emerged in unrehearsed sessions when I asked them "tell me your life story *or* tell me how you came to be a minister." Feminist ethnography, here designed as reciprocal, multilayered, and polyvocal, mirrors the text and subtext of the women's stories, which are equally multilayered and polyvocal. The spoken voices of the women interplay with other aspects of their own sub- (unspoken and/or muted) voices, with internalized male constructs of text and story, and with the stereotyped and misogynist demands of their cultural context, revealing in the end a rich harmony of experience and interpretation, of personal depth and political savvy, but a story that cannot and should not be understood on one level alone. The women in this study could have given me a standard, linear construction of their lives *or* related the unselfconscious "woman's" story, which would have reflected the relational aspects of their lives; instead, they gave me something else, stories that confounded and confused, stories that attempted to do both, by inclusion or by exclusion, by inversion and diversion. They related stories that incorporated self-interpretation and that demanded further collaborative interpretation, stories we came to understand together through discussion and dialogue.

In my work with female ministers, I have adopted what I am calling reciprocal ethnography. As I attempt to paint a descriptive portrait of women who are ministers, I have come to rely on a methodology that provides a way for my female collaborators to be involved in the collaborative process of gaining and sharing knowledge. At the beginning of this article, I posed the question about what reciprocal ethnography would provide for the scholar that she could not ascertain on her own; hopefully, this article has demonstrated the value of the methodology in expanding our understanding of how women construct a life story and why. In turn, the methodology provides a new frame for searching for meaning and collaborative interpretation; it also provides access to new theoretical perspectives about how social constructs of both lives and texts influence creativity and impulse, device and rhetoric. The metanarrational information provided through the dialogue sessions creates a lens through which to read and understand the stories the women actually told. There is not, at the present time, a perceived tradition of what a good professional woman's life story sounds like, at least as evidenced by these contemporary female ministers. They continue to seek the story script that will fully and accurately allow for all the different aspects of their lives. The integration and connection they seek in their lives have been represented here in their discussions about their stories. Reciprocal ethnography seeks this level of exploration and emergent knowledge sharing and deems it well worth the time and effort.[9]

Notes

1. The other participants of that panel were David Hufford, Diane Goldstein, William Wilson, and Leonard Primiano and Jeff Titon as discussant. All five continue to influence, support, and humanize my work with religion and belief, and I thank them for their continued critiques and friendship.

2. I am using "life story" as many scholars would use "life history" because I recognize this genre as both history and story. When I spoke to the women in this study about collecting the story of their lives, I used the term "life story" rather than "life history"; therefore, "life story" is the working term for this article. I do see the texts that they gave me as "stories," although I recognize that others will think of them as "histories" with stories embedded within. Recently, as I have begun to focus more sharply on single aspects of the larger story, I have had to speak about "life stories," as smaller, segmented stories within the total "life story," in the way that Sandra Stahl (1985) would. I will use "life story" as the larger texts that were collected in single settings and that the women and I recognized together as their "life stories."

3. To protect the lives and positions of the ministers included in this study, the location will be referred to only as "the upper Mississippi valley." All names of persons, places, and churches have been changed at the ministers' request. In most cases, references to actual denominations and seminaries have been retained as they may have bearing on the women's denominational experiences.

4. The longer I worked with this group of ministers, the more they have acknowledged the importance of my presence in their group and the effect that the "discussion sessions" have had on their group. They tell me that my work has drawn them closer together and has forced them to address issues on a much deeper level. They were genuinely dismayed when the group sessions had to end so that I could go back to teaching and begin to write my book. They opted to continue the sessions and discuss areas of interest they shared, as well as to embark on some group work on spiritual journeys. On infrequent occasions, I have taken or mailed my final drafts to them for their continued input.

5. This year, when I gave a version of this paper at the American Folklore Society, people seemed most eager to discuss it. I was frustrated, however, that even though I have made it clear that I am intentionally using the term "reciprocal," scholars then and now continue to refer to it as "reciprocity," which implies a connotation I specifically intend to avoid.

6. I have taken this notion of "scripting" women's lives from Rachel Blau DuPlessis (1985). I explored how Pentecostal women develop and tell oral narratives about their call to preach and about their lives in ministry in order to provide appropriate scripts both for themselves and for young women who may wish to follow in the ministry in Lawless (1988) and expanded that argument in Lawless (1991).

7. A "diaconal" minister in the Methodist Church is a consecrated minister who can preach and teach but cannot serve the sacraments or perform marriages. Anne-Marie serves as education director of a large Methodist church and preaches on a regular basis. While others question her choice because it seems less than an official, ordained minister, Anne-Marie justifies her choice by pointing out that as a diaconal minister, she is a free agent in the employment world of the church. Ordained ministers are moved by the church on a regular basis; she interviews for jobs and keeps them as long as she pleases.

8. I have often included comments about laughter because humor, joking, and loud, uninhibited laughter is an integral part of the women's interaction at lunch and in our group sessions. Because the topic and the discussions are quite serious and often emotional, and certainly because all are ordained ministers, I was not quite prepared for the levity of the group and the witty repartee that they have developed with each other. While the humor always serves to ease tensions and unite the group, it seems clear that it also helps this ecumenical group remain in a communicative mode, even when the discussions concern important theological differences.

9. The sociologist Howard Becker was present at Denzin's talk. Both Becker and Denzin responded with guarded enthusiasm to my description of my response to reflexive anthropology and thoughts about reciprocal ethnography, but Becker summed up their attitude, I think, by commenting that it sounded great, but "it would take too much time."

References Cited

Barbre, Joy Webster, et. al. The Personal Narrative Group. 1989. *Interpreting Women's Lives: Feminist Theory and Personal Narratives*. Bloomington: Indiana University Press.

Belenky, Mary Field, Blythe McVicker Clinchy, Nancy Rule Goldberger, and Jill Mattuck Tarule. 1986. *Women's Ways of Knowing: The Development of Self, Voice, and Mind*. New York: Basic Books, Inc.

Bennett, Gillian. 1989. "'And I Turned to Her and Said . . .': A Preliminary Analysis of Shape and Structure in Women's Storytelling." *Folklore* 100:167–183.

Briggs, Charles. 1986. *Learning How to Ask: A Sociolinguistic Appraisal of the Style of the Interview in Social Science Research*. Cambridge: Cambridge University Press.

Brodzki, Bella, and Celeste Schenck, eds. 1988. *Life/Lines: Theorizing Women's Autobiography*. Ithaca: Cornell University Press.

Clifford, James. 1988. *The Predicament of Culture: Twentieth-Century Ethnography, Literature, and Art*. Cambridge, MA: Harvard University Press.

Clifford, James, and George E. Marcus, eds. 1986. *Writing Culture: The Poetics and Politics of Ethnography*. Berkeley: University of California Press.

Crapanzano, Vincent. 1980. *Tuhami: Portrait of a Moroccan*. Chicago: University of Chicago Press.

Denzin, Norman K. 1989. *Interpretive Interactionism*. Newbury Park, CA: Sage Publishers.

DuPlessis, Rachel Blau. 1985. *Writing beyond the Ending: Narrative Strategies of Twentieth-Century Women Writers*. Bloomington: Indiana University Press.

Gilligan, Carol. 1982. *In a Different Voice: Psychological Theory and Women's Development*. Cambridge, MA: Harvard University Press.

Heilbrun, Carolyn G. 1988. *Writing a Woman's Life*. New York: W.W. Norton & Co.

Jelink, Estelle C., ed. 1980. *Women's Autobiography*. Bloomington: Indiana University Press.

Langness, L. L., and Gelya Frank. 1981. *Lives: An Anthropological Approach to Biography*. Novato, CA: Chandler and Sharp Pub., Inc.

Lawless, Elaine J. 1988. *Handmaidens of the Lord: Women Preachers and Traditional Religion*. Philadelphia: University of Pennsylvania Press and the American Folklore Society.

———. 1991. "Rescripting Their Lives and Their Narratives: The Spiritual Life Stories of Pentecostal Women Preachers." *Journal of Feminist Study of Religion* 7:53–73.

Marcus, George E., and Michael M. J. Fischer, eds. 1986. *Anthropology as Cultural Critique: An Experimental Moment in the Human Sciences.* Chicago: University of Chicago Press.

Mascia-Lees, Frances E., Patricia Sharpe, and Colleen Ballerino Cohen. 1989. "The Postmodernist Turn in Anthropology: Cautions from a Feminist Perspective." *Signs* 15:7–33.

Narayan, Kirin. 1989. *Storytellers, Saints, and Scoundrels: Folk Narrative in Hindu Religious Teaching.* Philadelphia: University of Pennsylvania Press.

Olney, James. 1980. *Autobiography: Essays Theoretical and Critical.* Princeton: Princeton University Press.

———. 1988. *Studies in Autobiography.* New York: Oxford University Press.

Reimer, Gail Twersky. 1988. "Revisions of Labor in Margaret Oliphant's Autobiography." In *Life/Lines: Theorizing Women's Autobiography,* edited by Bella Brodzki and Celeste Schenck, 121–132. Ithaca, NY: Cornell University Press.

Ruby, Jay, ed. 1982. *A Crack in the Mirror: Reflexive Perspectives in Anthropology.* Philadelphia: University of Pennsylvania Press.

Runyan, William McKinley. 1984. *Life Histories and Psychobiography: Explorations in Theory and Method.* New York: Oxford University Press.

Smith, Sidonie. 1987. *A Poetics of Women's Autobiography: Marginality and the Fictions of Self-Representation.* Bloomington: Indiana University Press.

Spacks, Patricia Meyer. 1972. *The Female Imagination.* New York: Alfred A. Knopf, Inc.

Stahl, Sandra. 1985. "A Literary Folkloristic Methodology for the Study of Meaning in Personal Narrative." *Journal of Folklore Research* 22:45–76.

Stanton, Domna, ed. 1984. *The Female Autograph: Theory and Practice of Autobiography from the Tenth to the Twentieth Century.* Chicago: University of Chicago Press.

Tyler, Stephen A. 1987. *The Unspeakable: Discourse, Dialogue, and Rhetoric in the Postmodern World.* Madison: University of Wisconsin Press.

Watson, Lawrence C., and Marie Barbara Watson-Franke. 1985. *Interpreting Life Histories: An Anthropological Inquiry.* New Brunswick: Rutgers University Press.

6

WRITING THE BODY IN THE PULPIT

Female-Sexed Texts

We wanted to call our newsletter *Naked in the Pulpit* because that was the way we were feeling much of the time, so since we couldn't, we called it *Notions 'n Pins*— the NIP still stands for "naked in the pulpit," but nobody knows that.

—Reverend Linda Stewart

A WOMAN IN THE PULPIT, DRESSED IN LITURGICAL vestments, celebrating the Eucharist, and preaching the word to a congregation of both men and women, threatens the very foundation of patriarchal order, but perhaps more significantly, such a woman exposes sexuality in a manner that cannot be denied or disregarded.[1] This article addresses the issue of sexuality in the pulpit, but it also seeks to examine and clarify the feminist admonition for women to "read/write the body." I will demonstrate that "writing the body" is a subjective experience, one that embodies rather than dismembers, and therein lies its power; if it is other than subjective, then the appropriation of "writing the body" becomes an objectified "mapping

---

Author's note: This article explores the various ways in which women in the pulpit threaten the patriarchal order by challenging models of God as asexual, inviting instead the possibilities of both a sexual God and a new model of Christianity focused on vulnerability and connection. In this article, I include the voices of the collaborating clergywomen in the study as we examine together notions of female sexuality from a subjective point of view borne of female experience. Their conclusions warn that the feminist injunction to "read/write the body" (Cixous's écriture feminine) is a far different matter than mapping the female body with an "Other's" (read: "male") gaze. This article was first published in the *Journal of American Folklore* 107, no. 423 (Winter 1994): 55–82.

the (female) body" that reinforces the fetishism of the female body that has served only to oppress, not liberate, women.

This article grew out of my field research with a regional group of mainstream clergywomen, most of whom are ordained, midwestern, Anglo American ministers.[2] I have long believed that notions of sexuality are at the heart of discrimination and misogyny in contemporary American Protestant churches, but the issue has proven to be a difficult one to explore because the discourse is complex—polyvocal and multileveled. However, it is my intention that this article celebrate and highlight the different discourses interacting in our collective endeavor to explore the issue of sexuality in the pulpit. The different discourses that appear in portions of this paper vary tremendously; I could have summarized and synthesized our journey exploring the issue of women's sexuality and religion, but I have chosen not to do that. I hope to demonstrate the evocative and evolving nature of the discourse on marked religious bodies among these clergywomen with myself as ethnographer.

Importantly, my personal commitment to *reciprocal ethnography* (Lawless 1991, 1992) and a shared dialogue of scholar and collaborators renders the task of presentation even more difficult in that I am determined to present the emergent, transmuted aspects of discovery inherent in any search for meaning and understanding—on the part of participants as well as scholars. Therefore, I do not offer this article as definitive. I offer my work as an endeavor shared with my collaborators, as an effort to discover and redress layers of religious, historical, and cultural beliefs and perceptions about women that have uniformly served to deny them access to both religious power and authority.

In this article I want to first outline some of the major issues I see involved in religious discrimination against women clergy. My discussion will then seek to reclaim the authority of experience and a subjective point of view. Finally, I will invite the voices of the women in my study to join in this dialogue to demonstrate how we worked together toward an emergent view of what they believe to be the validity of a woman embodied. A warning to the reader: scholarly discourse juxtaposed with ethnographic materials requires a shifting of perspective. This shift is immediate and distinctive in the researcher's fieldwork, but conveying the way in which field materials become transmuted into the fabric of scholarly discourse is tricky and requires the intellectual attention of both the writer and the reader. Rarely in our search for how people make meaning in their lives do we find finely tuned, well-articulated, formalized answers to our awkward, probing, and often insensitive questions. The theological concepts and belief systems of most ordinary people, and I include both the clergywomen and myself, are far from concretized. Discourse about meaning is often exploratory, ephemeral, tenuous, sketchy, emergent, evolving, and constantly changing. This is because meaning is derived from experience, and experience is ongoing, never static, and rarely replicated. Raw and subjective though it is, experience nonetheless holds the key to understanding meaning. Objective theological constructs tend to lie flat and remain unquestioned, rigid, and inflexible. But this excursion into the discourse of meaning based on experience will demonstrate the potential for dissonance, incongruence, and the inconclusive "feel" of it all—which only serves to demonstrate the chasm that lies deep between the social/cultural/religious constructions about women that have been invented and perpetuated by a gendered Other and the way women construct themselves, from the inside out, as subjects. In the end, their constructions about persons living a religious journey, one that includes both men and women, are healthier ones. They offer a holistic view of the world, the people in it, and of God: embodied, whole, and healthy.

What Is the Threat of a Woman in the Pulpit?

Religious men who have designed, perpetuated, and existed comfortably within a male-dominated patriarchal religious construction perpetuated and justified by divine right are threatened by the presence of an ordained woman in the pulpit. This threat can be recognized in at least five distinctive ways: as a threat to theological ordering and the divinely endorsed superiority of males, a threat to fixed gender roles, a threat to the male-dominated social order, a threat to the perceptions of God (and the male minister) as asexual males, and the threat of an emerging model of God as female. In many ways, these aspects are intertwined, and distinctions between them sometimes blur, but I shall discuss them individually here.

Threat to Theological Ordering

Female clergy first threaten male prominence in the theological ordering that has evolved into a concretized image of a male deity, a male savior, and a male Holy Spirit (the aspect, some have long argued, that initially represented the female aspect of the tripartite deity). The highly visible Roman

Catholic insistence that priests be male because only males have the physical characteristics of a male godhead and a male savior provides widespread validation of male domination and prominence in the larger Christian context, both Catholic and Protestant. This hierarchical, patriarchal structure pervades all of Western culture, even Protestantism, which has denied the viability of an all-male priesthood yet has historically shared an ambivalence about ordaining women to the ministry. Women in any pulpit, on the most obvious level, threaten and, indeed, usurp the exclusive rights of males to religious authority.

Threat to Fixed Gender Roles

A female in the pulpit also threatens the foundation of the dichotomous nature of fixed gender roles and traditional arenas for men and women. As long as the male claimed the sole religious authority, he could also lay claim to household authority and dominance over the other household occupants—women and children. Scholarship, such as Sherry Ortner's, exploring the historical roots of male activity centered in the public arena and female activity centered in the private provides one framework for understanding how women have been oppressed by a religiously inspired sociocultural system that has been reluctant to provide free access to spheres beyond the "hearth and home" for women (Ortner 1974). As Katie Cannon notes in *God's Fierce Whimsy*, "The Euromerican ruling class has attempted to contain women within a private sphere. Women, sexuality, bodies, feelings, and children have had no place in the public world of economics, politics, and 'matters of consequence'" (1985, 21). The most recent migration of women out of the cloistered home environment and into public professions, particularly in the ordained ministry, has threatened to rock the foundations of patriarchy, causing male dominance and oppression of women to shift, although by no means disappear.

Threat to the Male-Dominated Social Order

Ordained women gaining religious authority pose a new and penetrating threat to the male-dominated order. While women as lawyers, doctors, and college professors can remain in the public perception as (unauthorized) tokens, anomalies, freaks, and radicals who have no respect for the home and ideologies of family and tradition, they are often discounted with the line, "But they aren't *really* women." But an ordained clergywoman or priest has divine recognition; her authority is invested in her by God and is endorsed by the religious institutions that ordain her. In many cases she is a wife and mother; in other cases she is a lesbian; in others she chooses marriage without children. Whatever her choice, she is not actually perceived as a radical; more often than not she acknowledges the importance and primacy of family and/or relationship, home, and religion. Her position in the pulpit is nevertheless jarring, for it calls into question the makeup and the acting out of all the established sociocultural and religious constructs. The woman has divine authority; the woman has religious power; the woman preaches, teaches, travels, celebrates the sacraments, marries people, and buries people. Suddenly, the tidy configuration with a male at the head is called into question—exposed. Changes in the public social order are reflected, then, in the realities of the gender(ed) roles in the private order; new arrangements are necessary and endorsed: men cook; men care for children; women work; women travel; women counsel parishioners; men work; both work; both cook; women seek and find female partners. The patriarchal order does not prevail. Not only do males who seek to retain their dominating presence find this threatening, but women in congregations and local communities who have located themselves firmly, comfortably, and securely in the private arena and have participated in the construction of a patriarchal reality, *as well as the domestic model of reality for their own identity*, are equally threatened. It is always disconcerting when the comfortable social framework shifts and begins to reconfigure in new and unfamiliar ways. This aspect is not, of course, unique to clergywomen and to the other social participants in their life arenas, but it is true of any situation in which women enter the workforce and, by doing so, deconstruct and call into question the social frameworks and the human expectations of those involved. When the situation pivots around the church and is tied closely to religious beliefs, however, the impact is greater and the implications broader. What is unique to the situation involving female ministers is the *fact* of religious validation for this emerging social order, which comes on the heels of the ordination of a woman to the ministry. Could God possibly endorse such heresy? If God does, then must the patriarchy fall? How to maintain male dominance and absolute authority in the church, home, and social arena? Obviously, it cannot be done; the authority for the hierarchy has been rescinded. The ultimate threat to males is difficult to comprehend. It is not just that the absolute right of the male to the pulpit is being questioned; like a stacked line of dominoes, the effect could potentially invade every aspect of patriarchal authority and male dominance. In contrast to this frightened perspective, women in ministry claim that their presence is expanding perceptions of humanity as holistic, inclusive of all aspects of what it means to be a human being as created and encouraged by a concept of God that incorporates and celebrates the whole experience of every person—which, of course, includes the sexual.

Threat to Perceptions of God (and Ministers) as Asexual Males

A woman in the pulpit calls into question theological constructs or models of God that have for centuries claimed God as asexual. Like Catholics, Protestants have held firmly to the patriarchal construct that recognizes males as God's designated representatives on earth. While perhaps not articulated in the same fashion, the father-to-son male minister line of authority has survived centuries of hardline Protestantism. Most denominations did not authorize the ordination of women until this century, and some still will not. Protestant Christianity has never shared the Catholic belief that the minister of God ought to be celibate. Most have been a bit more realistic and have taken to heart the Pauline directive that it is better to marry than to burn. Nevertheless, for centuries, the prevalent image of a "minister of God" has been a (sexless) male image.

The Roman Catholic insistence on celibate male priests celebrates and upholds the line of divine maleness—from God the Father, to God the Son, to God the Holy Ghost, to the male priest. Father to Son to Spirit to priest, maleness is honored, celebrated, worshiped. At first glance, it is not clear— is this a gendered line of authority? Only (celibate or sexless) men may participate—is it not a *sexual* matter, then? Women are excluded from the hierarchical schema—femaleness simply does not appear as a component of the theological construct. Is it a sexual matter, then? But it gets more complicated. The Catholic Church deems that only an asexual male, a man who does not need to engage in sexual activities, is a pure and holy representative of the Holy Father (who, after all, did not actually copulate with Mary to conceive his son but sent his emissary the Holy Ghost to do the deed or whisper in her ear), and only men like this can be priests. The celibate male priest and the asexual virgin mother, then, become representatives of the ultimate human potential for godliness, and all participate in the pretense that this particular male (the priest) is asexual and therefore pure, holy, and above sin (then is sexuality sinful?). The priest dons long robes that hide the physical configurations and potential swellings of his body and pretends that he is (sexually) *unlike* other males or other humans. When he enters the pulpit, he is viewed as God's representative, the holiest human potential.

The Protestant minister, unlike the priest, can marry, and his wife can bear his children; thus, he has never participated fully in the pretense of pulpit asexuality. Yet his sexual nature is shielded. In the pulpit he may stand in vestments or in a business suit; he may be adored by some women in the congregation; he may even be the subject of innuendo or scandalous stories. But whatever the congregation whispers, the minister *should not signify sexuality*. He is suspect if he is openly perceived as a sexual being; he cannot celebrate sexuality; he cannot explore the sexuality issues of his constituents openly from the pulpit. By and large, sexuality is not a recognized aspect of religion because it is not a visible component of the male-dominated religious hierarchy. But, as Sallie McFague points out, to think of God as male is obviously to think in sexual terms, and yet in the efforts of early Christians to distinguish themselves from goddess religions and fertility cults, sexuality *was* an issue. Most importantly, the issue was that the god(dess) not be linked to the female: "the sexual implications of paternal imagery were masked. . . . Traditional language for God is not nonsexual; on the contrary, it is male" (McFague 1988, 98).

Daphne Hampson relates this to a social construct that posits men as good, strong, and more religious in contrast to women, who are seen as sinful, weak, and closer to things of the earth (especially reproduction) and the other worldliness of spirit: "What female and the feminine stand for thus becomes locked into a whole interpretation of reality . . . [in which] women and the feminine are conceived as inferior and sinful" (1990, 97). She notes that religious educator and writer Anne Wilson Schaef has, through her own work, determined how this internalized view of reality thrives and is perpetuated in Western social and cultural arenas. She aptly quotes from Mary Daly: "If God is male, then the male is God" (1990, 108). Obviously, these constructs serve to shut women out altogether and to deny sexuality as a religious issue.

If God is male and priests are male but neither signifies sexuality, then sexuality is part of the "Other," which is represented by the *female*. And femaleness has not been a recognized aspect of Protestant religion. The Virgin Mary has never enjoyed any power—overt or covert—in the Protestant Church. Any hint of iconography or intercessory power of a female has been historically eliminated. God the Father, God the Son, God the Holy Ghost, and the male minister have guided Protestants in a well-oiled patriarchal system that pervades every aspect of their public *and* private lives. Margaret Miles has pointed out that Thomas Aquinas's descriptions of Mary's talents indicate his awareness that, because Christ's power and the Virgin's power might easily be construed as competitive rather than complementary, her powers had to be deemphasized: "She possessed extraordinary gifts but could not use them publicly since it would detract from Christ's teaching" (Miles 1985, 201). Miles argues that women have had to be "guided to accept the model of the nursing Virgin without identifying with her power—a power derived from her body" (1985, 205). According to Hampson, male religious leaders in Western tradition have created a cultural "reality" that is aligned closely with Western theology: God has been conceived as particularly male, a transcendent being in an ordered hierarchy. Men see themselves as above women; thus, "humanity" has been designated as "feminine" in relation to God (Hampson 1990, 97).

Threat of an Emerging Model of God as Female

Female power, clearly recognized and defined in terms of women's sexuality, has never been recognized in a positive light in Protestant religious culture. A woman in the pulpit abruptly predicates a semiotic shift. Because the female has never been divorced from her sexuality, her presence as clergy forces a rethinking of the very perceptions of God. The predominant male images, so neatly configured in their interlocking hierarchy and their connection to an asexual supreme being, are rearranged and disengaged. The woman standing in the pulpit arrests the natural breathing of the now complacent and comfortable congregation. Both women and men must adjust their perspective, realigning their image of God with this female, this marginal Other. It is not an easy thing to do. Males are particularly uncomfortable because their divine-right status has been questioned openly, *in the pulpit*. Women are shocked, for the prospect of disruption of the order, and their place in it, is frightening. At first the question must be in everyone's mind: Is this a representative of God? The woman in the pulpit answers with a resounding yes; the rearrangement begins, and often bitterness and anger accompany the beginning of the new order.

If the priest/pastor/preacher can be a woman, then perhaps female images of God can be introduced and taken seriously. But McFague addresses the uneasiness that female metaphors for God elicit, telling us that "unlike the male metaphors, whose sexual character is cloaked, the female metaphors seem blatantly sexual and involve the sexuality most feared: female sexuality" (1988, 98). Importantly, McFague argues, "It is by introducing female metaphors for God that the sexuality of both male and female metaphors becomes evident, though it appears, because we are familiar with the male metaphors, that only the female ones are sexual . . . female imagery jolts us into awareness that there is no gender-neutral language if we take ourselves as the model for talk about God, because we are sexual beings" (1988, 98).

The Sexual in Religious Contexts

The sexual has been deemed inappropriate for religious contexts. Christianity has openly at times, more subtly in other times, decreed the flesh as sinful and denied the body—finding it the locus for all that is animalistic and "natural" in humans, as well as holding the potential power of the devil and of evil. Associations of the female body with the serpent, the (d)evil, and the loss of innocence have made it easy to persecute women and deny them access to the pulpit. The 1484 *Malleus Maleficarum* states that men are much less likely to associate with the devil in witchcraft than women because they belong to *Christ's sex* (Miles 1985, 206). Sexuality was relegated to the arenas of the flesh—sin and wantonness (associated with the female body) on the one hand and reproduction (also associated with the female body) on the other. The Catholic Church aligned celibacy with purity and divinity, a route chosen by male priests and nuns. This dichotomy between the flesh and the spirit parallels the perception of God as a transcendent being—separate from and on a higher plane than mere humans, separated from the body and the flesh of "lowly" humankind. This denial of the fleshly made it impossible to incorporate any potential for human divinity. Contemporary Protestant Christianity, too, fears the human capacity for debauchery and sexual lascivity, claiming the body as the "temple" of God but only if sexuality is tempered and pleasure is denied. Here sexuality is usually only condoned within heterosexual marriages and with the (implied) intent of reproduction. While celibacy has never been a restriction imposed on Protestant ministers, sexuality remains in Protestant socioreligious culture a danger to be checked, associating both sexual allure and danger with women. A female, then, in the pulpit raises the possibility, at the very worst, of polluting the pulpit, bringing nature, lust, lascivity, and temptation into "sacred" space, which has been purified by its insistence on an asexual constructed reality. At the very best, the woman presents a dilemma in that she forces a confrontation with sexuality for everyone involved—and dares to associate divinity with human desire.

An "Objective" View versus a "Subjective" View

With all of the above operating on a cognitive level, what, then, becomes the actual perception of a female who is ordained, dresses in robes, and stands before a congregation to speak for God? Who is looking at whom? Where does the power of "writing the body" reside? As I attempted to determine what a look at sexuality and the ministry would entail, particularly if I were writing about women clergy, I turned to some of David Hufford's thinking about how the terms *objective* and *subjective* are used, particularly in the arenas of belief and religion.[3] It is ironic and unacceptable that the "objective" view (that is, the impersonal outsider perspective) has gained validation over the "subjective" view, which is seen as personal and which is based on experience. How did we come to devalue the personal? When did experience cease to count for more than observation? Should we not question even a well-respected thinker like Walter Ong if he posits, in his discussion of why "learned Latin" was a significant boost to the elitist intellectual education of males in the Middle Ages, "Writing serves to separate and distance the knower and the known and thus to establish objectivity. . . . Learned Latin effects even greater objectivity by establishing knowledge in a medium insulated from the emotion-charged depths of one's mother tongue, thus reducing interference from the human lifeworld and making possible the exquisitely abstract world of medieval scholasticism and the new mathematics of modern science" (Ong 1982, 113)?

The clergywomen in my most recent study—all ordained in mainline denominations—say they feel "naked in the pulpit." They do not mean they feel stripped naked; they are not speaking from the outside purview of a woman's naked body. They are speaking about how they *feel* in the pulpit. What does that mean to the women who say it? Does it mean the same thing as how a woman in the pulpit is *perceived*—by those Others who can physically see her up there in robes, reading the scriptures, administering the sacraments, praying, blessing, baptizing, marrying, and burying congregation members? We have here the view from without and the view from within, and they are two very distinctively different views. Ironically, the view from the *outside* has been the privileged view. That is, the socioreligious (outsider) view of the female (as mapped by the male gaze) has determined her status and her limitations within the ordained ministry. From the outside (read: male) point of view (the authorized, empowered point of view), a woman's body *lacks* a penis; therefore, she is *not like* Christ; therefore, she should not be ordained as a priest. But also, and importantly, from this perspective, a woman *does have* (sensual) lips, long(er) hair, breasts, a vulva, (rounded) hips, and (alluring) legs. Her body has been perceived by those observing it, and her various body parts have been fetishized and loaded with semiotic and symbolic import.

On the other hand, the view from *within* the female body—from this side of the lips, the hair, the breasts, the vulva, the hips, and the legs—is considerably different. To "write" from this vantage point, to "write the body" from the pulpit, is to connect the knower with the known, the invert of Ong's premise. The *outside* view, based on observable data—reproducible, empirical, material, and tangible—refers to an object, the external, and is considered the more "objective" view. The view from *within*, based on the subject or one who experiences, is deemed "subjective" and automatically becomes suspect because we have been trained to trust the objective and mistrust the subjective. However, as Hufford cautions, the complexity of the connotations of the word *subjective*, reflecting its crucial historical role in the development of theories of knowledge, can be appreciated by a look at some of its dictionary definitions: "pertaining to the *real* nature of something; essential; proceeding from or taking place within an individual's mind such as to be unaffected by the external world" (emphasis added). "Subjective" is used pejoratively to connote privately arrived at judgments based on emotional or "prejudiced" grounds, as Ong has suggested. But this combining of the experiential mode with connotations of falsity flies in the face of the philosophical truisms that suggest that we are all *limited to and by* our own unique and peculiar perceptual (experiential) world. We cannot go beyond this world to know what the external world is like in itself; knowledge is inevitably structured in terms of our experiences and perceptions. Even the "objective" is reliant upon the "subjective" (or what we have experienced) to inform our interpretations of what we see.[4] The popular view of these terms has created a myriad of limitations and has hampered the world available to females; in this particular case it has worked to obstruct a woman's desire to be a priest with all the same rights and privileges as a man. The constructed reality of "female" from a male perspective actually can be viewed as a folk belief, in fact a belief that is perceived as authentic, validated, and objective and that has been codified as an official religious injunction against female priests.

In Protestant religions in which women can in fact be ordained, certain aspects of this particular folk belief are not shared by all persons, but the fetishization of the female body and the concurrent semiotic and symbolic overlays ("objective" reality) are clearly operating within the religious contexts in which these clergywomen serve. There are beliefs about women's bodies that dictate responses to her in the pulpit. On the other hand, the women also share beliefs about themselves ("subjective" reality), about their bodies, about the world, about religion, about their place in the pulpit, about God, and about humanity that are derived from their experience as female subjects. The result of their "writing the body" from the pulpit is a newly written text about God. But because this viewpoint has been disregarded as "subjective," it carries little or no authority or validation within the religion and culture.

I offer the argument that the female experience from within the female body is what is meant by "writing the body" and is more legitimate and should carry even more weight to what is perceived as the "objective" view from the outside. In fact, I find the subjective view closer to the dictionary perception, that is, "pertaining to the real nature of something; essential; proceeding from or taking place within an individual's mind," and find it to be more defensible because it is knowledge and belief constructed from actual experience and extended to interpretation, not knowledge and belief constructed from perception alone. How did we get to a place where perceived, objective knowledge is superior to and more trusted than subjective knowledge? How can we facilitate a "re-membering" of the female body that does not find nurturance in further violation and fetishization?

Clergywomen Speaking from the Inside

What I Mean by "Reciprocal Ethnography"

To gain access to the subjective view of female ministers and their interpretations of the female body in the pulpit—from the inside looking out—I have in my recent research developed what I have termed *reciprocal ethnography*, which means that my typical fieldwork has expanded from interviewing denominational clergywomen and recording sermons to group interviews, which I call *dialogue sessions*. In these sessions, the women in the study met together with me to discuss certain aspects of my research and our combined efforts at articulating meaning (Lawless 1991; 1992). Our dialogue sessions included (over the course of two years) discussions of women's life stories (and theirs in particular); their theology; their notions of spirituality, sexuality, and the pulpit; images of God; women's ministries; and other topics we, together, wanted to discuss. These dialogue sessions focused on the various aspects of their ministries that I had written about. I brought my writing back to them for their examination and discussion. This article relies heavily on three different sessions that we held to discuss the topic of sexuality and the ministry. Specific speakers have been quoted directly from the recordings of those sessions.

Sexuality and Gender Roles—What Is the Connection?

When I started writing about the topic of sexuality and the ministry, I thought it would be useful to discriminate between stories and experiences that depicted "gendered" situations and those that depicted "sexuality." This approach proved to be helpful at first, and some stories were fairly easy to place in one category or the other. The women told many stories about mixed messages from congregation members, stories that confirm the confused gender-role expectations that parishioners have with female clergy. When she cooks for church functions, Carter, an Episcopal priest, says her congregation members are astonished and say, "'You made this?' It is like they finally decided that I was in the role of a cleric, but obviously if I can do that, then I could not (also) cook!" Once, at a Bible study class, the church women were unable to light the pilot light on a stove and asked for the male priest to come help. Carter went instead, read the directions, and, to their amazement, she said, lit the pilot. "It was sort of my welcome to Faith Chapel. I could do what the priest could do. I could light the oven!"

Similarly, Maria laughed about how hard her female congregation members try to exclude her from the typical female expectations for pot-luck dinners and kitchen duties, insisting, "Oh, this doesn't mean *you*! You are the pastor!" In the process, however, she says, it becomes a "catch-22." At the same time that they insist that she need not participate, she is certain they are keeping an account of all the *female* activities that she does not share with them, and suddenly the gendered experience becomes potentially linked to Maria's sexuality; that is, if she does not bring salads and participate in the activities of the women, then her *femaleness* comes into question. This is an especially sensitive issue for this particular female pastor because she is, in fact, lesbian. She has not "come out" to her congregation and is overly conscious of how her behavior is directly related to perceptions of her as a woman.

Marsha told me about a "maddening" experience that "just continues to happen, over and over." She was called to officiate a wedding, and several women came up to her afterward, exclaiming about how they "had never seen a woman minister, wasn't that just amazing, a woman minister preaching a wedding! [They] had never heard a woman preach a wedding, but they thought it was OK; [they] thought she did a fine job." Marsha says she feels like she is in a zoo: "It's just an awful feeling to have to keep experiencing that! It gets to be a burden." Similarly, Constance laughingly recounted being at a funeral at which a female minister was officiating. A week later, she heard two older women discussing the funeral. One of the women was lamenting that no minister was there to conduct the funeral. "So," she told her friend, "some woman just got up there and did the talking. It was the darnedest thing!"

Somehow, the cognitive dissonance of seeing a woman in the pulpit under certain conditions and without explanation is something that many people cannot comprehend as legitimate. Sharing these stories led the women in the dialogue group into a long discussion of vestment catalogs and how they had changed in the past several years to include the *possibility* of female clergy. The clergywomen recalled that ten years ago there were no women pictured in the catalogs, nor were any women's measurements included. Then, for a time, there was a single-sheet insert that accompanied the regular catalog featuring choices for women. Gradually, pictures of women modeling only the vestments deemed "appropriate" for women to wear began to appear. Now, most pages of the catalogs include female models and this past year included a picture of a woman in a chassel, the symbol of the priest that is worn only by the celebrant of the Eucharist. Carter was delighted: "They finally put a woman in one!"

My neatly defined distinctions between gendered stories and sexual stories began to collapse, however, the more I listened to the voices of the women. I recall another very funny story that Carter shared in one of our dialogue sessions. The story was told as true but is one that I believe could be, and probably is, apocryphal: "I heard a story about a [male] priest, when he first went to be a director of a Newman Center. It was Christmas, and they were hanging things and all of that. The light bulbs needed to be changed; so he got a ladder, and someone came to him and said, "Oh, no, Father, let one of the *men* do that!"

This story actually helped me understand that gendered experiences and sexual experiences could not be separated so easily. Gendered roles and expectations are based on perceptions of sexuality. This story, then, leads us easily into an examination of beliefs about women and/or men—in the pulpit and the semiotic messages inherent in that "picture." This Catholic priest's *maleness* provided him access to the priesthood, yet in this anecdote it is clear that his *manhood* has been unwittingly questioned at the same time. While questions of appropriate gender-role differentiation continued to appear in the discussions of women in the ministry, it became apparent that gender was not at the heart of the issue. Sexuality was. Bold, raw, naked, open, embraceable, pure, but denied, human sexuality. Yet as we moved through the exploration of the issue, we found the lines blurred and sometimes indistinguishable. We came, I believe, to a recognition that gender is never really just gender, that gender is merely sexuality disguised and denied.

The Female Body in Vestments—Sexuality Embodied?

For many parishioners, the way their female ministers dress becomes a public issue, and it has to do with sexuality. Several women told stories of congregation members being upset by the shortness of their skirts; short skirts did not convey the proper image of the female pastor as demure and modest (nonsexual). Conversely, Anne-Marie told of an associate minister who lost her job because she wore pants to church a few times. Their stories illustrate how the issue of sexuality is certainly multileveled and takes us far beyond expectations of social behavior. Linda told a story about a female minister whose church-provided robes were too large for her. She therefore sought a robe that would neither hide her, nor reveal too much. Her stories led the women to talk about the denominational newsletter for female ministers, which the founders wanted to entitle *Naked in the Pulpit* because that was "the way we were feeling very much of the time." They concluded that the title would be too risqué and, instead, strategically chose the title *Notions 'n Pins*. This title preserves the abbreviation NIP but embeds their radical statement within an acceptable domestic image of sewing. Anytime they tell this, listeners often assume that "naked in the pulpit" has a sexual connotation. It does, and it doesn't—the lines of gender and sexuality are blurred. I shall return to this point later in this article.

Susan Suleiman, in *The Female Body in Western Culture*, tells us, "We find ample testimony to the fascination that the female body has exerted on our individual and collective consciousness. And simultaneously with its attraction, we find testimony to the fear and loathing that body has inspired: beautiful but unclean, alluring but dangerous, woman's body (. . . mother's body?) has appeared mysterious, duplicitous—a source of pleasure and nurturance, but also of destruction and evil. Mary and Pandora, in sum" (1985, 1). Women, in this view, are "embodied." Women cannot be asexual. They *signify* the sexual. No matter how young, old, large, small, provocatively uncovered or covered, the female body has come to signify sexuality: "The cultural significance of the female body is not only (not even first or foremost) that of a flesh-and-blood entity, but that of a *symbolic construct*. Everything we know about the body . . . exists for us in some form of discourse; and discourse, whether verbal or visual, fictive or historical or speculative, is never unmediated, never free of interpretation, never innocent" (Suleiman 1985, 2, emphasis in original).

This interpretation is, of course, political. That is, the persons in power, men by and large, are making these (objective) interpretations. This is what the female body signifies to them, and it references power and control within the society. In a disconcerting connection between the power of speech and women's bodies, George Steiner, in *After Babel*, states, "The alleged outpouring of women's speech, rank flow of words, may be a symbolic restatement of men's apprehensive, often ignorant awareness of the menstrual cycle [!]" (quoted in Brooke-Rose 1985, 311). Perhaps closer to the perceived reality, however, is Margaret Miles's comment that "women's mouths, tongues, and speech have frequently been associated with the vagina—open when they should be closed, causing the ruin of all they tempt or slander" (1989, 156).

Is "Writing the Body" a Subjective Endeavor?

How do we subvert the male gaze, taken to be the objective, valid, authorized view of the female body to a subjective one authorized from within the female experience? Do we turn to French feminists who are currently calling for an exercise that, they say, evolves from female experience? The call for "writing the (female) body" derives largely from the theoretical essays of Hélène Cixous, Julia Kristeva, and Luce Irigaray, who have been concerned with the body politic and who are encouraging *women* to "write" from their bodies (cf. Conley 1984; Daly 1978; Hite 1988; Jones 1981; Kristeva 1984, 1986). Drawing on her reading of Mariana Warner's *The Cult of the Virgin Mary*, Julia Kristeva, in her provocative essay "Stabat Mater," explores the proposition that today, due to the demise of the cult of the Virgin, and of religion in general, we are left without a satisfactory discourse on motherhood (Kristeva 1986, 160). According to Toril Moi, Kristeva asks what the "necessarily crumbling edifice [the cult of the Virgin] ignores or represses in modern women's experience of motherhood?" (Kristeva 1986, 160) In reply to her own question, Kristeva points to the need for a "new understanding of the mother's body. . . . There is, then, an urgent need for a 'post-virginal' discourse on maternity, one which ultimately would provide both women and men with a new ethics: a 'herethics' encompassing both reproduction and death" (Kristeva 1986, 160).[5] Kristeva's call, then, is one that would emerge from the female experience—although her language is firmly embedded in the female experience *as a maternal experience*. But her call is echoed in the work of Hélène Cixous, who, as Sandra Gilbert explains, tells us there is "a new voice crying in the wilderness . . . a voice of a body dancing, laughing, shrieking, crying. Whose is it? It is, they say, the voice of a woman, newborn and yet archaic, a voice of milk and blood, a voice silenced but savage" (Gilbert 1986, ix). Cixous's "newly born woman" writes in both milk and blood, although in her work, Cixous stresses more the importance of the woman writing as woman rather than woman as mother. The key to the feminist call for "writing the body," regardless of how the topic is approached, is the recognition of the primacy of female experience as the authentication of perspective; hence, the "subjective" is rendered more valid than the "objective." And in the study of women in the pulpit, "writing the body" poses for all humans involved in the endeavor to "write" their own experiences into a new text of God.

What Might a New "Herethics" Be/Look Like?

I would like to meet Kristeva's challenge, demonstrating how women in the ministry do provide a new "herethics" that not only encompasses reproduction and death but seeks to reunite the secular and the sacred, the temporal and the spiritual, the human and the divine, the flesh and the spirit—a new perspective that would, therefore, also reweave the natural connections between life and death and sever the lines that have connected sexuality, sin, and the female. If we continue to "map the body" through a patriarchal lens, however, the manifestation of this new herethics will remain on the level of signification rather than articulation and will fail to give voice to a herethics that will go beyond mapping the female body and demonstrate what might be called "writing the body." Allow me to demonstrate how our collective thinking came to question the productivity of "mapping the female body" in our search for a validation of female experience from the inside point of view, which will then be a viable example of *écriture feminine*.

As I sought a way to deal with sexuality and clergywomen, I listened to our recorded dialogue sessions with an ear toward what I conceived as "mapping the female body." Images of the female body and its link to sexuality led us to a semiotic and metaphorical examination. It seemed important in a discussion of sexuality in the ministry to map the female body in terms of its dissonance with the pulpit. Most of the ministers suspected the female body in general, complete with breasts, vagina, womb, sexual organs, long hair, and mouth (covered or uncovered), poses a problem for many of their congregants, perhaps more for the men than the women. In our discussions of sexuality and ministry, Linda Stewart, a United Methodist pastor, commented that when she was pregnant, she suspected her some of her congregation members felt very uncomfortable, largely because her pregnancy brought her sexuality to the forefront. The congregation had to face the fact that she and her (clergy) husband were engaging in sexual activity. Linda talked openly about how some of the men in her congregation often looked at her cleavage rather than at her face and noted that their interest in her breasts took an intriguing turn when she chose to breastfeed her son. She believed that many members of her congregation felt uncomfortable when she breastfed, and she suggested that many clergywomen choose not to breastfeed their babies because some parishioners find it inappropriate. Furthermore, it was her opinion that ancient Old Testament taboos about women being unclean during menstruation and, thus, unfit to serve the sacraments surfaced for some people when her pregnancy made it clear that at times previous she must have been menstruating when she served the sacraments. This discussion about breastfeeding and pregnancy led the women to acknowledge that the public display of pregnancy and breastfeeding posed a problem for some men because these images were the signifiers of what men could not do but also illustrated in an obvious way how the ministers were not men. Our first discussion, then, helped to map the female body in terms of sexual dissonance. Linda mapped the breasts, the womb, and sexual intercourse, which of course draws attention to the vagina and the sexual parts of the woman as well as her menses. Her story also draws the lines of sexual/textual dissonance that accompany this mapping.

It is important to point out here that the "dialogue sessions" we conducted allowed for diverse opinions to be expressed. The women by no means agreed on all the various points we discussed. In fact, it became quite clear to me that no one voice in this group could ever speak for all the other voices, thus confirming the notion that women's experiences are plural. We cannot presume to speak either "objectively" or "subjectively" about all women's experiences. Knowledge is gained through personal experience. Each woman seeks to authenticate her experience as real—as real as all of the others. Thus, in this discussion, no sooner had Linda concluded her account than others clamored to have their voices heard and acknowledged as well. Several claimed that their experience of being pregnant in a co-ministry situation "was nothing like that." Amy Seger, a young Disciples of Christ associate pastor, told a passionate story that counters Linda's experience of negative perceptions within the congregations she served. Yet Amy's story does not deny that she, too, was perceived by her congregation as an actively sexual being and that her pregnancy further exposed that aspect of her being: "It was almost the opposite of that: [it was] a celebration of sexuality and of creation of life. And I got none of that negative denial of who I was or that I was [not] a sexual being. There was none of that." She felt her pregnancy was noted and applauded as a celebration of sexuality and new life. In either case, the female body is mapped and noted as sexual and reproductive in its essence. As Miles notes, the connection between the female body and eroticism is ironic since female sexual arousal is not visibly apparent; furthermore, she notes, even though the male sexual organ displays the most visible "willfulness," it is the *female* who is identified with her sexual and reproductive organs (Miles 1985, 116).

The dissonance that exists between the female body and the pulpit is clearly associated with an "objective" view of the female body as potentially sexual and potentially pregnant. In one of our dialogue sessions, Marsha Johnston, a United Methodist pastor, repeated a story we had heard before about a Methodist district superintendent who had misled her about employment opportunities for her when her clergy husband had taken a church in the area. He had encouraged her to come talk with him and had suggested that he could help her find a church to pastor. Yet when she actually arrived, he said to her, "'Why do you want to be a minister? You are a woman. That's like bloodying your head against a wall.' He then began to laugh as he said, 'Can you imagine a pregnant bishop?'" He soon realized Marsha was not laughing with him. The group discussed why that was such a problematic image. For one woman, "It is a constant reminder of your sexuality. You cannot escape the fact that you were with a man. You did it at least once. You cannot be asexual anymore. You really cannot anyway. A man might be able to carry that off, but a woman never can."

As I asked the women to focus on these differences and on the perceptions of their congregations about them—either pregnant or not pregnant—my questions to the group centered around several aspects of sexuality and ministry that I had not been able to sort out. Some of these aspects included a question about why some parishioners would be hesitant to receive the sacraments from a pregnant minister or priest. Other questions focused on how congregation members perceived female ministers before they became pregnant, while they were pregnant, and then how they perceived them after their children were born. I wondered if congregations shared in the pretense that before the pregnancy, the minister was "just a person," not a woman, but that once she became pregnant, there could no longer be any denial of her gender and her sexuality. I further wondered if the female minister, like women in the general population, cease to be thought of as *sexual* once they become *mothers*.

Amy attempted to respond to these questions in terms of her own experience. She speculated that before her pregnancy:

> the women did not know how to respond to me as a professional woman. It doesn't take people long to figure out in my relationship with my husband that I'm not the person that cooks. He's the person who cooks in our family. So I was some kind of different breed, you know; I didn't have children; I didn't cook. They gave their pie recipes to my husband. And yet there was something affirming in my being pregnant, and there was something affirming in my having a child that said, "Yeah, she is a woman, and because she is a woman, I connect with her." And it opened doors; it opened intimacy—[doors] that were guarded before. But no one was ever appalled by my pregnancy. It was a celebration within the congregation. And no one was appalled that I nursed my child. The reality is that Linda had one kind of experience, and I had a very different kind of experience.

But once again, as in the case of unmarried or lesbian women, if she does *not* have a pregnancy, then her *sexuality is in question.* As Amy put it, they are asking, "Is she *really* a woman?" And what all of this reveals is that *sexuality* in this discussion and in the perception of most religious denominations means *appropriate and prescribed* sexual feelings for and with the opposite sex and for one's spouse.

In this discussion, I had to admit that I was still searching for the clue to how the body politic related to women in ministry and how the different stories might connect and guide us toward an understanding that would transcend the varied and different personal perspectives. Later, when Linda told how one of her pastor-parish relations committees had asked her to redesign her wardrobe to better cover her bosom, her story brought comic relief to a very difficult session. Both Marsha and Amy laughed and said, "That's why we've never had any of these problems. We don't have any breasts!" The entire group erupted in laughter at this remark and agreed that maybe it had something to do with just how large a woman's breasts were and how much the woman's configuration was revealed or hinted at under the ministerial robe. Breasts are mapped, noted, pondered. Breasts too large, too exposed, feeding children, protruding from the folds of the robe are dangerous, provocative, enticing, and sexual. Women without breasts are questionable as women. Ironically, the connection between all the stories becomes a perfect example of "damned if you do and damned if you don't." Either way the female in the pulpit loses.

Actually, when the laughter died down, several women in the group wanted to pursue this further and commented that, in fact, it did not matter how attractive a woman was, and it did not matter how much her body parts protruded from under the robe; what did matter was that she was a woman, in a robe, in the pulpit. Her presence is a signifier of *difference* and (I shall continue to argue) of sexuality. And this can occur because of her position in the society, because of the essence of the female as it has been cultivated in this culture. This is not biological determinism; this is an acknowledgment of the position of women in our culture and how their bodies are perceived. Margaret Miles argues in her book *Carnal Knowing: Female Nakedness and Religious Meaning in the Christian West* that "female bodies have not represented women's subjectivity or sexuality but have, rather been seen as a blank page on which multiple social meanings could be projected" (1989, 169).

Can Women Be Asexual? And/or Is This a Loaded Question?

We began to discuss the possibility that, in fact, women cannot be asexual. No matter how one approached the subject, we began to think aloud, it would be impossible for women and for the congregations of clergywomen to deny or ignore their sexuality. Women are embodied. They are flesh and blood and bodies that are sexual. But we felt the "dis-ease" of this kind of thinking. Considering *écriture feminine* as "writing the body" or "mapping the body" became uncomfortable. In fact, "mapping the body" is not what Cixous means by *écriture feminine*—a term Jane Przybysz has translated as "female writing" and interprets as "a cultural practice that is a body praxis some women use to alter patterns of female and male body use" (1993, 171). The power of this approach lies, Przybysz argues, in "destabilizing the ground of what is thought and said" (1993, 171). In her groundbreaking article about quilting as *écriture feminine*, Przybysz offers an explanation relevant to what happens in the pulpit: "Providing coherence and continuity to a fragmented and fragmenting experience of reality and self, and reclaiming/reframing the female body . . . quilt making potentially brings women to conceive of their single 'selves' as speaking subjects and marks their entrance into history as social and political agents" (1993, 171). Przybysz sees *écriture feminine* not as an essentialist, eternally "feminine" form of writing but rather as a "feminizing" cultural activity that has been "sustained and periodically revived by some women as a body praxis to cure their dis-ease with social relations under patriarchy" (1993, 172).

Mapping the female body brings us no closer to validating women's experience; it could serve, perhaps, only to reinforce the fetishism associated with women's breasts, legs, vaginas, and other body parts. As we talked, the women began to clarify their arguments, pointing out that what they were presenting were *cultural perceptions* of women as embodied, as always sexual, rather than suggesting that they themselves really believed that they personally were sexually embodied any more than their male counterparts. Women *are perceived as sexual*, they began to say, and therefore women, by their presence in the pulpit, force a confrontation with sexuality for everyone. They were in accord with the women who made up the Mud Flower Collective: "Sexuality and the reality of our sensual bodies, which women and gay men represent on behalf of all persons, is not recognized by most white or black males" (Cannon 1985, 20).

While the women in this group and I came to reject any categorical statement that insisted that women are more *embodied* and are, therefore, inherently more sexual than men, we did agree that women in ministry boldly confront the myth of the asexual minister (which forces every "body" to write itself): "Our being there changes the myth of asexuality. Because when they see a woman up there, they can no longer say that the priest has no sexual identity. In the ministry, it has been asexual. You can pretend a man is asexual, or a minister is, until you get a woman up there, and then that means the other one was a man and this one is a woman. And that means they have both have sexual identities."

The clergywomen struggled with why they felt this might be so: "If a male priest says he is celibate and that he never thinks about it [sexuality], which is unlikely, he is treated as though that were true." The others agreed, at least temporarily. Flannery, a lesbian minister, suggested that the male priest is expected to take this stance—asexual, celibate, never thinking about sex. "The male priest can really upset people by recognizing that he has sexuality and talking about it." In reality, she said, the male priest does not have to "buy into" the myth; he just has to recognize that the congregation needs to pretend that it is reality. A female in the pulpit, however, they all agreed, throws that myth into confusion. "We screw up the myth by appearing before a congregation. A woman can never be looked at as asexual. Therefore, the ministry can no longer be looked at as asexual because there is a woman in there. And if the woman is pregnant, there is no way they can fool themselves anymore—about either males or females." Until women entered the pulpit, no one was thinking about the male minister or priest as *male*. They agreed that there was no validation of the *reality* of men's sexuality. "By her presence the woman in the pulpit signifies 'I am woman,' and she forces the man and the congregation to say, then, 'This is a man,' because of the *difference*."

Some men deny their sexuality or are required to pretend that they deny their sexuality. In some religions, clergy are forced into celibacy and into a denial of their sexual natures and/or drives. There is a shared denial by many congregation members that the male pastor or minister is sexual. This is not, of course, always true, and we all know stories about the promiscuous minister, the ladies' man, the handsome minister who shares the pleasure of his sexual being with those to whom he ministers. Women, on the other hand, are perceived as sexual from the outset and therefore force a confrontation with sexuality by everyone. From the pulpit they "write the body," which is an insistence on the power of the presence of the body, in a kind of pre-language reality that some feminists claim as the seat of *écriture feminine*. While on the one hand this is a forced confrontation that is uncomfortable for both men and women and often makes them feel vulnerable, on the other hand, women who are recognizing it and carrying it to its fullest extension will, and are, humanizing religion by celebrating the full potential of what it means to *be* human—and to be sexual.

How Can We Offer a Subjective (Insider's) Point of View?

Yes, one can map the female body and its sexual/textual, semiotic, and metaphorical implications just as we have done here. Yet as I and the women in this study began to rethink such a dissection of female sexuality in terms of body parts, we began to ask: To what end do we offer such an analysis? Is this an approach from without or an approach from within? Is this sexuality from a female perspective or from a male perspective? Does this mapping highlight and illuminate the male idea of the provocative, alluring, and "dangerous" aspects of the female physique in such a way as to endorse and perpetuate the semiotic violation of women in the pulpit and elsewhere? While Hélene Cixous's directive to "write the [female] body" with white ink excites us in its potentials, we must heed the cautions as well. Helena Michie, in her book *The Flesh Made Word*, argues that "fetishization of parts of the body—breasts, legs, vulva, uterus—transgresses the body's integrity as subject," and she makes a point of differentiating between a "naked" and a "nude" body, where the latter is most definitely a re-creation intended for the male gaze (as quoted in Miles 1989, 181). Similarly, while acknowledging the potential importance of female body imagery in women's literature, Elaine Showalter concludes that "there can be no expression of the [female] body which is unmediated by linguistic, social and literary structures" (as quoted in Miles 1989, 181). According to Miles, Showalter would have us "gaze" at social contexts rather than female bodies.

Taking a female approach to the subject should not deny the stories related here nor the feelings shared by the women in our dialogue sessions. They and I know the mapping of the female body well, and we have all followed a prescribed path in these discussions. However, the women were also able to leave the mapping of the body and expand the discussion of sexuality in a way that would incorporate a female perspective not discernable as long as we remained preoccupied with sexuality in male terms. As Miles points out, generally women have not enjoyed the conditions necessary for formulating the self-representations that could have informed the collective male view of women; therefore, men have usually created representations of women out of their fears and fantasies. It will be difficult now, she argues, for women to offer acceptable alternatives based on female subjectivity and experience. But such a move toward self-description is absolutely necessary for the acquisition of political power. It is, however, difficult for us, as women, to move beyond "seeing ourselves as others see us" (Miles 1989, 170) Miles quotes Sandra Bartky, who writes, "a panoptical male connoisseur resides within the consciousness of most women" (Miles 1989, 170). Miles calls for a collective female voice to publicly begin to formulate new ways of perceiving the female body—offering perspectives from within rather than basing its formulation on the external male gaze. She denies that the female body has been irretrievably appropriated to a male agenda and is thus unavailable to women themselves for reinterpretation. In our dialogue sessions, the women ministers seem inclined, for the moment, to consider the mapping of the female body as a means for accessing female subjectivity and human spirituality; what I see them intuitively doing, is "writing (from) the body" and, hence, claiming the power. I hear them saying we need not try to de-eroticize the female body but to accept the equally erotic in all bodies. This is in many ways the message of Rita Brock's *Journeys by Heart: A Christology of Erotic Power* (1991) and Carter Heyward's *Touching Our Strength* (1989), although both Brock and Heyward go further in suggesting the erotic as a path to the divine. Cixous makes the connection between speech, the body, and life itself: "By writing herself, woman will return to the body which has been more than confiscated from her, which has been turned into the uncanny stranger on display—the cause and location of inhibitions. Censor the body and you censor breath and speech at the same time" (Cixous 1980, 250).

Here, then, is the voice, the Word, according to the women in my study, embodied in a herethics that validates difference and human wholeness. The message cannot solely be played on the level of signification and semiotics; it is a philosophical and theological discourse that refuses to deny *any* aspect of sexuality, male or female, but that strives to articulate beyond the sign, the signifier. In a radical turn on the Lacanian denial of the female access to language and the symbolic, women in ministry challenge what being sexual and spiritual are taken to *mean*. According to Suleiman, Luce

Irigaray rejects the Freud/Lacan "erection of the phallus to the status of transcendental signifier" and the subsequent exclusion of women from the symbolic and from language. She posits instead—in opposition to a "phallic" discourse, characterized by linearity, self-possession, the affirmation of mastery and authority—a feminine discourse that must "struggle to speak otherwise . . . to *write* a 'feminine' text" (Suleiman 1985, 13). Women, Suleiman argues, must cease to be *objects* and become *subjects*: "Reclaim your body" (1985, 13). Miles quotes Jean-Paul Debax: "To reduce woman to silence is to reduce her to powerlessness; that is how the masculine will to castrate operates. Lavinia's tongue is cut off, as are her hands, a symbol of total powerlessness. Thus, perhaps because of this, women's will to revolt necessarily passes through the use of language, the tongue. Language, the tongue, is women's weapon" (Miles 1989, 74). Rebecca Chopp, in *The Power to Speak: Feminism, Language, God*, speaks of language as a political activity, noting that God has long been associated with the Word, while women have been opposed to the Word: "As Word, God has traditionally been prevented from being represented by woman, while woman has been configured as taboo and placed on the margins of the Word" (1989, 3). Yet, as Chopp acknowledges, women do speak from the margins, and they speak of the Word. Thus, she seeks to reconstruct in a "theological semiotics the proclaimed Word as the perfectly open sign that funds multiplicity and otherness in and through feminine discourses" (1989, 7). Like Rosemary Radford Ruether (1986), Chopp finds in "women-church" the basis for a community that lives in and for the proclamation of God in the world—formed in and through the Word. Chopp's description proposes a new discourse based on new ways of being human, which include the desires of women and what women have experienced and what they know.

Reciprocal Ethnography at Work—
I Ask the Women in the Study . . .

At first, Anne-Marie put it this way:

> I am uncomfortable with the equation of men with asexuality, but I do think that . . . the fact of women being there somehow triggers more thought about sexuality. And, furthermore, the women who are up there [in the pulpit] are, for the most part, doing a lot of rethinking and deconstructing of the traditional ways in which we understand the body and sexuality. Sex is so different for men because it's almost like—it's just different for them. There's this thing, this member, outside their bodies that you do this other thing with,

and then you feel better, but for women it's so intrinsically integrated, and it involves your whole body, not just one part. And so, if it triggers—it partly has to do with the very, very different ways in which women and men are sexual or know sexuality, and it is so intrinsically who women are.

Amy agreed and went on to explore this line of thinking:

I think for women the sexuality has always been there. It may not have been there for the men, because there were men in the pulpit, and there's such a denial, such a phobia—so a woman in the pulpit has opened the door to sexuality in a broader way for men.

This brought agreement:

The kind of sexuality we are calling for now is a whole one, a healthy one, where sexuality is intimately connected with God and God's grace in our lives rather than the dirty thing you do off in the dark.

Interestingly, Amy pointed out that Protestant churches are currently treating (male) sexuality in a negative way. Conferences often deal with sexuality, but the focus is "sexual abuse by the clergy." She lamented, however, that the churches are not dealing with sexuality as a wholeness issue but as a male power issue: "We're not dealing with the wholeness of sexuality, but rather we're talking about the abuse of sexuality—and it is a way to continue to distance ourselves from dealing with our sexuality."

Anne-Marie tried to articulate some of what she felt was at the root of this belief:

I think it's more than pregnancy and menstruating. I do not feel as though I am free to admit to or express any kind of sexual feelings. Now, probably, men aren't either. But I think it is a part of the *wholeness* that I am striving for—to be able to be sexual. I don't mean unpleasantly exposing yourself. What I mean is to be able to say or to intimate that one has truly sexual feelings and that they play a part in the way we relate to the altar. And I don't feel free to say that. And I guess no one does, in fact; hardly anyone in our culture can say that. But we preach—we are very revelatory in our sermons about a lot of things that are very deeply important to us, but there is never a hint of that! This is a long way from where the church is right now, but it is something that I feel, that I feel called to work toward.

At this point, Amy remembered a sermon that her male co-pastor preached, "and he said in his sermon that the reason he enjoyed sex so much is because it takes us beyond ourselves. The minute he said that, he could see people's heads go [*Amy mimics a double-take*]. Think of the shock value of that coming out of the pulpit!" Anne-Marie responded, "But, you see, when we're pregnant, that it is almost as if we have said something like that because it is a physical manifestation of it."

Telling this story helped Amy articulate the theology of sexuality as she sees it: "And I think that there's power in that, to say that *God is a part of all of that*. So I don't see that as a negative, and I think people's reactions to it can be really positive."

Anne-Marie agreed: "Humanity and sexuality are a part of this business of being called to the ministry as women. Justice is a part of the wholeness ministry that the church needs to face. There are lots of contradictions, even in our own stories. The call for wholeness and embodiment is coming from feminist theology, which, of course, includes both women and sympathetic men."

Kathleen added, "It's wider, in the sense that . . . I see women . . . calling for and, simply by their presence, forcing the recognition of all the stories of individuals, the recognition of individuality, [and] the recognition that each person is an important entity, an important being, and that making the generalization, the theological overview, isn't what religion is about."

And, finally, Anne-Marie said, "So what we're doing is calling—is bringing the emphasis back not just to sexuality or on being women but bringing back that it's the person that's holy, and the person is whole, and the person has a story, and the story matters enough that you just don't put it in the back and extrapolate out of it to make generalizations. And so that wholeness has to do with the value of a person." Margaret Miles would agree with Anne-Marie that this view calls the Christian Church back to an earlier notion of the human body: "The first theological meaning of nakedness in Christian tradition was the innocence, fragility, and vulnerability of human bodies in their initial creation" (Miles 1989, xi). Anne-Marie concluded, "I think sexuality is at the heart of who we are as human beings and that, as we search for this wholeness in the midst of a call to ministry, we've got to deal, then, with what it means to be sexual human beings who are called to ministry. It is a theological issue as well as a political issue. That's me! That's my one voice."

What, Then, Is a View from This Side?

I want to return now to the newsletter title that did not get used: *Naked in the Pulpit*. The women who proposed this title said they wanted to use this phrase because "that's how we were feeling most of the time." Yet, ironically, the title and their feelings had nothing to do with sexuality as we normally perceive it or the semiotic images and messages that such a linguistic turn of phrase might conjure. The image "naked in the pulpit," for them, rather, embodied their feelings of vulnerability, of being stripped naked, indefensible, attacked, denied, violated, and disconnected. The newsletter, designed for women only, was an attempt to "re-member" the female constituents and help them feel less vulnerable, to serve as a corrective, a move toward connectedness. Furthermore, as I listened to the women talk about sexuality in these sessions, it became clear that, for them, sexuality is intricately bound up in their notions of what it means to be a spiritual being. Being naked meant being vulnerable, taking risks, and acknowledging their femaleness in the pulpit. The reason this position feels threatening is that sexuality is inherent in their presentation of self in front of a congregation, while the presentation of a male can deny his sexuality, what Cixous claims is his "niggardly lip service which engages only the tiniest part of the body, *and the mask*" (1985, 286, emphasis added). Their theology and spiritual aspirations include a broader notion of what it means to be a sexual being— *being human in all the manifestations of what that means includes being sexual.* The "wholeness" of which they speak comes to embody all bodies in all their aspects. Being a spiritual being means learning to be vulnerable, to take risks, to acknowledge who you are in all the ways in which you are human—such a stance, then, becomes a directive for inclusivity. Women who are lesbian, males who are gay, women who are mothers, women who are unmarried, women who are barren, men who are caregivers and cooks, women who minister and pastor, women who marry, people who live and love and *be*. "Naked in the pulpit" then becomes the paradigm for a message of vulnerability and trust. It is not that women are inherently more sexual than men; it is that culturally the female body has been so intrinsically linked to sexuality that its presentation becomes the signal for recognition of sexuality for all the participants. The response to this message has been predictable: the mapping continues, and men retreat further rather than expose themselves as equally vulnerable. Anne-Marie says the denominational concern with abuse of sexual power by male ministers is an indication of the reluctance to face sexuality head on and acknowledge its power in the lives of all the members of a congregation rather than to approach the issue by exploring what it means to be a sexual human being, laity or clergy. Her approach is clearly aligned with Sallie McFague's when

McFague argues that "female sexuality would not be so feared or found so fascinating if sexuality, both female and male, had been accepted in a more open and healthy manner both as a human good and as an important way to model the activity of God in relation to the world" (1988, 98).

Conclusion

In truth, women are no more "sexual" than males, but the patriarchy *sees* the female body as sexual. Women in the pulpit, in the vestments, delivering the sacraments, have re-energized religion, have reinserted the human, in all its aspects, into the imagery of the divine. Because women signal the sexual, they "write the body" from the pulpit. The presence of the female within the sacral splits open the myth of asexuality in any human and affirms the right and beauty of the divine to exist and thrive within and through the corporeal. To return to Kristeva's challenge, it is in this way that religion becomes accessible, pertinent, relevant, and meaningful as worshipers discover, through the human, a relaxation of the dichotomy between the sacred and the secular, the spiritual and the temporal, the flesh and the spirit. While some progressive theologians and these women ministers alike would agree, Christ's message embodied this "incarnation theology," which humanizes religion through the image of Jesus. But as Anne-Marie has suggested, women are calling the church *back* to an acknowledgement of that. "I think the larger issue is not just with sexuality but being in touch with the concrete, the real, the everyday, the tangible. Of course the sexual is a part of that." Others agreed: "Sexuality is definitely a piece of it and probably the most inflammatory piece of it, but in a much larger sense we are calling the whole church into wholeness."

Kristeva calls for a new herethics, Mary Daly speaks of a "metaethics of radical feminism" (1978), and Sharon Welch writes of a "feminist ethic of risk" (1989). They are all redefining the notion of ethics as vulnerability and acknowledging the importance of a more holistic concept of being that encompasses all aspects of what it means to be human, which of course includes sexuality. Daly explains, "When I use the term *mythic* to describe the depths of meta-patriarchal Self-centering/being, I mean to convey that the Dreadful Selves of women who choose the Wild Journey participate . . . in a sense of power, not of the 'wholly other,' but of the Self's being. Metapatriarchal mythic amazing means repudiating saintliness and becoming wholly haggard, Holy Hags. As such, women are 'wholly other' to those who are at home in the kingdom of the fathers" (1978, 50). Daly's "wild journey" is a different journey from most of the women in this study; all of them, thus far, remain within the perimeters of Christian denominational religions. But with Daly, they do seek a new and sometimes wild journey that goes beyond the "kingdom of the fathers." And clearly they extend an invitation to all men to join them in this journey into (w)holiness and well-being.

Notes

1. I first presented this article at the American Folklore Society meetings in October 1991 in St. John's, Newfoundland. I want to thank David Hufford for sending me some of his teaching materials and for our conversations that greatly aided me in thinking about this article. I also want to thank Katharine Young and Barbara Babcock for their encouragement and perceptive readings of this paper and for working to make this theme issue a possibility. I also need to thank my colleague Charlie Shephardson at the University of Missouri for allowing me to sit in on his theory course this fall and my graduate students, especially Virginia Mueller, for many cogent and helpful conversations on these subjects.

2. My work is based on field research that I have been doing for several years with clergywomen in what I am calling "mainline" denominations in a specific region in the upper Midwest. The denominations represented are all contemporary noncharismatic religions, including Episcopal, United Methodist, Christian Church-Disciples of Christ, American Baptist, Unitarian, and Unity. At the request of the women, no actual geographic locations are given; names of persons and churches have been changed; names of specific denominations have been retained. The basis for this article stems from interviews, dialogue sessions with the women, and field research in all of their respective churches.

3. I am relying here on unpublished classroom materials for a graduate seminar on belief and religion that Hufford teaches at the University of Pennsylvania. My thinking has also been aided by David's published works and our extensive conversations on these issues.

4. Taken from classroom materials shared with me from David Hufford.

5. The women in this study pointed out that this is only one letter away from *heretical* and thought that, because it is a heretical ethic, Kristeva possibly intended this.

References Cited

Brock, Rita Nakashima. 1991. *Journeys by Heart: A Christology of Erotic Power*. New York: Crossroad.

Brooke-Rose, Christine. 1985. "Woman as Semiotic Object." In *The Female Body in Western Culture*, edited by Susan Rubin Suleiman, 305–316. Cambridge, MA: Harvard University Press.

Cannon, Katie G., and the Mud Flower Collective. 1985. *God's Fierce Whimsy: Christian Feminism and Theological Education*. Stanford, CA: Stanford University Press.

Chopp, Rebecca S. 1989. *The Power to Speak: Feminism, Language, God*. New York: Crossroad.

Cixous, Hélene. 1980. "The Laugh of Medusa." In *New French Feminisms: An Anthology*, edited by Elaine Marks and Isabelle de Courtivron, 245–264. Amherst: University of Massachusetts Press.

Cixous, Hélene, and Catherine Clement. 1986. *The Newly Born Woman*. Translated by Betsy Wing. Minneapolis: University of Minnesota Press.

Conley, Verena Andermatt. 1984. *Hélene Cixous: Writing the Feminine*. Lincoln: University of Nebraska Press.

Daly, Mary. 1978. *Gyn/Ecology: The Metaethics of Radical Feminism*. Boston: Beacon Press.

Gilbert, Sandra M. 1986. "Introduction: A Tarentella of Theory." In *The Newly Born Woman*, edited by Hélene Cixous and Catherine Clement, translated by Betsy Wing, ix–xviii. Minneapolis: University of Minnesota Press.

Hampson, Daphne. 1990. *Theology and Feminism*. Oxford: Basil Blackwell.

Heyward, Carter. 1989. *Touching Our Strength*. New York: HarperCollins.

Hite, Molly. 1988. "Writing—and Reading—the Body: Female Sexuality and Recent Feminist Fiction." *Feminist Studies* 14:121–142.

Jones, Ann Rosalind. 1981. "Writing the Body: Toward an Understanding of 'L'Ecriture Feminine.'" *Feminist Studies* 7 (2): 247–263.

Kristeva, Julia. 1984. *Revolution in Poetic Language*. New York: Columbia University Press.

———. 1986. *The Kristeva Reader*, edited by Toril Moi. New York: Columbia University Press.

Lawless, Elaine J. 1991. "Women's Life Stories and Reciprocal Ethnography as Feminist and Emergent." *Journal of Folklore Research* 28:35–61.

———. 1992. "'I Was Afraid Someone Like You . . . an Outsider . . . Would Misunderstand': Negotiating Interpretive Differences between Ethnographers and Subjects." *Journal of American Folklore* 105:302–315.

Miles, Margaret. 1985. "The Virgin's One Bare Breast: Female Nudity and Religious Meaning in Tuscan Early Renaissance Culture." In *The Female Body in Western Culture*, edited by Susan Rubin Suleiman, 193–208. Cambridge, MA: Harvard University Press.

———. 1989. *Carnal Knowing: Female Nakedness and Religious Meaning in the Christian West*. Boston: Beacon Press.

McFague, Sallie. 1988. *Models of God: Theology for an Ecological, Nuclear Age*. Philadelphia: Fortress Press.

Ong, Walter J. 1982. *Orality and Literature: The Technologizing of the Word*. New York: Methuen.

Ortner, Sherry. 1974. "Is Female to Male as Nature Is to Culture?" In *Women, Culture and Society*, edited by Michelle Rosaldo and Louise Lamphere, 67–87. Stanford, CA: Stanford University Press.

Przybysz, Jane. 1993. "Quilts and Women's Bodies: Dis-eased and Desiring." In *Bodylore*, edited by Katharine Young, 165–184. Knoxville: University of Tennessee Press.

Ruether, Rosemary Radford. 1986. *Women-Church: Theology and Practice of Feminist Liturgical Communities*. New York: Harper and Row.

Steiner, George. 1975. *After Babel*. New York: Oxford University Press.

Suleiman, Susan Rubin, ed. 1985. *The Female Body in Western Culture*. Cambridge, MA: Harvard University Press.

Welch, Sharon D. 1989. *A Feminist Ethic of Risk*. Philadelphia: Fortress Press.

7

WOMAN AS ABJECT

Resisting Cultural and Religious Myths That Condone Violence against Women

*W*HEN *I* WAS NINE YEARS OLD, MY MOM *called me a "whore" one day, and I had no clue what the word meant. So I looked it up, and I read the definition. I don't remember what the definition said, but what I remember was this horrible sense of shock that came over me that this was the reason*

Author's note: Chapter 6 in this volume illustrates the development and implementation of my concept of reciprocal ethnography. My work with the mainline women ministers was effective because they were interested in what I was trying to do and were willing and able to read what I was writing, discuss it with me in the dialogue sessions that I was also able to record, and assist me in constructive ways as I attempted to provide a richer ethnographic experience for all of us.

Conversely, the work with women living in shelters posed many particular, and at times overwhelming, difficulties for this kind of ethnographic work. Certainly, my work in the shelter was long-term and extended over several years, and my research was enhanced by my daily attendance at the shelter, answering the hotline, intake procedures, conversations with law enforcement and court representatives, casual conversations with the residents in the various rooms of the shelter, the interviews I did with the women, and the conversations in the support groups that were held with community members and residents in the evenings, which I could not record. In addition to the requirement that all my interactions with the residents must be confidential and their words anonymous, free of all identifying markers, the women I was interviewing were in crisis mode, having just left their homes, often with their children in tow, and, quite honestly, had no time or energy to read what I was writing. They were, however, very interested in what I was thinking and what I intended to write about them. Although the rules about confidentiality and anonymity were restricting, the women's shelters actually provided many ideal situations for my ethnographic research. In this context, I was able to share with them what I was "hearing" in their stories, the ways in which their stories were similar, the ways they were different, and what I felt might be important for me to write about their lives and their stories. Verbally, they were able to respond to what I was thinking and writing and often interjected their own opinions about these aspects of the research. At times they were eager to agree with what I was saying, and sometimes they were quick to tell me how I was wrong or was missing some aspect they felt was important.

that my uncle had done these things to me all my life, that basically men treated me the way that they did because somehow I was born that way, that it was a condition you were born with and that's what was wrong with me. And I internalized that very much, I guess because my mother said it to me.

Steven had some hang-ups about sexuality. I wouldn't say we "dated," because we didn't go to the shows or anything. We would ride around in his truck a lot, and then, after things developed, we started petting. Or let's say he initiated petting, and I enjoyed it even though I didn't really feel right about it, not being married, but I still enjoyed it. But after we were finished, he would say, "You know, I really think that Satan is influencing you in letting me do this, and you need to pray about this because you are the woman, and you really have the control." So every time that we would pet, then I would have to get on my knees and ask God to forgive me. And he would say things to me like, "Well, maybe you have been chosen as a vessel of dishonor. Maybe God chooses some people to be vessels of honor, and maybe you are one of dishonor." He would put just this little twist on scripture. So I began to think of myself as, maybe, not so good.

I don't understand why they get as destructive as they do—like is it stamped here [motions to her forehead], I mean is it stamped here, you know, "abuse me"? I mean, why can't they [men] just leave me alone? I want to know why I keep doing the repeats [abusive relationships] all the time. Is it me? Do I do these things to cause it? Sometimes I think, yeah, I do.

The religious and cultural significance of the biblical story of Adam and Eve and their behaviors in the Garden of Eden has had serious repercussions even in the postmodern context of contemporary society.[1] Both "religious" and nonreligious citizens in the United States, and certainly many persons even globally, know this story and could recite a version of it without much

---

Although it was not really possible to utilize my own ideal conception of reciprocal ethnography in this particular context, I later did ask several former residents of the shelter who served on a local community service board with me to read my chapters and articles and respond to what I was writing. In this way, I felt the residents' discussions, combined with the responses I received from those who were better able to find both quiet space and time to read, provided an acceptable way to adapt a modified version of reciprocal ethnography. The key for this methodology is, after all, to share our thoughts, ideas, and conclusions with the participants in our studies, to be willing to listen and actually hear their responses, and to locate ways to include their voices, their acknowledgment when our assertions are accurate and sensitive, and to include their concerns about what we have missed. This article was not written as an argument for the value of reciprocal ethnography, but it stands as an excellent example of how we can utilize the methodology, adapt it, and reap the benefits in our work. This article first appeared in *Western Folklore*. 9, no. 4 (2004): 12–22.

trouble—whether it is part of their "creation myth" or not. What is more surprising, perhaps, than its tenacity is the continued potency of this story, one of the oldest religious creation stories that has its roots in both oral and literary art and culture, particularly in the ways it prescribes beliefs about women. Even as the various versions of this story are questioned, the power of the core story remains intact. Rereadings of the Genesis creation texts point to the fact that there are actually two distinct narratives in these passages: one that posits Adam's creation first, with Eve's creation as a second thought and a companion for Adam, plucked from his rib; the other narrative, also in the canonical texts, tells about how God created both creatures, male and female, at the same moment "in his image." Not surprisingly, the first telling has received far more attention historically and religiously than the second. As for who ate the apple first and caused the "downfall" of humanity, the interpretation that Eve ate first and lured Adam to follow has acquired more potency than the suggestion that Eve's curiosity was not weak at all but a healthy curiosity that brought about humankind's liberation from the passivity of the pastoral. Arguments such as these, however, tend to get played out in the journals of religious academic journals; few of the suggestive rereadings have actually been absorbed into the cultural and religious consciousness of the lived lives of people in the American cultural landscape or examined through on-the-ground research.

This article is a theoretical exploration based on ethnographic field research that I believe substantiates my basic propositions that many cultural perceptions of women as abject continue to stem from this most basic Genesis story. The propositions I make will not apply to all persons, religions, or contexts within the boundaries of the United States, the Americas, Europe, Asia, or beyond. Yet I do believe my propositions can be applied to many cultural contexts globally, particularly in terms of attitudes and beliefs about women. I will argue that the first and most popular interpretation of the biblical story of Adam and Eve in the Garden, particularly the parts that locate the blame for disobedience and the subsequent expulsion from the garden squarely on Eve, is firmly entrenched in contemporary culture to such an extent that the view of Eve as the sinner who causes problems for men and for all of humankind pervades mental and cultural constructs. It is my argument that these shared constructs of Eve as Evil=Woman as Evil continue to support a view of women as *abject*—that is, whatever is deemed polluted, dirty, and sinful—to such an extent that violence rendered against women is often construed, consciously or not, as justifiable given the defiled status of women within various cultures. Furthermore, it is my argument that women who are fleeing violence in their lives know how the construct of women as abject gets played out in the sociocultural and religious contexts of their lives. It is also my argument that through the enactment of their own agency—that is, leaving their violent partners and telling their life stories—women are able to identify and isolate the view of women as abject and identify its dangers, while they simultaneously resist this reading of women's roles and worth for their own individual lives. Some women's words and actions defy the "woman as abject" trope as they dare to redefine themselves in ways that interrupt and critique cultural and religious myths about women. The three women's voices that are "heard" at the beginning of this article are only a few of the stories I have recorded in my work with battered women who have escaped violence in their homes and lives. I will return to their stories in the pages that follow.

In my ethnographic work with women who are beaten, raped, and (sometimes) killed by their husbands and partners, I have recorded many life stories of women currently living in shelters trying to escape abuse (Lawless 2001). In this article, I will explore how religious concepts that connect women with sin, such as the Adam and Eve story and the religious implications for Eve's sin and women's defiled nature, affect many women's everyday lives in the twenty-first century.[2] While no life story is truly "the whole story," the women's life stories told to me do provide an effective backdrop for understanding their present predicament and their sense of self as unworthy. Without a doubt, the women's early years set the stage for later relationships that led them to emergency rooms with broken bodies, clinics with shattered minds, and shelters, hiding with their children in order to stay alive. From their stories, I have come to understand how the belief that females are dirty, sexualized, abject beings is transmitted to small girls at a very early age and is endorsed through religious, cultural, and social discourses throughout their lives. The message girls receive and internalize is articulated either through language ("you are a whore") or through defilement: girls are raped, molested, abused, *and then silenced and/or ignored* at a very early age because they are often seen as sinful objects of desire. These early encounters lead young women to internalize the belief that they represent what is abject. They may even come to believe that they do, in fact, deserve what they get. However, I read their personal narratives as a continued resistance to this defining religious and cultural narrative; by leaving the violence and telling their stories, women are calling into question the viability of the "woman as evil" concept in a world where women's consciousness can be raised and rallied.

Traditions of Women as Evil

Twenty years ago, feminist anthropologist Sherry Ortner posed the question: how is it that women are relegated to an inferior position in nearly all cultures and are consistently aligned with "nature" in ways that enforce their submission to the power brokers of culture, that is, to men (Ortner 1974)? An extension of her question is, of course, how did the equation of "female is to nature, while male is to culture" come to direct so much research and scholarship? And how is it that the association of female with nature comes to be also associated with the base, the polluted, the animal, the defiled, even what is evil? Ortner poses more questions than she answers, and certainly other scholars have resisted the dichotomies she outlines in her article (Jacobs 1997, 178). But following Ortner's argument, I want to explore how it is that beliefs about women as evil prevail in many contemporary Jewish, Christian, and Islamic societies and how these beliefs serve to reinforce the attitude that the abuse of and violence against women is expected, even acceptable, male behavior. Using the Midwestern women living in a shelter to escape men who are violent toward them as the basis for my examination, I will explore the ways in which beliefs about women as evil, polluted, and "lures" for sin get conflated with actual violence against women's bodies. I ask whether the perception and treatment of women by men is identifiable as a predictable consequence of the deep-seated prejudices and beliefs about women as evil that appear as far back as the Bible, and, further, I ask how can and do women resist these perceptions and the effects they have in their lives?

Many scholars over the years have addressed the history, theology, and significance of the Genesis story of Adam and Eve. In her book *Adam, Eve, and the Serpent*, Elaine Pagels presents the Adam and Eve story as an ancient, orally transmitted religious myth that delineates, as thousands of other "creation" myths do, a story about the creation of people on the earth, humans created by a superior being (God, in this case) who first created the earth, all the "animals" on the earth, and then, lonely and dissatisfied, created two creatures "in his own image"—creatures distinct from the other "animals" who have inferior brain power, emotions, memory, and conscience (Pagels 1988). Different exegesis of this story abound, and with each interpretation different subtle aspects of the story have been end-lessly queried: Did God create a male and a female simultaneously, and did that indicate there should be equality of the sexes? Whose "crime" was the greatest—Eve's for letting the snake seduce her and then seducing Adam in turn or Adam's for succumbing to Eve's wiles? Was eating the apple a terrible misdeed that destroyed humankind's access to the pure Garden of Eden, or was Eve, in fact, courageous in opening the door to knowledge and consciousness as well as mortality? If Eve was punished with child-birth pains for her crimes and a longstanding tradition that views her as duplicitous, wily, luring, and evil, man's equivalent punishment of toiling the earth seems mild by comparison. Pagels reminds us that through the ages, several different interpretations of the Genesis story(s) have prevailed in varied religious circles. Extending to the social society, laws have been passed based on these interpretations; new interpretations became popu-lar, while others declined in importance when other ways of thinking pre-vailed. But throughout the ages, one belief has remained fairly stable: Eve disobeyed God's admonition in the Garden to not eat the fruit of the one designated tree; the snake (Satan) tempted her into taking a bite of the now totally symbolic apple. Eve, in turn, tempted Adam to eat of the apple as well (for which there is no small stretch to an interpretation in totally sexual terms that posits the wily, seductive (male) serpent as having intercourse with Eve). At any rate, Eve seduced Adam to have sex with her: as such, sexual knowledge was what was learned in the Garden of Eden. Their dis-obedience caused God to become angry; they (for the first time) realized what they had done, recognized both their nakedness and their vulnerabil-ity, hid from God, and covered their nakedness. Finally, God, in his anger at being disobeyed, banished them from the Garden forever with specific admonitions about what they would suffer in the time to come.

During different epochs, this story has been referred to variously as the "Genesis Story," "The Garden of Eve Story," "The Sin [or Fall] of Adam," "The Sin [or Fall] of Eve," and "The Seduction of Eve by the Serpent." But no matter how it has been referenced, the guilty party, the one we love to hate and blame, is Eve—certainly more than the serpent, the snake, the devil in disguise, the banished angel, Satan, and certainly more than the first man, the good guy Adam. Eve, as the "original" woman, has come to personify all that is base, lustful, untrustworthy, wily, beguiling, deceitful, seducing, and evil in the universe; in many visual depictions of the ser-pent, in fact, the face of the snake looks eerily like Eve herself, offering a "tempting" opportunity to posit Eve and the devil as one and the same creature or at least sharing the same characteristics. And Eve, as this religio-cultural myth confirms, resides in all females; she is in evidence all around us; she works her evil magic. She is mysterious, insatiable, greedy, lusty for sex, beguiling, and all that men cannot control—although they had best try to control and restrain her by all means at their disposal, including mores, rules, decrees, laws, and the use of force.

Folklore motifs recorded from around the world attest to the nearly universal portrayal of women as the equivalent of evil, not just possessing evil powers.[3] It is telling that the first entry for "woman" in the *Dictionary of Mythology and Folklore* (Leach 1949) *begins* with this: "Woman—as evil." The entry outlines Eve's deceitful nature, the lure of sirens, adulterous women, and the untrustworthiness of a plethora of women in mythology and Judeo Christian religious historiography, iconography, and theology. This volume, as well as several others, also notes the traditional Jewish story of Lilith, purported to have been Adam's first wife. Lilith is depicted as independent, strong, and demanding. She and Adam had evidently already discovered the act of sexual intercourse, but Lilith refused to allow Adam to dominate her in the so-called "missionary position" (male on top) and insisted that she, too, should be able to hold that position (female on top). Apparently, both Adam and God were furious with Lilith for her insubordination, so God banished her to the caves along the sea, where (as some tell it) she still resides, wailing and cursing both God and man. According to legend, she occasionally also ventures into human abodes and takes the breath from sleeping babies because she recognizes that she will have none of her own (this can be compared with the traditional La Llorona legends popular in Latin culture), hence the amulets that adorn Jewish cribs to guard the child from Lilith's rage in the night. Of course Lilith's story was never included in the canonized books of the Bible; in fact, it does not fit well with the other Genesis creation stories. Therefore, it was simply ignored in most Judeo/Christian official documents. Oral tradition, however, has not abandoned Lilith entirely, although her story has evolved most popularly into yet another sad story of a woman expelled from grace for her daring. Her story is consistent with Eve's—both were disobedient to God and man, and for this they are equally associated with that which is *abject*.[4]

The Adam and Eve story, according to Pagels, serves to support a gendered view of the creation story and "man's" fall. Her careful historical work points out that there was a brief time when the first Genesis story was more popular than the second. That is, the narrative depicting God as simultaneously creating male and female in his own image out of clay was apparently regarded as the official creation story for much of the civilized world for some time. It seems plausible, however, that as church fathers and male patriarchs yearned to enforce the rights of men to dominate the world and the church, the emphasis on the "other" creation story—the one that explains how God created Adam and then, realizing Adam was lonely, caused him to sleep so that God could take one of his ribs to create Eve and "give" her to Adam as his helpmeet—was favored and eventually dubbed the "official" creation story in the ensuing eras. This version enabled priests and male leaders to enforce male rule in the home, community, and church—a theological premise that persists into present time. Furthermore, Eve's transgression is even greater in this version because here she was purportedly created to stand beside her partner or stand in submission to him, but she seduced him instead, birthing the concepts of sin, evil, and death—notions that would forever be associated with *woman's sin*. Understanding that most biblical narratives are metaphorical in nature, it has been understood that the "knowledge" Eve discovered was *sexual* knowledge. She and Adam became ashamed of their nakedness, covered themselves, and fled from God's wrath. It was in this manner, then, that sexual knowledge and desire came to be associated with sin—and *woman* represented that sin. If women were not around to tempt, lure, beguile, seduce, and cause men to lust after them, then men would simply not sin is the thinking. By her presence, woman has come to signify and symbolize both sin and evil—or *the abject*. As Pagels and others have noted, certain historical periods and various religious authorities have insisted that even sex *in marriage* is acceptable *only* for procreative intent (hence the Catholic prohibition of birth control, which placed some early sects at risk for annihilation, in fact, when celibacy was required for all its members).[5] Clearly, this association of sexuality with sin, and abstinence as a "purer" state, directs priests to never marry. It is no surprise that in certain eras, all the attributes of a feared "witch" are associated with *women* who are deemed dangerous, endorsing the view that persecution, battering, banishment, and even death be rendered against them. It is no surprise that the story of Eve and Adam in the Garden of Eden has come to influence so many conceptions of woman as evil and capable, by her mere presence (particularly if "uncovered"), to cause men to lust and sin. The "evidence" is clear: woman represents all that is *abject*. And as long as we can blame *her*, men are off the hook. The discourse that prevails in this vein goes something like this: Men are not sinful by nature—they are, in fact, close to God; as such, their sins are caused by the evil inherent in woman. No one will blame him; in fact, other people (especially other men) will probably understand if he lashes out and beats her to a pulp. After all, women are all alike, and they are all evil.

No other single story has influenced more cultures to think as single-mindedly as has the Adam and Eve story. Mary Daly devotes an entire chapter in her book *Beyond God the Father* to "Exorcising Evil from Eve: The Fall into Freedom," arguing that the story has had tremendous power to shape perceptions of "women," perceptions that are imbedded in contemporary Western culture and certainly seem to shape cultures' views of women in various parts of the world (Daly 1973). The myth of Adam and Eve has, she argues, "projected a malignant image of the male-female relationship and of the 'nature' of women that is still deeply imbedded in the modern psyche" (Daly 1973, 45). Later, Daly states, "The point is simply that by its built-in bias and its blind reinforcement of prejudice the myth does express the 'original sin' of patriarchal religion. The message that it unintentionally conveys—the full implications of which we are only now beginning to grasp—is that in patriarchy, with the aid of religion, women have been the primordial scapegoats" (47). The dangers of these implications are many, but perhaps most destructive *for women themselves* is that women who also know this pervasive myth often come to believe the message is true: "It happens that those conditioned to see themselves as 'bad' or 'sick' in a real sense become such. Women who are conditioned to live out the abject role assigned to the female sex actually appear to 'deserve' the contempt heaped upon 'the second sex' " (49).

Women and the Abject

The lives of women in the contemporary world are deeply influenced by traditional beliefs about man as pure and woman as evil. Viewing the Edenic narrative of Adam and Eve through the aid of Julia Kristeva's work in *The Powers of Horrors: An Essay on Abjection* (1982) has helped me theorize that it is *Eve's* disobedience and "sin" that has led to a dichotomized view of male as *pure and clean,* on the one hand, and female as *loathing and defilement,* on the other. In one reading of her work, we might see the speaking subject as male and the semiotic unspeakable object as female. Kristeva claims the *abject* is a part of the subject that the subject considers "detachable";

it confronts the subject as alien and external (70). Although Kristeva insists upon the connection of the abject with the *maternal*, rather than the *female* in general, I want to expand upon these notions of the *female as abject* as a way of suggesting a rationalization for men (subjects) to beat women (the abject). According to Elizabeth Grosz, Kristeva connects the "clean and proper" body, access to symbolization, and the speaking subject to the male, but she portrays the "underside" of a stable subjective identity, unable to utilize symbolization and language, as female—as "an abyss," a "hole into which the subject may fall when its identity is put into question" (72).

Using Kristeva to understand the concepts of the abject and abjection and their connection to the female body, I see this ancient biblical narrative and these discourses still having distinctive performative power in contemporary life—that is in accepted behaviors of male violence against women and in the legal policies and practices that allow for the perpetuation of what Mary Daly has termed the "malignant image of women" (1973, 45). Again, we can relate this image back to Kristeva, who claims, "Abjection is a sickness at one's own body" (1982, 82). My extension of her discussion, then, is to claim that male lust and loathing is associated with defilement and transferred onto and signified by the female body. The physical manifestation of lust (the erection) cannot be controlled: since "he" cannot control his desire, he can feel cleansed if he can attack the signifier, that is, "he" can feel cleansed if he beats her, berates her, calls her the names that he has transferred (with his loathing of his sinful self) upon *her* (whore, cunt, pussy, siren, witch, bitch, lusty, insatiable, seductress), and, thus, defers her semiotic "reality" from woman to evil woman.

The traditional master narrative of woman as sinful, evil, and responsible for that which is abject is told, retold, reinforced, and played out upon the nascent bodies of young girls, as well as seasoned wives, by men who are "unable to help themselves." On the other hand, by leaving the violence and telling their stories, women are sometimes able to turn this narrative on its end, subvert it, and, thus, resist it. But before they can reject the myth, they first have to recognize it and perceive how it serves as a prescriptive in their daily lives.

Clearly, the symbolic transference of the *abject* upon the female body has lasting and dangerously deleterious effects on both the speaking subject and the semiotic object. Females come to absorb and "believe" that they are "bad," "evil," and "deserving of punishment," while males come to abhor the desire of their own uncontrollable bodies—the material, the corporeal, the semiotic—and try, in the end, to obliterate that which is perceived as *not* believed to be "clean and proper" by expunging evil out of woman, she who is defiled and defiles. A way of making this connection is revealed in my women's studies classes. We may use the term "misogyny" but fail, perhaps, to explain exactly what that word means or how it operates in the world. Often, my undergraduate students ask, "Why would men *hate* women? I don't think you can say that. I don't think my father hates my mother; I don't think my husband [boyfriend] hates me." They are insulted, confused, even frightened by these implications. And they should be. Often residing alongside a more subverted misogyny are cultural icons that appear to put women on a pedestal, notions such as the beloved *mother*, which successfully divert attention away from the anger and hatred of women. My research with battered women presents ethnographic evidence of how misogyny actually operates, and it demonstrates just how deep-seated and *real* this hatred of women can actually be. Furthermore, the prevalent discourse of violence against women is often rationalized by the very theology(ies) that grounds their being on the earth. Defying evil, then, can be rationalized as a religious act, one worthy of execution; to remove defilement, to erase ambiguity, to banish lust and desire, to die whole, clean, and proper is justifiable.

Placing Women's Stories in Context

The stories I use to support my argument that women represent the abject in contemporary Midwestern American culture demonstrate how this perception determines violent male attitudes and behaviors toward women. The women's stories I have collected illustrate how they themselves learn to recognize the cultural representation of "women as evil" even as they recognize they must resist it—by leaving their abusers, by refusing to accept the violence inflicted against them, and by sharing their stories. These stories were recorded from women living in shelters for battered women from 1997 to 2000.

As an ethnographer trained in both oral/verbal traditions (folklore) and literature, I have devoted my career to scholarship and teaching about women's lives and narratives, both oral and literary. Although the field of folklore studies has long recognized how certain stories gain traditional cachet over the years and in different cultures, our discipline has also, in more recent years, recognized the significance of personal-experience stories as narratives that rely on traditional story tropes while at the same time maintaining validity as original and unique life experiences. I asked women living in shelters to share their life stories with me. I found their stories to be similar, parallel, and predictable on the one hand as well as unique, individual, and dynamically different on the other. Most told their stories in a recognizably linear, chronological manner, beginning with their earliest memories (although not all told their stories this way). In these accounts, the women often reported that their own mothers and grandmothers were also terrorized, beaten, raped, and emotionally battered most of their lives. In general, I recorded mostly sad and traumatic stories—narratives that often go far beyond any violence I could have ever imagined. Many times, I noted that their narratives were truncated, paused, cut off just at the moments when the trauma became too difficult to articulate, too "unspeakable" to share (Lawless 2001, especially chapter 3).

Many of the stories that women told to me refer to how they were treated from an early age as though they were defiled, polluted, and dangerous, and they were beaten for it (for defilement and pollution of the female, see Douglas 1976). Few of them felt secure, wanted, or loved. Most of the narratives that will follow in this article reveal how utterly alone the women felt as girls. As they move into young adulthood, among many other aspects of their lives, the women often talked about how they felt "religious" themselves (often asking for personal guidance from God), but their religious denomination and "the church" generally did not assist them in any constructive ways in their efforts to change or escape the violence in their lives. Too often the reluctance to get involved with domestic abuse is shared by the church as well as the police force, the school systems, and the community at large. Questioning what goes on "behind closed doors" or the rights of the "heads of households" to control families (read "wives and children") threatens religious and cultural norms that support male dominance and control—whether the "control" is claimed by a father, a husband, a partner, or even a brother or a son. Many aspects that emerge in these stories expose some of the profound dangers of the traditional cultural and religious maps when the cartology involved is the female body.[6]

As a folklorist and ethnographer, I am interested in women's personal experience narratives, the language the narrators use, how and when the women tell what they tell (and what is not told), when women use disclaimers, and when they can articulate their own theories about how violence operates and how they might locate avenues of resistance against it. From the start, I recognized the importance of the women's early years, noting how they talked about their childhood memories and how they narrated aspects of their lives with their family and community. I wanted to know whether or not women would render themselves as "victims" in their narratives and how they would portray their own subjectivity. I wanted to hear the stories of how they dealt with their abusive partners and how they conveyed the terror of the incidences that compelled them to finally leave and seek the safety of the shelter. Certainly, the stories shape the way women have framed their lives in order to keep living; even more significantly, the stories also portray how the women are able to move (through the telling of their stories) beyond a victim stance and seek a more independent, defiant, resisting voice. They must sort out their life experiences in such a way that makes sense given where they are now residing in a temporarily safe space.

Women's Stories/Women's Experiences

At this point, I will share excerpts from several different life stories I recorded from women living in shelters. All of them, in one way or another, point to the pervasive belief shared by families and communities that women are defiled and/or evil. The stories imply that girls, even at a very young age, are rejected because of their femaleness; their bodies are seen as polluted and dangerous. The ways in which the culture provides the leap from women's bodies as defiled to how female bodies mark the sin of sexuality is clearly evident in these narratives. The first story illustrates how small girls (and older ones, as well—that is, their mothers) are subjected to the rhetoric that claims they are defiled and unclean even before they understand the implications of those accusations. Girls come to internalize the belief that they are, by their *nature*, sinful, evil, and unworthy. In this first account, both of this girl's parents adhere to and support the belief that their daughter represents the *abject* and, therefore, must be controlled, repressed, rejected, and even, if necessary, beaten.

> The first, one of the first, memories that I have is of my mom trying to choke me and me almost dying. And I was preverbal. I was in a crib, and I just had this memory a few years back. And my mom had no one to help her; she was alone with my brother and me most of the time when my father was gone. My brother is two and a half years older than me. But my mom was alone with us, and she sort of didn't have any emotional coping mechanism for us, and that's what life was like with my mom from as far back as I can remember. She was just very verbally and emotionally abusive. My mom just scared me, and she

> sort of kept me in line by constant threats, but my father was the one who beat me. My father used to beat me with a belt, and he would beat me for anything. If I didn't eat all of my dinner, if I spoke out of turn, if I embarrassed him. . . . I was the most—everybody always said that I was the most well-behaved kid they had ever seen. And [laughing] there was a damn good reason for it.

How this early "preverbal" experience gets sexualized as the girl grows up is revealed when she begins to talk about her preteen years:

> So I believed for years that that wasn't really my mother—that God had taken my mother away because I was so bad. And so I really hated God, and I just felt really empty inside. . . . Once I started having sex (and I did at a very early age), I figured I could just suck somebody in, and they would take care of me. So, then, I would just tell my mom, "Do whatever you want." Well, it was all about all this torture, and I literally could not shit. I would hold on to my shit. I just couldn't go to the bathroom for weeks on end because I was so uptight.

Are we surprised, then, when this girl gets married at a young age, only to find her husband equally despises and tortures her? Why would she expect anything else?

> And the night we got married, it was the first time he had ever gone off on me. He went off on me. He was a terrorizer. He would just get in my face, and he would throw stuff, and he would break stuff, and he just terrified me. And he would keep me in line by terrorizing me. He would terrorize me for hours on end. He wouldn't hit me here [gestures to her face]. He would hit right here [her chest], and he would hit right here [her belly]. He would threaten to kill me, and he would tell me that I was a whore and a slut and blah-blah-blah.

This woman was willing to believe the things her new husband told her about her own base nature because little in her early life had prepared her to think any differently about herself. Most of her girlhood experiences convinced her that she could expect nothing better. She also told me about her encounter with an "older" Christian man (twenty-three to her sixteen years) who had befriended her at a religious retreat before her marriage. She found him to be compassionate, gentle, loving; he seemed to actually care for her in a way that was not sexual. Sometime after the retreat, however, he visited her on her seventeenth birthday and brought her a wood carving that he had made for her. She was overwhelmed by his generosity. She was full of hope that he saw her differently from all the other men in her life, that he cared for her as a human being, not as an object of desire or loathing. But she was mistaken, and her encounter with him set the stage for a life of living as the abject:

And we sat in his car, and we talked. And I felt so loved by this man and so comforted by this man until he attacked me. And it was like—he had me pinned down in his little VW Volkswagen, and he had his hands all over me, and his tongue was all over me, and it was just like—that was probably the worst—I don't know what it is, but all my life, all this molestation and sexual abuse was always gross to me.

Years later, as she sat with me at the women's shelter, trying to stay away from her abusive husband, she claimed,

And that has been my life—very slowly, I have tried to gain a voice. Very slowly, I am learning to forgive myself. . . . And the only thing that holds me back in my life today is me—and my fears and my own self-loathing.

Girls Growing Up Wounded

I want to share other examples from the narratives of women living in shelters that confirm the deep-seated belief transmitted to them as girls that they are evil and sinful in order to illustrate how these beliefs eventually translate into violence against them by fathers, brothers, uncles, husbands, and, unfortunately, by mothers, aunts, and grandmothers as well. The first is the extended version of one of the stories at the beginning of this chapter.

When I was nine years old, my mom called me a "whore" one day, and I had no clue what the word meant. So I looked it up, and I read the definition. I don't remember what the definition said, but what I remember was this horrible sense of shock that came over me that this was the reason that my uncle had done these things to me all my life, that basically men treated me the way that they did because somehow I was born that way, that it was a condition you were born with, and that's what was wrong with me. And I internalized that very much, I guess because my mother said it to me. She had knocked me down on the floor, and she took off her shoe and raised it up to hit me with it, and that was when she said—when she called me "a little whore." My mom was sexually abused by her father, too, who was an alcoholic when she was growing up, which I didn't know until many years later. And so when I was fourteen, I just finally decided that it was time for me to prove to myself that I was the person that I believed that I was, not the person everyone—everyone meaning my family—was telling me that I was. And I ran away from home.

Of course, knowing that the narrator is now living in a shelter for battered women, the reader will realize that this young girl's resistance to the notion that she was *evil* was not able to sustain her, at least not for a long time. In fact, to follow her life is to follow the pattern typical for so many women. The accusations that she was a "whore" (by her mother) at a young age carried through into an abusive marriage, where she was beaten black and blue on a regular basis. She finally left her abusive and violent husband only when he held a cocked gun to her head and said, "I *am* going to kill you." She believed him and left. The fact that she *did leave* her abuser and she did *tell her story* (to me as well as to others in the shelter) demonstrate her ability to find avenues of resistance that can hopefully sustain her into the future.

Almost without exception, most of the stories in my study included accounts of molestation by fathers, stepfathers, brothers, uncles, and neighbors. Minimal in their detail, the accounts are told in a matter-of-fact manner that belies the intensity of the encounters. Since many of the women's early experiences were, as the young woman above suggests, "preverbal," or preconceptual, the narrators do not attribute adult feelings to the childhood accounts. But the message that the female body is dispensable, available, detachable, alien, external, disposable, accessible, and always the object of male sexual drives is undeniable. For a young girl, Kristeva's notions of the ambiguity of internal and external, the marked space on the "threshold of language and a stable enunciative position," are denied, erased; a girl is unable to claim her own body and gain symbolization. As the object of male desire *and* loathing, she is kept prisoner in the semiotic, which enables *him* to successfully maneuver his own symbolic subjectivity at the expense of her own. He can incorporate the abject at the same time he rejects it as outside his own body, as only embodied in hers. The girl absorbs the message, the belief, that it is her body that has "caused" the desire to be manifested. For example, the following story illustrates how another girl, Cathy, came to "own" the blame:

> My earliest memories are of an uncle that I had who, I guess, spent a lot of time with our family, although I don't know why. He was actually abusive. To the best of my knowledge, that started about the time I was three or before, but that is the first memory that I have of it. And I can remember when it used to happen, thinking even as little as I was that he can hurt my body, but he can't hurt me, and I always had this sense of kind of being outside of myself, watching what was going on. And I don't know if he threatened me. I don't know how I knew that I had to cover this up or hide it, but I do know that when I was sort of outside of myself watching what was going on, I would think things like, "Oh, that is going to leave a bruise. I'll have to cover that up. I can't let Mom see that"—those kinds of things. And I really believe that has caused a lot of dysfunction in my life. I have tried over the years to put that sexual abuse into its perspective in my life. It went on until I was about probably thirteen or

fourteen years old, sporadically. It wasn't constant. But it was at least probably three or four times a year. It was more often when I was younger because we lived closer to them, and then we moved farther away, so it didn't happen as often.

Later, in a different session, Jennifer tells me her story, although it could be the same woman continuing to talk about the abuse in her life, the words are so familiar:

It seems like my whole life, men have—when I was in my teens, friends of my family that were older, men, would always try to kiss me inappropriately or touch me or whatever. I had the sad misfortune, when I was nine years old, I started filling out; I was wearing a bra before any of my other friends . . .

I was anywhere between five and ten those summers, and so they were very, very mysterious and scary and with adrenalin running all the time, and I was stealing and doing all this stuff, and I'm a good little Catholic girl and being beat if I speak out of turn and with my uncle dealing drugs and doing all this other stuff, and so it was—I had a pretty schizophrenic life. My dad's brothers—one of them—my Uncle Bob and my Aunt Martha—they were heavy-duty alcoholics, and they lived near us, and her parents were also alcoholics, and we would go visit them a lot, and they would just sit around, and everybody would just get wasted, and then my dad would just sort of pass me around between my uncle and her father, and everybody—I was just handled a lot. Everybody was drunk, and nobody knew what was going on except me. And nobody really paid attention to what was happening, and it was just gross. My Uncle Bob was a pretty angry drunk, and if I wouldn't go sit on his lap and kiss him and let him feel me up and all this stuff, I'd get in trouble. And so I was sort of in the middle of all this with no ally.

And Marcie's story further illustrates the similarity of the stories.

He, my stepdad, didn't bother us girls too much the first year. The second year, he started messing with me, sneaking into the bedroom. And every night at the same time when he started messing with me, it was right around *Jeopardy*. When *Jeopardy* would come on [the TV]—and still to this day, when *Jeopardy* comes on, I start shivering and have to leave or turn it off or something—he would come in there in the bedroom, and he would mess around with me quite a bit. Make me do this to him, and he was doing that to me and just off and on did this stuff. That went on for probably a good two years. And he was threatening me. You know, "If you say anything, I'm going to hurt you and hurt your mom," and I remember dreading—being scared to go to bed because I knew what was gonna happen when I did. So I got to the point where I would wrap myself up in sheets and blankets, thinking that was going to protect me, and it never did, but I was a child, you know; you think of anything you can to try to protect yourself.

At this point in Marcie's story of abuse, she is not able to say exactly what her stepfather is doing to her or forcing her to do to him. She is vague here, either because she does not actually remember the details or because she is not able to articulate what he did to her because, as a silenced child, she cannot tell. She does not, of course, feel that she can talk to her mother about this situation. Not only is she terrified of what her stepfather may do to her (and to her mother) if she tells, she certainly is not convinced that her mother will be supportive even if she tells her. Finally, her mother asks her about a sore that has developed on her mouth as a result of the oral sex she has been forced to perform for her stepfather:

> I think it was on a Saturday—I was sitting on the porch, and I remember this real clearly. She was sitting on the swing, and I had formed a sore around my mouth. It looked like a huge ringworm is what it looked like. And my mom asked me, "What's wrong with your mouth?" And I wouldn't answer her. I wouldn't even look at her. And she picked me up, and she turned me around, and she said, "What is wrong with your mouth?" And I told her. I said, "Michael is doing bad things." I would never call him Dad. Never. And she said, "What do you mean Michael is doing bad things?" And I told her—I was crying—I remember crying and telling her I couldn't tell her because he was going to hurt me and her, and she started shaking me, and she was like, "What do you mean, what do you mean?" And finally I told her. She had shook me and slapped me so many times that I just told her that he was making me have oral sex with him and that was causing it—and she beat me. She beat me bad. She didn't believe me. She said I was a lying, instigating little bitch—just beat me bad, bad.

We have to wonder if Marcie, at this young age, actually said to her mother, "He's making me have oral sex with him." In the context of her story, her words seem like adult words. We might guess that she probably told her mother exactly what Michael was making her *do*—like put his penis in her mouth. In any case, Marcie's instincts about her mother's reaction were correct. She remembers this day very, very clearly. She learned several lessons about trust and support and how not to get beaten in the future. Silence is enforced. She will not turn to her mother again. In truth, her mother must have partially believed Marcie's story, even though she beat her, because a few nights later, she actually spied on her husband and caught him in the act of molesting her younger daughters. Mustering all her strength, she did an amazing thing that even Marcie admires, although her own beating was never addressed.

> There was one night she didn't go to work, but everybody in the house thought she did. She didn't go to work, but she went downtown to the bar and was

waiting for dark—for it to get dark—and she snuck back to the house, and she looked in the bedroom window—us girls' bedroom window—and she saw for herself what was going on because he would always leave not the big light itself but the nightlight on, and she saw for herself what he was doing, and she come in with—I'm not sure if it was a sledgehammer or something—it was a hammer but one of those big hammers—but she come in, and she started raising all kinds of hell, and she ended up leaving, making him leave.

This statement is a remarkable narrative sentence, long, extended, adding on the events one after the other, building to a crushing blow of a large hammer. All in one breath, Marcie recalls in her little-girl voice what her mother did that night. She cannot actually recall whether her mom left or if she forced her husband to leave, so she mentions both. What is clear, however, is that this act of strength on the part of her mother does not absolve her of not "hearing" and sympathizing with her daughter's dilemma. What Marcie does recall is that her mother never talked with her about it; she has never forgiven her mother for beating her and not being there to support *her*.

And I think it was a few years later they finally got divorced, but the whole time she never did apologize to me for beating me or anything. She just said, "Lesson learned."

For yet another girl, Shirley, it was her father who was abusing her. One day, she told me, her father (who was estranged from her mother, whom he had beaten for years) had picked her up after a basketball game, saying,

"You and I got some business we got to take care of." Well, I didn't think anything about it. I figured we were going to do something with my car, or, you know, I didn't think anything about it. So we go home, and I've still got my uniform on, my basketball uniform, and I went in the house and fixed me a glass of tea, and I sat down on the couch, and he sat down beside me. And I'm thinking, "Oh, great. Here we go with a lecture or some kind of daughter/father talk." That's what I'm thinking. And he sat there, and he just glared at me, and he just kept staring at me. And I said, "Stop it. You're making me feel uncomfortable. Why are you looking at me like that?" And he said, "You remind me so much of your mother. Your looks, your actions . . . everything." Next thing I knew, boom, he had me down on the couch and was kissing me all over my neck. I can remember feeling whisker burns on my face and on my neck and everything, and he was fondling me and everything, you know, and I'm kicking and screaming and telling him to get off me, and I finally got him off me, and I didn't have no shoes on because I had took my shoes off, and I just ran out the door, and I went to my boyfriend's house, and I told him what happened. And he's like, "Are you serious?" I said, "Look . . ."—because I still had red marks—whisker burns—you know, I said, "Look what he did to me." And he ripped my uniform shirt, and my boyfriend just couldn't believe it. I mean, he could not believe it.

As with this story, the ways in which girls come to believe they embody both lust and desire create a no-win situation from which they often cannot escape. No girl should have to suffer what this girl did at the hands of her own father. *She* is not guilty of anything, yet she carried the guilt of *his desire* the rest of her life. Standards about female behavior are confusing and often carry implications that are not always articulated but nevertheless seethe beneath the surface and directly affect how girls learn that they must watch what they wear, where they go, how they speak, who they choose for friends, and how they relate, especially, to men. Girls often learn these rules by unwittingly breaking them. They are not privy to these rules in childhood; rather, they stumble upon them, are startled by them, react in various ways to what they interpret as contradictory in them, and, in most cases, are condemned by them before they even know what they have done "wrong."

One girl's story demonstrates just how pervasive and destructive the belief is that women and girls cause sin and how parents reinforce this message for their daughters. Janie was home alone; she opened the door and welcomed her brother's friend, who asked for a dry place to wait through a thunderstorm. After requesting a glass of water, he raped her at knifepoint. She was terrified *when her parents returned* because she somehow believed that her parents would blame *her* for the rape. And she was right. The boy left via the back door, and she had to face her parents alone. They were outraged, not because she had been raped but because they were angry with her disobedience in allowing the boy into the house in the first place. This girl learned the hard way that for her own parents, rape is not male responsibility—it is female responsibility.

> But what ultimately happened was my parents—Eddie was nineteen years old, and I was only thirteen—and my parents called his parents, and they came over to our house. And his parents basically had the attitude that, well, I should know better than to let people into the house when I'm there by myself. And, ultimately, I ended up having to apologize to his parents for having let him in the house and that kind of thing. I was never—there was never anything done about him raping me. My parents were very angry with me for having let him in the house and brought this embarrassment onto our family. And so I apologized to his parents for what I had done, and that was that.

This woman recalls her girlhood experience vividly, telling about the storm that was fast approaching, how the boy ran to the door to get in out of the rain, how he politely asked for a glass of water before putting a knife to her throat and guiding her down the hall to the perfectly white bedspread on her parents' bed. It is clear in her account that she internalized the guilt, the blame, and the implication of *her body* as causing sin. However, her words belie the significance of the moment when she must apologize to the boy's parents. In summation of the state of things, she says "and that was that"—the damage has been done, "lesson learned." Deep-seated beliefs about the female body as seductive and eliciting sin perpetuate violence against women, perhaps most noticeably in the way meaning is constructed and perpetuated in quiet and insidious ways, such as the parents' behavior in these story of rape and blame.

The Female Body as Signifier

The belief that women, in general, are evil and that individual women are evil often seems to solidify as women mature—based on their personal experiences. They are forced to accept responsibility for their own participation in the transcription of their body as abject. Many women come to feel responsible for their lives in violence because somehow taking responsibility provides at least one identifiable reason for the battering—maybe it is something "I have done wrong." However, if and when they come to realize that the violence against them has *nothing* to do with their own behavior (that is, recognizing that his rage and his behaviors are *not* about whether or not the food was cooked correctly, whether or not dinner was ready the moment he walked in the door, whether or not it was the right kind of food, how she dressed, where she had gone that day, what she said), only when they realize his behavior and hers are not linked, then, sometimes, the women are able to stop blaming themselves. When they can name the violence as *his problem*, it seems to mark a moment for possible escape. But the transformation is not instantaneous. The woman speaking in the following story is still confused about just who is at fault, and she continues to wonder what she needs to do about the various conflicted feelings she is having:

> Every relationship [I've ever had] has been abusive. I've had knives pulled on me. I've been hit. I've had my teeth knocked out. I've had black eyes. Ribs cracked. I've had all that done to me. I've been suffocated, choked, had my hair pulled, thrown in the wall. But the only abuse that I'm focusing on now was why I'm here. His. But there's still some sick part of me that can't let go. [Crying] And I try hard, OK. I miss him. And I know—I miss what we had at first. You know, I would give anything, like they always say, to go back because I feel like I'm responsible in some parts. I guess probably I am, you know.

> I don't understand why they get as destructive as they do—like is it stamped here [motions to her forehead], I mean is it stamped here, you know, "abuse me"? I mean why can't they [men] just leave me alone? I want to know why I keep doing the repeats [abusive relationships] all the time. Is it me? Do I do these things to cause it? Sometimes I think, yeah, I do.

Not only has Delores internalized the belief that she is the cause of the violence, but she even poses the question "What, is it stamped here [on my forehead] 'abuse me'?" She examines this question in different ways. She realizes that, in fact, in her body language, in the ways in which she reveals parts of her life to the new men she meets and tells them of past abuse, in the ways in which she accepts her role as the object of male desire and hatred, she does, in fact, have semiotic messages scripted on her own body— signs "read" by the men in her life. Only when she can remove herself from the intimacy of the beatings (in the shelter and beyond, in a free landscape away from violence and abuse) can she become the speaking subject and reject the status of her body as sinful and deserving of the violence bestowed upon it.

Delores's story, as she gave it to me, is a long and convoluted one that portrays a complex and violent existence. She would often tell a portion of her story, stop, and loop back to pick up a thread she had forgotten to tell or that needed to be explained and rewoven into the larger tapestry of her life. Delores told me of her early body maturation ("I had huge breasts by the time I was nine") that she seemed to link with early childhood molestation by her uncles. When she was about fourteen, her father "disowned" her because he thought she was sexually active; she was not, but she could not convince him of this. In fact, her own ignorance about her sexuality made her think she might get pregnant if she let a boy "touch her down there." She left home at a very young age, moved to another town, and worked in a factory where she sewed faux fur onto winter coats during the hot summer months. She joined a local Pentecostal church to meet people; it was there, in fact, that she met the man who would become her first husband. Sex and religion, already encountered but misunderstood in her younger years, now combined to confuse her even further. Confused she might be, but Delores's husband was quite clear in his assessment of her sexual powers as dangerous:

> Steven had some hang-ups about sexuality. He was twenty-eight years old, had never dated anyone, still lived at home. I wouldn't say we "dated," because

we didn't go to the shows or anything. We would ride around in his truck a lot, and then, after, things developed, we started petting. Or let's say he initiated petting, and I enjoyed it even though I didn't really feel right about it, not being married, but I still enjoyed it. But after we were finished, he would say, "You know, I really think that Satan is influencing you in letting me do this, and you need to pray about this because you are the woman, and you really have the control." So every time that we would pet, then I would have to get on my knees and ask God to forgive me. And he would say things to me like, "Well, maybe you have been chosen as a vessel of dishonor. Maybe God chooses some people to be vessels of honor, and maybe you are one of dishonor." He would put just this little twist on scripture. So I began to think of myself as, maybe, not so good.

Delores says she recognized immediately that she had made a huge mistake in marrying this man. The litany of his abuse began with his demands that she pray for forgiveness for his own lust even before they were married. Over the years, Delores encountered Steven's anger and violence manifested in myriad ways. Always, after sex (even in marriage), he demanded that she get down on her knees and beg for God's forgiveness for causing lust in her husband's heart.[7] She called her mother once and asked if she could come home. Her mother told Delores that she would have to clear it with her father, but she never returned Delores's call. Eventually, Delores did leave her husband, but her pastor threatened that God would punish her if she did not return home and try harder to be a "good wife." Like many other women in this study, the advice she received from her minister was for her to "go home and search your heart to try and discover what you are doing to provoke your husband." Delores was conflicted and, as most women do, went back to her husband several times before finally leaving him for good.

What eventually propelled Delores out of this abusive marriage was not her own well-being and survival but her suspicions that Steven had begun to molest her daughters. When she observed how he caressed the girls at bedtime and during their baths, she was quick to anger and to denounce his behavior. She moved out, filed for divorce, and went back to school to get some education. Eventually, she landed a job in a prison facility, where she met her second husband, who turned out to be at least as abusive as the first one. In the beginning of this new relationship, however, she had found this man to be sympathetic and attentive. She later believed that telling him the stories about the abuse of her first husband was a big mistake and eventually led to his own violence against her.

> It didn't take long, and he became really abusive. He was a really big guy, but the other officers would tease him about being "pussy-whipped," saying he didn't wear the pants at home. So he would bang my head against the floor. He made me sit in a chair while he dumped beer and cola on my head, made me say, "I'm the squaw; you're the chief." And so it was another experience of someone dominating me and telling me I had no worth and me being in a position to survive I had to go ahead and do what he said. So I numbed myself.

After years of therapy and shelter support groups, Delores also left this man only to enter into a third abusive relationship. I met her in the shelter after she left the third abuser. She is now in a fairly secure place in her life, trying to connect and build a relationship with her two daughters, who are "too mouthy," she says, laughing, "but thank God they can speak their mind." Her last comments to me were about spirituality and resilience:

> But all this has given me a lot of empathy for other women. I've learned that I can't judge other people and what they're going through. And spiritually, I've had a lot of people judge me about my spiritual life, and we all go through things at different stages, and I've become more spiritual actually through all of this. I know now that a church cannot tell me that I'm good or bad. I will never let anyone else control my life. I still work at becoming more spiritual, and when I say more spiritual, [I mean about] becoming more aware of how my life can help other people through their struggles. And you know I haven't completely healed myself, so there's not a whole lot I can do. I try to figure out—as I get more power in my life, how can I help other people regain power in theirs.
>
> We have to learn to trust our intuitions. You know as a child, I was always taught, I learned, not to face people, not to make any waves, to please, to be invisible.

And she was invisible. That her spirituality survived is a testament to the strength of the mind's imagination to conjure a better life, a better reason for living. Unfortunately, her remarks are typical. She blames herself for not trusting her intuitions. God was trying to warn her, she said; she just did not listen. Even though this may still be her opinion, she can now articulate how her body, both female and maternal, is in defiance of the speaking subject and *has become one herself.* In so doing, she has disrupted the abuser's "stable subjective identity," defied his orders, insisting that she can claim her own symbolic self and reject the role of the abject.

In time, some of the women I interviewed in the shelter came to recognize that their abused and battered bodies ought not to be read as a confirmation of their own defilement but rather as bodies in evidence of unprovoked male violence against their bodies and against their minds.

This is a difficult and nearly impossible transformative move. To refuse the notion that one's body is the semiotic sign of the abject and then to more toward thinking the battered body might carry a different kind of semiotic evidence is a big leap. One woman's attempt to use her broken and bruised body as evidence of *his crime* against her becomes a powerful act. In many cases, simply speaking the truth suffices to bring a woman across Kristeva's "threshold" of "language and a stable enunciative position" (73). Yet, in many cases, this assertion from the newly emerging female self is not sufficient to provide a new script for public "reading" of her body, particularly by police and prosecutors.[8] An illustration of this will make my point.

Cathy has also been in three abusive relationships. Her marriage to her husband of nearly twenty years ended with death threats, a gun to her head, a fairly typical scenario for these women. She continued to get protective orders against him, but he continued to break them. She changed the locks on the doors of their house; he would break in, find her, and beat her senseless. Eventually, she found her voice, denied his view of her, and embraced the reality of her own body as evidence against his brutality. In a session with their court-ordered therapist, both she and her husband were asked what they each thought was the problem in their relationship. Her husband attended the sessions but refused to speak openly; he gestured that she was free to tell the therapist what she thought was the major problem.

> So I said [to him], "What would you say was our most immediate problem?" And he said, "Oh, I don't know. You go ahead. What do you think it is?" So in a very bold move, I stood up, raised my shirt up, undid my pants, showed them all my bruises, and said, "As far as I'm concerned, this is my most immediate problem." He went ballistic. He jumped up, turned over the coffee table, said, "You're just trying to get me arrested, you bitch." I guess it didn't cross his mind if wanted to get him arrested, I would have done it while he was at work that day. I would have gone and reported it.

This woman's bravery in the display of her wounds and bruises was actually not enough to get him arrested, as she quickly learned. Her continued frustration with the police is summed up in the following account:

> The county sheriff's department was not cooperative with me at all as far as keeping him away from me, honoring the *ex parte* orders. He came back about two months after he had left, came in his mom's car because he knew they were watching for his truck and came in his mom's car because I wouldn't let him in the house, knocked me down in the driveway, gave me a concussion, fractured my collar bone, broke two of my ribs, and then proceeded to try to run over me with his mother's car. And I rolled out of the way, which I was hardly capable

of doing. I couldn't breathe very well at the time. And I went to the doctor the next day. I went to the police station to file charges and then went to talk to the prosecuting attorney. And he said, "I'm not going to file these charges."

And I said, "Why not?"

And he said, "It's just your word against his. You don't have any witnesses or anything."

Cathy's body, battered as it was, bruised and bleeding, should have provided ample evidence, not of her defiled and abject nature but of his brutality and uncontrollable violence against her. Yet in the ways in which the semiotic and the symbolic get played out in the real world, the "word" here holds more power, of course, than the beaten body. The prosecutor says, "It's your word against his," which is to say her bruised body is not evidence of his brutality. In fact, it signifies nothing about him; it only holds signification about her. Unfortunately, to argue, again, about the pervasive power of the Edenic story, we can better understand how her bruised and broken body is "read" as evidence of her abject nature, and the self-righteous husband too often may be perceived as taking appropriate steps toward its eradication.

What Life Stories Can Tell Us

Orally constructed *life stories* are a particular type of narrative.[9] Unlike literary autobiography or memoir, or the shorter oral stories told spontaneously in the shelter, the life stories the women gave to me have not been self-consciously rendered or honed, although certain stories within their larger life narrative (or life story) certainly have been recounted many times. Consciously or unconsciously, the narrators are crafting a story for immediate consumption by the other women in the shelter and for me, the researcher. I am aware that the simple fact of my requesting their story imbues it with an importance they have probably never encountered before nor ever expected. I believe the time each woman spends telling her story is a time that is empowering for her. I make it very clear that I am not a therapist, and this is not therapy in any professional sense of what that typically means. But when they agree to "give" me their story, I agree to sit alone with them and listen attentively to the life they have lived—or the version of that life they choose to share with me. Some of the women in this study are not very well educated; all of them have been abused most of their lives; most of them are in a position of extreme imbalance at the current moment in terms of their living conditions and the level of anxiety, fear, and pain they are enduring. Yet every one of them who agreed to participate has taken time out of her chaotic current situation to calmly tell me her story. The miracle is that most of the stories I recorded are extraordinarily coherent by any measure. It is not so much what we can learn about a life of violence by listening to the women's stories, although certainly we learn a great deal about that in the process, but more importantly is what we can learn about the significance of articulation: the act of telling our stories becomes the significant moment, the *now* of the process.

In general, what I heard from the women in this project is that religion, the culture, society, the family, the community, and the church have failed them miserably in their darkest moments. A frank and bold assessment of the ways in which beliefs about women negatively shape the cultural contexts that allow for violence against women is long overdue. The potential for beliefs about women as evil to shape their experiences and "unmake their worlds," as Elaine Scarry points out, is revealed in their own stories—some insinuate the negative beliefs, and some articulate the pain inflicted on them clearly.

Enunciating the Self

Sally Robinson, in *Engendering the Subject: Gender and Self-Representation in Contemporary Women's Fiction*, makes the essential point that if women do not begin to represent themselves, then the representations of women historically presented and enforced will prevail:

> . . . "representation" is an act of violence, perpetrated by the self-present and knowing subject against, one can only assume, the Others that that subject desires to know and control. Thus, representation is a form of colonization, an imperial move on the part of the subject. Yet representation . . . has another, and contradictory, meaning: representation must also be made to signify the process by which ("invisible") subjects "legitimize" themselves by inscribing their experience, their desires, and their "reality" into discourse. The difference between these two meanings of representation, both political, is in the conceptualization of the subject of representation. . . . That subject is akin to the humanist "self." (1991, 190)

Robinson's argument, which draws on the work of gender theorist Judith Butler, is that this "humanist self" has been limited by the normatized, inscribed Western discourse as the story of the privileged, white, male subject. Women's stories have been "delegitimized," and, thus, the woman as subject has been left out of the history of (hu)mankind. The possibility of women as subjects in world discourse(s) and in history can only be realized through women's *self-representation*. In self-representation, argues Robinson, women become (engendered) subjects. It is Robinson's hope and desire that these actions, this reinscribing of the female subject, will *disturb* the dominant discourses. The inability to accomplish that enabling act dooms the subject to a terrified site where "self" can never be realized. This is, of course, the goal of the oppressor, to stifle the emergence or development of more positive "selves," women who might challenge or subvert the status quo.

During my time at the shelter, Cathy (a resident quoted above) began to organize the women living there to develop an activist group that would serve all the women in the shelter as well as those who came regularly on the evening of the support group. It is significant, I believe, that Cathy named the organization she envisioned EVA—for Empowering Victims of Abuse. This group, named intentionally after Eve, was designed to help women deal with the immediate contingencies of leaving their abusers. Cathy was furious when she discovered that all her joint bank accounts with her husband had been cleaned out by ten o'clock on the day after she arrived at the shelter. The night she arrived, I remember that she had to visit the emergency room three times during the late hours because she had severe headaches, nausea, and probably a brain concussion. Why they did not just keep her at the hospital I cannot say, unless it was because she was unlikely to be able to pay for her stay. She had a broken nose, several broken ribs, and a serious bump on her head. She had taken a taxi to the shelter. It was not until the next morning that she even thought about her bank accounts and drawing out money for her own expenses. Her husband sold her car, her furniture, cashed in all their CDs, and changed the locks on the doors of her house during her first days in the shelter. Cathy was concerned because she knew that most of the women coming into the shelter would not, as she had not, think about the importance of these kinds of things as they nursed their bruised and battered bodies. Yet she wanted them to "think," she said, "about all the possibilities." She would go with women to the nearby ATM at midnight to withdraw money from bank accounts. I know several instances when she helped women "steal" their own cars out of their driveway. She had all the phone numbers of the local sympathetic police officers, the court advocates, and the food bank in her purse and shared them freely. She made flyers with important information and posted them all over the walls of the shelter; she copied her phone numbers and put them under every door. Eventually, Cathy moved out of the shelter with another shelter resident, Hannah, and they set up housekeeping in a small house in a fairly safe neighborhood. They were like giggling children buying groceries for their new place, finding pots and pans, a sofa, a chair, and a bed for each of their rooms at the Salvation Army. Cathy got a "temp" job, and her roommate began working at the bakery of a local grocery store. I still occasionally see her there. They swore to protect each other from their abusers and help each other through the next difficult months. This conscious transformation of Eve's heritage (negative) to EVA's (positive) resistance to violence marks the essence of the process of how women can and do redefine their roles and their intrinsic worth in ways that defy the power of the master narrative of woman as evil. Of course, I know how many times Cathy came into shelter before she found a path that she could walk alone or with her new friend; I am also aware that many women will not be as successful in reinscribing their bodies and their lives. But the reality is that many women do leave the violence and are able to tell their stories in ways that project a different choice for other women to follow.

I found the battered women's shelter to be an extremely rich arena for women's storytelling, sharing, and discussions about how to combat violence and where to find resources and strength. It is a haven for escaping violence, and the residents' reactions to me, and my interest in their stories, were generally positive. After all, they *did* want to talk about what they were doing and feeling. They had escaped. They had a story to tell. They needed to think through where they had been and where they were going. My research and my interest in them offered a safe space for them to explore what was, after all, on their minds. Most women fleeing violence bring only a few belongings into shelter, usually in black plastic bags, along with their children. It is, in fact, a place for reflection, albeit not often quiet or free from chaos and confusion. They come broken, broke, and vulnerable into what they hope will be safe shelter. The past must justify and explain this present moment, the "now" of where they are today. Telling their story, that is, framing their life for me sitting together in a back room of the shelter actually seems to help them determine how they got here and how they will approach tomorrow. The story they tell is a story that crafts a "self"—a self evolving from their earliest memories to this present moment. The telling provides a kind of remembering of the parts of their "self," a making sense of the past, a restructuring of what seem to be disparate parts of their being into the construction that is now the "I" of their voiced narrative. Their voice, then, becomes the embodiment of their "self." I see this act of voicing the self as a healthy one. Otherwise, each woman must carry around in her mind, isolated in her consciousness, on her flesh and bones those disembodied, separate encounters of violence. The telling becomes the glue to holding some of her memories together, assessing the damage done, and then creating a newly constructed holistic self that defies and subverts the dominant trope of woman as evil, abject, and victim. As Cathy asserted when she finished her tape, "That's my story, and I'm sticking to it." The telling of her story has made a difference in how she sees herself. The telling gives her the opportunity to craft a narrative self that has cohesion and meaning, with reference to past and future, one that can rationalize and justify her agency, her story, and her very being. She is, in essence, saying, as one woman did, "This is who I am. Thanks for asking." She walks out different from when she walked in.

The value of ethnographic work that allows for the emergence of a new and different, more positive, female symbolic, the speaking self, should be apparent from this article. Both the telling of and the listening to women's stories are avenues toward healing and escape for women who choose not to live with violence and want to claim their rightful place in the world. I end with the words of one woman who reflected upon her act of telling her story to me and in so doing validated my own work in this endeavor:

> One of the cool things about this [telling her story for my recorder] for me is that in my house, we were told never to talk about anything, and after I talked about all this yesterday, I called my sponsor and just said, "I'm just so terrified that I'll be struck with lightning. I've had a really hard time separating God and Mom and God and Dad out." I still struggle with that. I think that that's why this was given to me to do. That I have to know that I'm not lying and I'm not crazy and I'm not going to die and I still have some—I still have some time to sort this all out and move on.

Notes

1. This paper was originally written as the 2002 "Paine Lecture in Religious Studies," an endowed lecture series held by the Religious Studies Department and the Center for Religion and the Professions at the University of Missouri, Columbia.

2. The field research for this study was conducted in shelters for battered women in the midwestern United States. I worked at one shelter for over a year before attempting to record any stories of the women who were living there. By working in the office and taking calls on the hotline, I became acquainted with the staff and the residents. To solicit their stories, I

put signs up in the living quarters announcing that I was doing research on violence against women and would like to record their stories for my intended book. Some women were quick to let me know they were interested in giving me their stories on tape; others never did volunteer; several women waited until they received positive reactions from those who volunteered before they agreed to give their stories to me. I heard women talking within the residence quarters about how the telling of their stories to me was insightful and helpful for them as they tried to sort out where they had been and where they might be going after the shelter. This kind of confirmation not only enabled my field research, but it supported my contention that the telling itself is cathartic and meaningful for the women who are finding their voices. All the women whose stories were recorded volunteered. As per their request, I promised to remove all names of persons, places, and other identifying characteristics. All quotes used in this article are verbatim (with the noted exceptions) from the recorded stories; no stories have been conflated; all names are pseudonyms.

3. Folklorists are familiar with the many indices of folkloric types and motifs; the best-known and most frequently referenced are *The Types of the Folktale* (Aarne/Thompson), the six-volume *Motif Index of Folk Literature* (Thompson), and the *Dictionary of Mythology and Folklore* (Leach). Although this kind of global counting and identification of shared motifs identified in oral narratives is not at the core of folkloristics in the present century, these indices nevertheless still serve as compendiums of shared beliefs and evidence of persistent, widespread motifs, personages, and symbols.

4. Equally disconcerting, a quick glance at the "religious" motifs in the six-volume *Motif Index* provides references to the Adam and Eve story and its variants around the world in stories that have been collected and documented as similar and repeated. Mythological (religious) motifs appear first in this index; hence, we find these motifs identified as follows: A63.6 "Satan tempts woman," A1376 "Origin of mental and moral characteristics" and "Man excels woman," A1371 "Why women are bad," A1371.1 "Woman is bad because of head exchanged with devil," and A1371.2 "Bad woman combination of nine different animals." This litany of "bad women because" motifs continues for several pages, including motif G303.12.6 "Devil disguised as a woman," D658.3 "Devil transformed to a woman [in order] to seduce," T337 "Man tempted by fiend in woman's shape," G303.12.6, "Man marries she-devil," and G303.12.7, "Satan's sexual intercourse with Eve." A1372.1 begins a series to explain "Why women are prattlers," "Why women are roving," "Why women are deceitful," "The origin of pleasant and unpleasant women," "Why women never have leisure" (they were deceitful to God), and "Why women are subservient to men," among others. It needs to be pointed out that there are no equivalent etiological entries about why men display negative characteristics; only women's deplorable traits are outlined, and all are linked to *Eve's sin* in the Garden, that is, A1384.1 "Origin of evil; punishment for fall of man via Eve's response to Satan."

5. Motif T330-360 is identified as "woman as source of all sin"; T332.1-T333.5 traces some of the ways that men are led astray by the female form: "man self mutilates when tempted by woman," "sight or touch of woman as source of sin," "woman's girdle as source of sin," "woman's voice as source of sin," and "virtuous man seduced by sinful woman." These short entries are often extended to give an abbreviated tale synopsis: "Husband puts out wife's eyes at night because he has heard that a beautiful wife is his enemy" (J2462.3), or "A boy who had never seen a woman, when he sees a girl and asks his father what it is, the father tells him it is Satan" (T371). The index is full of "woman" as witch, devil, treacherous, adulterer, imprisoned, raped, banished, tar and feathered, exposed, head shaven, thrown into the sea,

blinded, committed to the devil, and sometimes even killed: K944 "Deceptive agreement to kill wives," K1394 "Friends agree to beat wives," K941.1.1 and K944 include "wife killed by husband," and K951.0.0 is "mistreated wife choked and killed."

6. Although nearly all of the women in this study were Christian, not all were. Both Muslim and Jewish women resided at the shelter while I was there and participated in my study. The patterns I have identified in their stories were in evidence across religious boundaries. Rachel Adler (1988) uses the story of "Matiyah ben Heresh: The Eyes Have It," which appears in the *Midrash Aseret Ha-Dibrot* (*The Midrash of the Ten Commandments*), to illustrate "present motifs about the otherness and dangerousness of women in an extreme form." She writes:

> This particular story focuses upon a psychic struggle between woman and the holy text for the scholar's attention. This psychomachia is dramatically externalized, and its threat to the autonomous masculine self is resolved in shockingly literal terms. The story is set in the beit midrash, the paradisiacal world without women. . . . To tempt Matiyah, whose purity is reflected in his angelic beauty, Satan takes the form of Naamah, sister of Tubal-cain, whose evil is embodied as beauty so great it caused the fall of angels. Male beauty, as a reflection of moral and spiritual perfection, is a recognized motif in midrashic and aggadic literature. Female beauty, on the other hand, is considered to have great potential for evil because it heightens the possibility of female visibility and, hence, rivalry with the [holy] text. (12)

Later, Adler wryly comments, "Female visibility is not even female; it is Satan in drag, the personified evil impulse whose power will *mitgaber,* 'overman,' rise, swell, and dominate its object. Satan outmans man because desire feminizes, placing man, like Eve, at the mercy of her own desire and thus dooming him to be ruled over. Sexual sin is here defined as the wish for merger that threatens to undo autonomous [male] selfhood by restoring the original identity with *woman* [read: state of sin]" (13). When Matiyah cannot resist looking upon the beauty of Naamah, he "called to the student who served him and said, 'Bring me nails.' . . . He put the nails in the fire until they glowed and then put them in his eyes." In the end, Matiyah is rewarded for his feat; he is healed both of the mutilation and of all desire to merge with the feminine (13).

7. This motif of asking God's forgiveness for lust caused by a woman appears in various guises, of course, in literary texts (both fiction and nonfiction). It has, furthermore, been the basis for religious debate since ancient times, influencing religious and legal decrees concerning rape, premarital sex, adultery, rules about sex for procreation only, celibate clergy, and modesty coverings to hide the female body to prevent male lust.

8. In other published material, I have examined in detail how women learn—from other women, from counselors, lawyers, from the police, from advocates, from public defenders, prosecutors, and judges—that their actual stories may not assist them positively in their efforts to gain shelter or protection (*ex parte*), win lawsuits, get their violent partners arrested, or other services they are entitled to receive. Rather, they learn quickly the language for the script that is more likely to assist them than the one that is closer to the "truth." This reality about the legal system and services meant to help women living with violence only exacerbates and reinforces the status quo and fails to help move women and their experiences from the semiotic into the symbolic (see Lawless 2001).

9. Certainly oral life stories have been of interest to scholars in psychology, communications, theater, literature, and folkloristics for several decades. Reed-Danahay (1977) points to new ways in which this study has become interdisciplinary and significant in many fields.

References Cited

Aarne, Antti, 1961 (2nd ed.). *The Types of the Folktale: A Classification and Bibliography* [orig: *Verzeichnis der Märchentypen* (FF communications no. 3)]. Translated and enlarged by Stith Thompson. Helsinki: Suomalainen Tiedeakatemia.

Adler, Rachel, 1988. *Engendering Judaism: An Inclusive Theology and Ethics*. Philadelphia: The Jewish Publication Society.

Daly, Mary. 1973. *Beyond God the Father: Toward a Philosophy of Women's Liberation*. Boston: Beacon Press.

Douglas, Mary. 1976 [1966]. *Purity and Danger: An Analysis of Concepts of Pollution and Taboo*. London: Routledge and Kegan Paul.

Jacobs, Sue-Ellen, Wesley Thomas, and Sabine Lang, eds. 1997. *Two-Spirit People: Native American Gender Identity, Sexuality, and Spirituality*. Urbana: University of Illinois Press.

Grosz, Elizabeth A. 1989. *Sexual Subversions: Three French Feminists*. Sydney: Allen & Unwin.

Kristeva, Julia. 1982. *Powers of Horror: An Essay on Abjection*. NY: Columbia University Press.

Leach, Maria, ed. 1949. *Funk & Wagnalls Standard Dictionary of Folklore, Mythology and Legend*. NY: Funk & Wagnalls.

Ortner, Sherry. 1974. "Is Female to Male as Nature Is to Culture?" In *Woman, Culture and Society*, edited by Michelle Rosaldo and Louise Lamphere. Stanford: Stanford University Press.

Pagels, Elaine. 1988. *Adam, Eve, and the Serpent*. NY: Random House.

Reed-Danahay, Deborah E. 1977. *Auto/Ethnography: Rewriting the Self and the Social*. NY: Oxford.

Robinson, Sally. 1991. *Engendering the Subject: Gender and Self-Representation in Contemporary Women's Fiction*. Albany: State University of New York Press.

Thompson, Stith. 1989 [1956]. *Motif Index of Folk Literature: A Classification of Narrative Elements in Folktales, Ballads, Myths, Fables, Mediaeval Romances, Exempla, Fabliaux, Jestbooks, and Local Legends*. Bloomington: Indiana University Press.

APPENDIX: SELECTED PUBLICATIONS BY ELAINE J. LAWLESS

Books

God's Peculiar People: Women's Voices and Folk Tradition in a Pentecostal Church. Lexington: The University Press of Kentucky, 1988.

Handmaidens of the Lord: Pentecostal Women Preachers and Traditional Religion. Publications of the American Folklore Society. Philadelphia: University of Pennsylvania Press, 1988. Reprint, Eugene, OR: Wipf and Stock, 2010.

Holy Women, Wholly Women: Sharing Ministries through Life Stories and Reciprocal Ethnography. Publications of the American Folklore Society. Philadelphia: University of Pennsylvania Press, 1993. Reprint, Eugene, OR: Wipf and Stock, 2010.

The Liberation of Winifred Bryan Horner: Writer, Teacher, and Women's Rights Advocate. Bloomington: Indiana University Press, 2017.

Troubling Violence: A Performance Project, author with M. Heather Carver. Jackson: University Press of Mississippi, 2009.

When They Blew the Levee: Race, Politics, and Community in Pinhook, Missouri, author with David Todd Lawrence. Jackson: University Press of Mississippi, 2018.

Women Escaping Violence: Empowerment through Narrative. Columbia: University of Missouri Press, January 2001.

Women Preaching Revolution: Calling for Connection in a Disconnected Time. Philadelphia: University of Pennsylvania Press 1996. Reprint, Eugene, OR: Wipf and Stock Publishers, 2010.

Documentary Films

Joy Unspeakable, produced with Elizabeth Peterson, a television documentary on southern Indiana Pentecostalism, 1981. Available on Folkstreams.org.

Taking Pinhook, produced with D. Todd Lawrence, a documentary film on the destruction of Pinhook, Missouri, by the Army Corp of Engineers, 2014. Available on YouTube and at ReBuildPinhook.WordPress.com.

Chapters in Books

"Brothers and Sisters: Pentecostals as a Religious Folk Group." In *Folk Groups and Folklore Genres: A Reader,* edited by Elliott Oring, 149–163. Logan: Utah State University Press, 1989.

"Heal Thyself: Healing Women in mid-America." In *Diagnosing Folklore: 21st Century Health Systems, Belief and Practice,* edited by Trevor Blank. Jackson: University Press of Mississippi, 2015.

"Images of God in Women's Sermons." In *Gender and Belief Systems: Intersections of Women and Language*, edited by N. Warner, J. Ahlers, L. Bilmes, M. Oliver, S. Wertheim, and M. Chen , 403–411. Berkeley: University of California Press, 1997.

"The Issue of Blood: Reinstating Women into the Tradition." *Women Preachers and Prophets Through Two Millennia of Christianity*, edited by Beverly Kienzle, 1–18. Berkeley: University of California Press, 1997.

"Not So Different a Story After All: Pentecostal Women in the Pulpit." In *Outside the Mainstream: Women Leaders in Marginal Religious Groups*, edited by Catherine Wessinger, 34–62. Bloomington: Indiana University Press, 1993.

"Performing Ecstasy across a Thin Line; Pentecostalism in the Deep South." In *Moving Boundaries: American Religion(s) through the Louisiana Purchase*, edited by Richard Callahan, 34–56. Columbia: University of Missouri Press, 2007.

"Tradition and Poetics: The Sermons of Women Preachers." In *A Memorial for Milman Parry*, edited by John M. Foley, 269–313. Columbus, OH: Slavica Press, 1987.

"Troubling Violence through Performance: Community Responses to Local Stories" (chapter 9; volume 4). In *Violence against Women in Families and Relationship: Making and Breaking Connections*, edited by Evan Stark and Eve Buzawa. Westport, CT: Greenwood/Praeger, 2009.

"Women's Folk and Popular Arts: The Need for a Grounded Theory." In *The Material Culture of Gender/The Gender of Material Culture*, edited by Kenneth G. Ames and Katharine Martinez, 197–217. London: University Press of New England and the Henry Francis du Pont Winterthur Museum, 1996.

Articles in Journals

"Ars Rhetorica en Communitas: Reclaiming the Voice of Passionate Expression in Electronic Writing." *Rhetoric Review* 16, no. 2 (Spring 1998): 310–327.

"Brothers and Sisters: Pentecostals as a Folk Group." *Western Folklore* 43 (1983): 85–104.

"A Call for Action: Improving Community Awareness of and Responses to Local Violence against Women." *Peace Studies Journal* (Fall 2007): 66–80.

"Claiming Inversion: Lesbian Constructions of Female Identity as Claims for Authority." *Journal of American Folklore* 111, no. 439 (Spring 1998): 1–20.

"Connecting with God: Christian Women's Sermons and the Revisioning of the Divine," *Southern Folklore* 53, no. 2 (1996): 113–135.

"The 'Cycles of Violence' Narrative Prototype as a Folk Story: Recognizing Folklore Where It Works for Justice." *New York Folklore Quarterly* 8 (Spring 2004): 18–25.

"Folklore as a Map of the World: Rejecting 'Home' as a Failure of the Imagination," [AFS Presidential Address]. *Journal of American Folklore* 124, no. 493 (Summer 2011): 127–146.

"'I Know If I Don't Bear My Testimony I'll Lose It': Mormon Women's Testimonies." *Kentucky Folklore Quarterly* 30, nos. 1 and 2 (1984): 32–49.

"Joy Unspeakable as Folklore Documentary" (with Larry Danielson and Elizabeth Peterson). *Western Folklore* 42, no. 4 (December 1982): 320–327.

"Make a Joyful Noise: An Ethnography of Communication in the Pentecostal Service." *Southern Folklore Quarterly* 44 (1980): 1–32.

"The Monster in the House: Legend Characteristics of the 'Cycles of Violence' Narrative Prototype." *Contemporary Legend* 4, no. 2 (2002): 21–38.

"Narrative in the Pulpit: Persistent Use of *Exempla* in Vernacular Religious Contexts." *The Journal of the Midwest Modern Language Association* 20, no. 1 (Spring 1988): 48–64.

" 'The Night I Got the Holy Ghost . . .': Holy Ghost Narratives and the Pentecostal Conversion Process." *Western Folklore* 48, no. 1 (January 1988): 1–21.

"Oral 'Character' and 'Literary' Art: A Call for a New Reciprocity between Oral Literature and Folklore." *Western Folklore* 45 (1985): 77–96.

"Performing Fiction(s)/Performing Folklore: 'Magical Realism' as a Literary Trope/Folklore as Embedded Belief." *Louisiana Folklore Miscellany* IX (2009): 1–22.

"Peirce, Semiotics, and Strange Tongues: A Folk Religious Theory of Signs." *Semiotica* 99, nos. 3/4 (1994): 273–295.

"Piety and Motherhood: Reproductive Images and Maternal Strategies of the Woman Preacher." *Journal of American Folklore* 100 (1987): 469–479.

"Place, Space, and Disruption: A Response to the Question 'Why Doesn't She Just Leave?' " *Western Folklore* 67, no. 1 (Winter 2008): 35–58.

" 'Reciprocal Ethnography': No One Said It Was Easy." *Journal of Folklore Research* 37, nos. 2/3 (May–December 2000): 197–207.

"The Silencing of the Woman Preacher: A Vindication of Dinah Morris in George Eliot's *Adam Bede*." *Women's Studies* 18, nos. 2–3 (1990): 116–136.

"Traditional Women Preachers in mid-Missouri." *Missouri Folklore Journal* VI (1984): 47–60.

"Transformative Stories: Women Doing Things with Words." *Journal of Applied Folklore* 4, no. 1 (1999): 61–78.

"Transforming the Master Narrative: How Women Shift the Religious Subject." *Frontiers* 24, no. 1 (Spring 2003): 61–76.

"Weaving Narrative Texts: The Artistry of Women's Sermons." *Journal of Folklore Research* 34, no. 1 (1996): 15–43.

" 'What Did She Say?' An Application of Pierce's General Theory of Signs to Glossolalia in the Pentecostal Religion." *Folklore Forum* 13, no. 1 (Spring 1980): 23–38.

"What Zora Knew: A Crossroads, a Bargain with the Devil, and a Late Witness." *Journal of American Folklore* 126, no. 500 (Spring 2013): 152–173.

" 'Your Hair Is Your Glory': Public and Private Symbology for Pentecostal Women." *New York Folklore Quarterly* 12 (1986): 33–49.

INDEX

ELAINE J. LAWLESS is Curators' Distinguished Professor Emerita of English and Folklore Studies, Women's and Gender Studies, and Religious Studies at the University of Missouri. She is author of ten scholarly works, including *Women Escaping Violence: Empowerment Through Narrative*, *The Liberation of Winifred Bryan Horner: Writer, Teacher, and Women's Rights Advocate*, and *When They Blew the Levee: Race, Politics and Community in Pinhook, Missouri*, as well as numerous published articles. Lawless continues to write and publish in Folklore and Ethnography, as well as mentor graduate students both in the United States and abroad.